Lecture Notes in Computer Science 9857

Commenced Publication in 1973
Founding and Former Series Editors:
Gerhard Goos, Juris Hartmanis, and Jan van Leeuwen

Stefan Schiffner · Jetzabel Serna
Demosthenes Ikonomou · Kai Rannenberg (Eds.)

Privacy Technologies and Policy

4th Annual Privacy Forum, APF 2016
Frankfurt/Main, Germany, September 7–8, 2016
Proceedings

 Springer

Editors
Stefan Schiffner
ENISA
Athens
Greece

Jetzabel Serna
Goethe University Frankfurt
Frankfurt am Main
Germany

Demosthenes Ikonomou
ENISA
Athens
Greece

Kai Rannenberg
Goethe University Frankfurt
Frankfurt am Main
Germany

ISSN 0302-9743   ISSN 1611-3349   (electronic)
Lecture Notes in Computer Science
ISBN 978-3-319-44759-9   ISBN 978-3-319-44760-5   (eBook)
DOI 10.1007/978-3-319-44760-5

Library of Congress Control Number: 2016933473

LNCS Sublibrary: SL4 – Security and Cryptology

Printed on acid-free paper

This Springer imprint is published by Springer Nature
The registered company is Springer International Publishing AG Switzerland

Preface

It is our great pleasure to present the proceedings of the 4th Annual Privacy Forum (APF), which took place in Frankfurt am Main, Germany, during September 7–8, 2016, organized by the European Union Agency for Network and Information Security, the European Commission Directorate General for Communications Networks, Content and Technology, and Goethe University Frankfurt, as host.

The history of the 2016 conference venue, Goethe University's Westend Campus with the buildings of the former IG Farben headquarters, may well remind us how important the right to privacy is for a free and democratic society. And indeed privacy is mentioned in the European Human Rights Charter. Nowadays, in a world that moves ever-faster digital, we need to work on the implementation of privacy in electronic services. This means not only providing technological solutions but also setting up a viable policy framework. Earlier this year, the data protection regulation was approved by the European Parliament. Therefore, we focused on the implementation aspects of a sustainable future data protection framework. APF continues striving to close the gap between research, policy, and industry in the field of privacy and data protection. This includes presentations on privacy impact assessment, data lifecycle, and privacy challenges of new technologies.

We received 32 submissions in response to our call for papers. Each paper was peer-reviewed by at least four members of the international Program Committee (PC). On the basis of significance, novelty, and scientific quality, we selected six full research papers. In order to support less experienced researchers, an additional seven papers were selected to undergo shepherding, i.e., a PC member was in close contact with the authors advising how to improve the paper. Six of these seven papers eventually met our quality standards. Thus, this book presents twelve papers organized in three different chapters corresponding to the conference sessions.

The first chapter, "eIDAS and Data Protection Regulation," discusses topics concerning data life cycle agreements, processes for privacy impact assessment and electronic IDs in a policy and organisational context. The second chapter, "IoT and Public Clouds," discusses privacy and legal aspects in IoT, cloud computing, and their associated technological domains. Finally, the third chapter, "Privacy Policies and Privacy Risk Representation," takes the user on board, discussing privacy indicators to better communicate privacy policies and potential privacy risks to users.

In addition, three panels were organized. "Online Privacy Tools for General Public" – to examine the availability of reliable online privacy tools today, the information that is provided to end users, the potential of self-assessment of privacy tools by PETs developers, as well as the level of awareness of Web and mobile users on PETs. "Appropriate Security Measures for the Processing of Personal Data" – to further explore a risk based approach, which should also support organizations to select appropriate security and organizational measures to mitigate the identified risks. "Building a Community for Maturity Evaluation of PETs" – to discuss a structured community approach on the evaluation of the technology readiness and maturity of current privacy-enhancing technologies.

APF 2016 would not have been possible without the commitment of many people around the globe volunteering their competence and time. We would therefore like to express our sincere thanks to the members of the PC – and especially to those who carried out shepherding tasks – and to the authors who entrusted us with their works. Many thanks also go to our sponsors and to all conference attendees, who honored the work of the authors and presenters. Last but not least, we would like to thank the Organizing Committee led by Elvira Koch. Their excellent and tireless efforts made this event possible.

September 2016

Stefan Schiffner
Jetzabel Serna
Demosthenes Ikonomou
Kai Rannenberg

APF 2016

Annual Privacy Forum
Germany, Frankfurt, September 7–8, 2016

organized by

European Union Agency for Network and Information Security
(ENISA)
European Commission Directorate for Communications Networks,
Content and Technology (DG CONNECT),
and
Goethe University Frankfurt

Organization

Program Committee

Sven Wohlgemuth	Independent Consultant, Germany
Bernhard C. Witt	it.sec GmbH & Co. KG, Germany
Diane Whitehouse	IFIP and ICT, UK
Andreas Westfeld	HTW Dresden, Germany
Stefan Weiss	Swiss Re, Switzerland
Jozef Vyskoc	VaF, Sloakia
Carmela Troncoso	IMDEA Software Institute, Spain
Morton Swimmer	Trend Micro, Germany
Jan Schallaböck	iRights.Law, Germany
Angela Sasse	UCL, UK
Kazue Sako	NEC, Japan
Heiko Roßnagel	Fraunhofer IAO, Germany
Vincent Rijmen	KU Leuven, Belgium
Kai Rannenberg	Goethe University Frankfurt, Germany
Charles Raab	University of Edinburgh, UK
Christian W. Probst	Technical University of Denmark, Denmark
Joachim Posegga	University of Passau, Germany
Siani Pearson	HP Labs, UK
Aljosa Pasic	Atos Origin, Spain
Peter Parycek	Danube University Krems, Austria
Sebastian Pape	Goethe University Frankfurt, Germany
Jakob Illeborg Pagter	Alexandra Institute, Denmark
Gregory Neven	IBM Research, Switzerland
Chris Mitchell	Royal Holloway University, UK
Vashek Matyas	Masaryk University, Czech Republic
Fabio Martinelli	IIT-CNR, Italy
Daniel Le Métayer	Inria, France
Gwendal Le Grand	CNIL, France
Stefan Köpsell	TU Dresden, Germany
Sabrina Kirrane	WU Wien, Austria
Els Kindt	KU Leuven, Belgium
Dogan Kesdogan	University of Regensburg, Germany
Florian Kerschbaum	SAP, Germany
Stefan Katzenbeisser	TU Darmstadt, Germany
Sokratis Katsikas	NTNU, Norway
Marko Hölbl	University of Maribor, Slovenia
Marit Hansen	ULD Schleswig-Holstein, Germany

Lorena González Manzano	Universidad Carlos III de Madrid, Spain
Simone Fischer-Hübner	Karlstad University, Sweden
Mathias Fischer	University of Münster, Germany
Hannes Federrath	University of Hamburg, Germany
Thomas Engel	University Luxembourg, Luxembourg
Prokopios Drogkaris	ENISA, Greece
Josep Domingo-Ferrer	Universitat Rovira i Virgili, Spain
Roberto Di Pietro	Bell Labs, Italy
José María De Fuentes	Universidad Carlos III de Madrid, Spain
Malcolm Crompton	IIS, Australia
Fanny Coudert	KU Leuven, Belgium
George Christou	University of Warwick, UK
Claude Castelluccia	Inria Rhone-Alpes, France
Valentina Casola	UNINA, Italy
Pompeu Casanovas	UAB, Spain
Bettina Berendt	KU Leuven, Belgium
Luis Antunes	University of Porto, Portugal

General Co-chairs

Kai Rannenberg	Goethe University Frankfurt, Germany
Demosthenes Ikonomou	ENISA, Greece

Program Co-chairs

Jetzabel Serna	Goethe University Frankfurt, Germany
Stefan Schiffner	ENISA, Greece

Publication Chair

Ioannis Prinopoulos	ENISA, Greece

External Reviewers

Christian Roth	Universität Regensburg, Germany
Hernando Ospina	Goethe University Frankfurt, Germany
Eugenia Nikolouzou	ENISA, Greece
David Harborth	Goethe University Frankfurt, Germany
Pedro Faria	HealthSystems, Portugal
Toralf Engelke	Universität Regensburg, Germany
Fabina Dietrich	Fraunhofer IAO, Germany
Bud P. Bruegger	Fraunhofer IAO, Germany

Authors

Jasper van de Ven
Tsung-Ying Tsai
Sih-Cing Syu
Ali Sunyaev
Gion Sialm
Chuang-Ming Shiung
Stefan Schiffner
Jose Fran. Ruiz
Martin Rost
Henrich C. Pöhls
Marinella Petrocchi
Anil Ozdeniz
Hannah Obersteller
Jonida Milaj

Jeanne Pia
   Mifsud Bonnici
Ilaria Matteucci
Mirko Manea
Tzu-Ching Liu
Thomas Länger
Kay Kühne
Barbara Krumay
Silvia Knittl
Marit Hansen
Joel Hansen
Solange Ghernaouti
Carmela Gambardella
Michael Friedewald

Mathias Fischer
Frank Dylla
Tobias Dehling
Gianpiero Costantino
Li-Da Chien
Shi-Cho Cha
Niklas Büscher
Thomas Brüggemann
Luca Bolognini
Camilla Bistolfi
Christoph Bier
Felix Bieker
Jürgen Beyerer

Sponsors and Organizers

Contents

eIDAS and Data Protection Regulation

A Lifecycle for Data Sharing Agreements: How it Works Out   3
Jose Fran. Ruiz, Marinella Petrocchi, Ilaria Matteucci,
Gianpiero Costantino, Carmela Gambardella, Mirko Manea,
and Anil Ozdeniz

A Process for Data Protection Impact Assessment Under the European
General Data Protection Regulation   21
Felix Bieker, Michael Friedewald, Marit Hansen, Hannah Obersteller,
and Martin Rost

Bring Your Own Identity - Case Study from the Swiss Government   38
Gion Sialm and Silvia Knittl

The E-Waste-Privacy Challenge: A Grounded Theory Approach   48
Barbara Krumay

IoT and Public Clouds

Challenges of the Internet of Things: Possible Solutions from Data Protecy
and 3D Privacy.   71
Luca Bolognini and Camilla Bistolfi

Smart Meters as Non-purpose Built Surveillance Tools   81
Jonida Milaj and Jeanne Pia Mifsud Bonnici

Consumer Privacy on Distributed Energy Markets.   96
Niklas Büscher, Stefan Schiffner, and Mathias Fischer

Selected Cloud Security Patterns to Improve End User Security and Privacy
in Public Clouds   115
Thomas Länger, Henrich C. Pöhls, and Solange Ghernaouti

Privacy (Privacy Policies and Privacy Risk Representation)

PrivacyInsight: The Next Generation Privacy Dashboard   135
Christoph Bier, Kay Kühne, and Jürgen Beyerer

A Framework for Major Stakeholders in Android Application Industry to
Manage Privacy Policies of Android Applications   153
Shi-Cho Cha, Chuang-Ming Shiung, Tzu-Ching Liu, Sih-Cing Syu,
Li-Da Chien, and Tsung-Ying Tsai

Qualitative Privacy Description Language: Integrating Privacy Concepts,
Languages, and Technologies   171
    Jasper van de Ven and Frank Dylla

An Information Privacy Risk Index for mHealth Apps   190
    Thomas Brüggemann, Joel Hansen, Tobias Dehling, and Ali Sunyaev

Author Index   203

eIDAS and Data Protection Regulation

A Lifecycle for Data Sharing Agreements: How it Works Out

Jose Fran. Ruiz[1], Marinella Petrocchi[2(✉)], Ilaria Matteucci[2],
Gianpiero Costantino[2], Carmela Gambardella[3], Mirko Manea[3],
and Anil Ozdeniz[1]

[1] Atos, Madrid, Spain
{jose.ruizr,anil.ozdeniz}@atos.net
[2] IIT CNR, Pisa, Italy
{m.petrocchi,i.matteucci,g.costantino}@iit.cnr.it
[3] Hewlett Packard Enterprise, Milan, Italy
{carmela.gambardella,mirko.manea}@hpe.com

Abstract. An electronic Data Sharing Agreement (DSA) is a human-readable, yet machine-processable contract, regulating how organizations and/or individuals share data. In past work, we have shed light on DSA engineering, i.e., the process of studying how data sharing is ruled in traditional legal human-readable contracts and mapping their fields (and rules) into formats that are machine-processable, leading to the transposition of a traditional legal contract into the electronic DSA. However, the definition of an electronic DSA is only the starting point of a complex DSA lifecycle, driving the contract from its creation to (1) an analysis phase, where the DSA rules are checked against conflicts; and (2) a mapping phase, where the analysed rules are transposed into privacy policies expressed in enforceable languages. This paper presents our vision for the architectural definition of a DSA system, where a lifecycle manager orchestrates: an authoring tool for legal experts, policy experts, and end users; an analyser for checking consistency of the DSA rules; a mapper for encoding rules in a low level language amenable for enforcement.

1 Introduction

Nowadays, highly-connected systems exchange a large number of data, being either internal or belonging to clients. Additionally, due to reduction of costs and functionalities, companies prefer to use cloud infrastructures for storing their data. In this context, it is mandatory for companies to have a way to store and exchange data internally and externally in a secure and private way in the cloud, being it private, public or hybrid. The aim of Coco Cloud project (http://www.coco-cloud.eu) is to fulfil this security and privacy issues, by providing a framework that allows the storing and exchanging of data using (a) secure storage of data and (b) enforcement of policies for accessing and storing objects. This

---

The research leading to these results has received funding from the European Union Seventh Framework Programme (FP7/2007–2013) under grant no 610853 (Coco Cloud).

S. Schiffner et al. (Eds.): APF 2016, LNCS 9857, pp. 3–20, 2016.
DOI: 10.1007/978-3-319-44760-5_1

last property is supported by the concept of Data Sharing Agreement (DSA). DSAs specify policies that are applied for accessing the object they are linked to. In this sense, policy experts, when creating the DSAs, can specify not only user or role-based access and usage control rules, but also, e.g., location, time and other complex constraints. The main objective of this paper is to present the lifecycle for managing DSAs and the methodology and tools we have designed and developed. We have identified the different phases of DSA design, development and use and its status: (i) DSA Template, which provides the basis for creating a DSA and (ii) the DSA itself. Following, we started developing tools for its different necessities and defined their interactions. This resulted in a DSA Authoring Tool, DSA Analysis and Conflict Solving Tool and a DSA Mapper Tool. We then noticed the need for a component that could integrate and allow working with all the different tools in a unified way together with a repository for DSAs and a way to communicate easily with them through the different tools and unified framework. The resulting framework was the DSA Lifecycle Manager, which encompasses all the tools as building blocks and provides a very user-friendly way of working with the DSAs in a transparent way for the different users. The structure of the paper is as follows: Sect. 2 presents Data Sharing Agreements characteristics and goals; Sect. 3 describes the DSA System, where the tools, roles, functionalities are presented. Section 4 presents more in detail the tools and components of the DSA System; Sect. 5 presents the related work and, finally, Sect. 6 describes the conclusions and future work.

2   State of the Art

Here, we provide the state of the art solutions for the management of DSA, from their specification, to their validation and refinement to enforceable languages.

Specification. [3] investigates platform-independent policy frameworks to specify, analyze, and deploy security and networking policies. In particular the authors describe a scenario-based demo of a portal prototype for usable and effective policy authoring through either natural language or structured lists that manage policies from the specification to the possible enforcement. [22,23] specifically focus on DSA. They model the agreement as a set of obligation constraints. Obligations are expressed as distributed temporal logic predicates (DTL), a generalization of linear temporal logic including both past-time and future-time temporal operators. Attempto [7] advocates the idea of formalizing English language to be able to write Semantic Web content in a controlled, user-friendly, and yet logically precise way. [5] presents a logic-based policy analysis framework which (i) is expressive, (ii) considers obligations and authorizations, (iii) includes a dynamic system model, and (iv) gives useful diagnostic information.

Analysis and Conflict Solver. Analysis of privacy policies is essential to detect inconsistencies and conflicts before the actual enforcement. [15] presents an analysis tool to identify possible conflicts or incompatibilities among the DSA clauses. A subsequent report in [4] describes the integration of authoring and analysis tools into a working enforcement framework tailored for Cloud systems. The authors of [12] apply the policy analysis framework in [15] to detect conflicts among medical data protection policies. Work in [11] distinguishes between unilateral and multilateral DSAs (the latter being agreements constituting of data sharing policies coming from multiple actors) and proposes a conflict detection technique. In [2], it is shown that the Event-B language (www.event-b.org) can be used to model obliged events. The Rodin platform provides animation and model checking toolset to analyse specifications in Event-B leading to capability of obligations analysis [1]. Relevant work in [16] proposes a formal definition of conflicting permission assignments is given, together with efficient conflict-checking algorithms. [6] considers policies that restrict the use and replication of information, e.g., imposing that certain information may only be used or copied a certain number of times. Related to the sharing of data, but not strictly related to analysis, [9,20,21] present on opportunistic authority evaluation scheme for sharing data in a secure way in a crisis management scenario. The main idea is to combine two already existing data sharing solutions to share data in a secure way through opportunistic networks. Policy conflict detection is generally followed by conflict resolution. The approach adopted by the eXtensible Access Control Markup Language (XACML) [17] is a very general one. In fact, XACML policies (or policy sets) must include a combining algorithm that defines the procedure to combine the individual results obtained by the evaluation of the rules of the policy (of the policies in the policy set). [8,13] proposes to resolve conflicts by evaluating the specificity level of the elements constituting the policies. Such an approach evaluates how much a policy is specific in identifying the subject, the object, and the environment to which it is applicable. The basic idea is that policies that are applicable to smaller set of subjects, objects, and environmental conditions should have the priority on the others [19].

Mapper functionality. Once policies are specified in high-level language, they need to be automatically transformed into enforceable policies. It is an instance of a problem of refinement that has been studied for a number of years in various areas of computer science. The action refinement theory [18] is typically used in formal methods for converting the specification of an (abstract) action into a (concrete) process. [10] addresses this theory and provide a mechanism for transforming high-level primitives/actions into lower level processes, in such a way that some security properties are preserved within the transformation.

3 Data Sharing Agreements

Data Sharing Agreements (DSA) are electronic documents consisting of:

- the DSA title, a label which could be used to identify the DSA.
- the parties involved into the DSA. For each party, we need to specify its role in the DSA and its responsibilities, which are the duties of the organisations

that cannot be expressed in terms of authorisations, obligations, and prohibitions by a data sharing rule, and for which the compliance checks cannot be enforced automatically (e.g., the role that each party will play in terms of gathering, sharing and storing the relevant data). Regarding the roles of the parties, we mainly consider Data Controllers, Data Processors, and Data Subjects. A Data Controller can be a natural person or a single legal entity, in private sector, rather than an agency or a division within an institution, in the public sector. It is responsible for identifying the purposes and the manner in which any personal data are processed, according to national and/or international (e.g., European) regulations. Data Processor is entrusted by the Data Controller (e.g., a hospital) to process personal data of the Data Subject (e.g., patients of a hospital). The latter is a natural person or one who can be identified as the subject the personal data are referring to, in the scope of the agreement.

– the validity of the DSA states: its start and end date, and the duration of offline licenses for data access. The latter information allows the DSA actors to manage some particular scenarios, as for example, when the data are accessed by a mobile without Internet connection: it means that, in certain circumstances, data may be kept by the recipient also after the contract expires, for a predefined time.

– the vocabulary used for the DSA, which provides the terminology for authoring DSA rules. The vocabulary is defined by an ontology, a formal explicit description of a domain of interest.

– the data classification, describing the nature of the data covered by the DSA. We consider two main data categories: personal data and non-personal data. Additionally, we can propose deeper data taxonomies for each of these classes to identify better the object of the DSA. A (not exhaustive) example of non-personal data are business data (Highly Confidential, Confidential, etc.) and administrative data. Personal data are, e.g., contact details, common personal data, etc. Additional data categories are, e.g., sensitive data (medical data), judicial data (data relating to offences or criminal convictions), etc. This data classification has been provided by legal experts of the Coco Cloud project focusing in the main three areas we work with and presented as a result of the project [24]. Unfortunately due to the limitation of size of the paper we are unable to include more information about it.

– the purpose of the DSA, which is linked with the data classification. There is only one purpose for a DSA. If more than one purpose is needed, another agreement is made. According to the data classification, the purpose can be:
  • Administrative and Accounting (e.g., for booking, for payment)
  • Healthcare services (e.g., for diagnoses)
  • Scientific Research
  • Statistical (e.g., public costs control, epidemiological)
  • Marketing (e.g., for commercial proposal of services/needs)
  • Profiling (e.g., aggregation/grouping of users depending of certain user characteristics to propose specific products/services tailored to those characteristics)
  • Fulfil law obligations (e.g., to access data in case of public authorities)

DSA are also made of some optional sections containing the data sharing rules:

- the authorizations section contains rules on permitted operations for each party;
- the prohibitions section contains rules on prohibited operations for each party;
- the obligations section contains rules about the duties of each of the parties in relation to the data sharing.

Note that, to have a significant DSA, at least one rule must be filled.

4   DSA System

The DSA System is in charge of the creation and management of the DSA, providing tools and a framework for these functionalities. We define a DSA specification to be encapsulated (or wrapped) as an XML (eXtensible Markup Language) file. The XML format facilitates the task of programmatically accessing and working on the different DSA sections defined in the previous section; furthermore the XML fosters the interoperability with different components of the DSA system. The different components of the DSA System (described in details in the next section) are the DSA Authoring Tool, the DSA Analysis and Conflict Solver Tool, the DSA Mapper Tool, the DSA Lifecycle Manager and the DSA Repository. More specifically:

- **DSA Authoring Tool:** this tool is in charge of creating and managing DSA. The rules included in the DSA are created using a language called Controlled Natural Language for DSA [14], or, more concisely, CNL, based on pilot-specific dictionaries (ontologies). The tool is available as a graphical web application to provide an easy to use interface for end users.
- **DSA Analyser and Conflict Solver:** these tools take care of analysing the rules in the DSAs and detecting potential conflicts using a semi-automatic process. In particular, the DSA Analyser checks that DSAs have no conflicts among their rules and it can be invoked as remote component using a simple URL plus the identifier of the DSA to analyse. The DSA Analyser detects a conflict when two policies simultaneously allow and deny an access (or usage) request under the same contextual conditions. In case no conflict is found, the DSA does not notify the presence of conflicts to the DSA Lifecycle Manager and does not invoke the Conflict Solver. On the other hand, if the Analyser reveals conflicting rules, the Conflict Solver will drive the Mapper in its translation from CNL to the enforcement language by suggesting how to prioritize the rules relying, e.g., on the freshness and/or the issuer of the rules.
- **DSA Mapper:** this component translates the DSA rules from CNL into an enforceable XACML-based language. This translation happens on CNL rules that have been previously checked by the DSA Analyser and Conflict Solver Tool and the mapping process takes into account the prioritization outcome of such tool to include an appropriate combining algorithm in the enforceable policy.

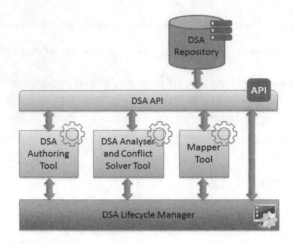

Fig. 1. DSA system high-level architecture.

- **DSA Lifecycle Manager:** this component orchestrates all the DSA System components. Different roles are assigned to users of such system, i.e., Law Expert, Policy Expert and End User. The DSA Lifecycle Manager provides specific functionalities according to the specific role of the user. Such specific functionalities refer to methods provided by the tools of the DSA System (DSA Authoring Tool, DSA Analyser and Conflict Solver, and DSA Mapper) and the DSA Repository (see the following item). Thus, users do not interact directly with those tools but via the Lifecycle Manager.
- **DSA Repository:** it is a repository where the DSA are stored and requested by the tools presented before. The access to the DSA Repository is implemented through the DSA API, which provides methods for accessing and retrieving DSAs using a unique identifier or a set of metadata used to identify the correct DSA by means of attributes such as level of security, creator, validity, etc. In case of multiple organizations managing the same set of DSA, only one organization owns the repository, and then it will give appropriate access to the repository.

Figure 1 shows a high-level architecture of the DSA system and the communications of the tools. As depicted, the DSA workflow, from authoring to mapper, is coordinated by the DSA Lifecycle Manager. The DSA Lifecycle Manager communicates with all the components of the DSA subsystem. Then, they perform their actions and return the control to the DSA Lifecycle Manager. The DSA Repository stores the DSAs, which can be retrieved using the DSA API.

4.1 Roles of the DSA System

Users can log into the DSA system under three different roles. In the following of this paper, we will refer to the DSA system roles as DSA roles or, simply, roles.

Each of the roles features specific goals and functionalities. A user that is logged with a specific role can use specific components of the system for achieving those goals and performing those functionalities. A description of each role follows:

- **Law expert:** the user logged with such role is familiar with legal and contractual perspective content of agreement, for example a lawyer. Such a user is in charge of creating and managing DSA Templates through the DSA Authoring Tool.
- **Policy expert:** the user logged with such role is responsible for defining business policies and DSA metadata, for example a company policy expert. She uses DSA Templates to create DSAs (e.g., company specific agreements).
- **End user:** the user logged with such role can either extend, if requested, the DSA of the Policy Expert with her user-specific input or simply review and accept a DSA created by a Policy Expert for being used for her data. An example of such a user is a patient in a hospital.

4.2 DSA Status

Within the DSA lifecycle, various states are defined and set to DSA, according to the specific lifecycle phase the DSA is into. That way, specific functionalities can only be applied when the DSA is in a specific status. Figure 2 shows a diagram of the different states of a DSA. Arrows represent DSA status change, the component responsible for that change, and the action through that component that let the DSA change the status.

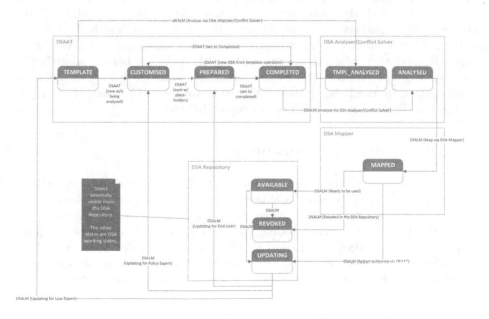

Fig. 2. DSA status diagram.

The first phase is the creation of the DSA Template. The component in charge of that is the DSA Authoring Tool. The Law Expert creates the DSA Template by inserting the data classification, the purpose of data sharing, the DSA roles, and the rules derived from terms of law (the DSA is in the Template status). Then, the Law Expert can launch the DSA Analyser and Conflict Solver to check that such rules have been well edited. That way the expert obtains the DSA Template in TMPL_Analysed status. This status means that the DSA Template can be used for creating a DSA. The Policy Expert can now pick the DSA Template and starts creating a DSA from it. The status of this new DSA is Customised, as it is not yet completed. The Policy Expert can start adding specific information of her company (like the name of the company, and the data sharing rules that specifically apply for her organization). When adding elements and working on it the DSA status changes to Prepared when the End User still has some information to add to the DSA. This status means the DSA has already some information but is not final yet. However, it could also be possible to pass directly from Customised to Completed. This status means that the DSA has all the required information (either the End User has filled all the necessary information, thus, the status passes from Prepared to Completed).

When the DSA is Completed, then it can be analysed. The Policy Expert uses the DSA Analyser and Conflict Solver tool for checking if there exists any conflict in the DSA rules, as described in the following sections. Once the analysis process terminates, the DSA status changes to Analysed. In this status, the high level DSA rules can be mapped to enforceable rules via the DSA Mapper component. When the rules have been mapped, the DSA status changes to Mapped. The DSA Lifecycle Manager can change a Mapped DSA into three of the following states: Available, Revoked, Updating. Available means that the DSA is available in the DSA repository and is ready to be enforced. Revoked means that the DSA is still in the DSA repository, but it is no more valid (because, e.g., the DSA validity is expired). Updating means that some parts in the DSA are being updated. The update can be performed either by the Law Expert (that will work to update a template), or by the Policy Expert, (that will work on a Customized DSA), or by the End User (that will work on a Prepared DSA).

5   DSA System Components

Hereafter, we describe the different tools of the DSA Subsystem together with their requirements, goals, functionalities, and main use. These tools are complementary and support each other in order to allow the creation, management and use of the DSAs. As aforementioned, the DSA Lifecycle Manager is the main orchestrator of the DSA System and provides the functionality to work with all the different tools in an integrated way. That way, the interactions, dependencies and work done for creating, managing and using DSAs is done thought it.

5.1   DSA Authoring Tool

The DSA Authoring Tool (DSAAT) is a Web application that supports the user for the creation and management of Data Sharing Agreements. The application is available as a SaaS Cloud service, employing the standard best practices of access protection (including password based control and TLS channel). The authoring of a DSA follows a multi-step design phase. We have considered a three-step authoring process. First, legal experts create and fill DSA templates (i.e., a generalized and to be completed DSA version for the use case), then business-specific policy experts complete the templates and give life to DSA, by instantiating it with use case specific details. Optionally, in a third phase, the end user can add information (as defined by the policy expert) to pinpoint data privacy preferences, such as the consent for data treatment, the identities of doctors or relatives that can access their medical investigations in a health scenario, and the like. According to the three identified steps, the users of the DSAAT can assume one of the roles presented in Sect. 4.1. The DSA creation is supported by an ontology-based vocabulary (specified in OWL format) defined specifically for a business domain. It describes terms (like categories of data, roles of subjects, identifiers), actions (like read, print, write), and relations between them for the specific reference context (i.e., healthcare, mobile, public administration, etc.). Ontologies used have sufficient expressive power to describe the terms and relations between them in the reference domain; their expressiveness is not very high so that the analysis phase is simple and not error prone, also due to the reduced grain of the ontologies. DSA templates include information about data category, role of the parties, purpose of use, and the rules from legislation that shall apply among the parties (i.e., data controllers, data subjects, data processors). DSAs are instantiated using an already existing DSA template and augmented with business-specific rules. Additionally, the DSAAT allows the data subject, identified as an end user to specify user (privacy) preferences. For example, if a rule regarding the access to radiological examinations involves a doctor belonging to a hospital, a patient can constraint the doctor(s) she would like to have access to her data. The DSAAT allows users to access the content of an existing DSA depending on their role, retrieved from the list of available DSA, by either viewing the raw DSA data (in XML format), or a user-friendly graphical form.

Figure 3 shows the GUI prototype where the user can set the DSA properties described above. The specific names of the parties can be filled by a Policy Expert when instantiating the DSA template for specific organizations. According to the vocabulary, the DSAAT assists the user in writing the rules, by suggesting only valid terms and actions in an interactive and dynamic process that guides the construction of the statements in a controlled yet natural way. As an example, Fig. 4 shows the composition of an authorization rule where the DSAAT is suggesting a list of predicates that can be joined to Data. Such predicates shows up on a pop-up window that follows the writing of the rules.

The legal rules, which are set at template level by the legal expert cannot be changed by the policy expert. The rationale behind this choice is that those rules encode specific terms of law that are not under the expertise and duties

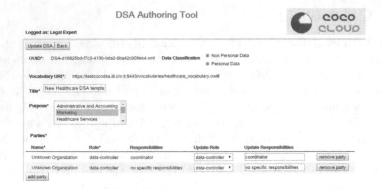

Fig. 3. DSAAT interface for creating a DSA template.

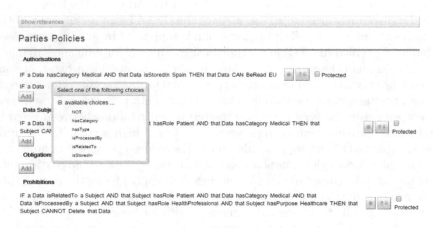

Fig. 4. Assisted definition of rules.

coverage of the policy expert. As the DSAAT is delivered as a service, it easily provides support to the DSA creation and management to external applications, like the DSA Lifecycle Manager (DSA LM). The DSA LM redirects the user to the DSAAT at certain phases of the DSA lifecycle, in particular, when either legal experts, policy experts and end users create and edit DSA templates and DSA, with an integrated and seamless user experience.

5.2   DSA Analyser and Conflict Solver

The objective of the Analyser is to take as input a DSA and verify that their rules are not in conflict against the same access request. To perform this step, the Analyser scans the DSA and extracts all policies among Authorizations, Obligations and Prohibitions xml-tag. In the following, we show two simple rules, one authorization and one prohibition:

```
<authorization>
   <expression language="UserText" issuer="Legal Expert">
```

```
    IF a Data isStoredIn Belgium THEN Subject CAN Read that Data
    </expression>
</authorization>
<prohibition>
    <expression language="UserText" issuer="Legal Expert">
    IF a Data isStoredIn Belgium THEN Subject CAN Read that Data
    </expression>
</prohibition>
```

The above rules are expressed in a friendly-easy language understandable by humans, however the DSA expresses the same rules also in the Controlled Natural Language for DSA (CNL). An example of an authorization written in CNL is:

```
<expression language="CNL4DSA" issuer="Legal Expert">
IF isStoredIn(Data, Belgium)
AND
    hasLocation(Subject, Africa)
THEN
    can [?X_4, Write, ?X_2]
</expression>
```

The Analyser leverages on MAUDE, which is a rewriting logic-based framework specification of complex systems and properties verification, to find conflicts among rules. When the analysis phase starts, the Analyser first extracts all the CNL rules in the DSA and stores them into dynamic arrays. Then, those rules are converted in the MAUDE syntax. In addition, the Analyser prepares a set of other variables and data that MAUDE needs to correctly evaluate the rules under a specific context. An example of context, expressed in MAUDE, saying that it is true that the data is stored in Belgium is:

```
eq eval (isStoredIn(data,belgium)) = true
```

When MAUDE evaluates the DSA rules, it will consider that context to provide the evaluation result in a Boolean format (true or false) for each rule defined into the authorization, obligations, and prohibition xml-tag of the DSA. True means that the rule is valid for that context, false the opposite. The Analyser collects all the evaluation results, for each rule specified within each category (authentications, obligations and prohibitions), for all the possible combinations of contexts that are formed starting from the vocabulary associated to the DSA. To detect a conflict, the Analyser compares the evaluation results of the authorization set with the prohibition set, and of the obligation set with the prohibition set. If we consider the toy authorization and prohibition rules at the beginning of this section, we observe that a conflict exists. In fact, the authorization states that if data is stored in Belgium, then subject can read it, instead the prohibition states the opposite. In the same fashion, the Analyser compares the output of each authorization rule with each prohibition rule, and if there are two rules, in the different sets, that return true as result of the evaluation, then we know the rules are in conflict. Once a conflict is detected, a possible solution is provided. The solution strategy is parametric. As an example, the current version of the solver indicates as priority those rules written by the end-users, then those by the legal experts, and finally those by the policy experts. This is only an example of strategy that we may implement to prioritise conflicting rules detected by the Analyser.

5.3 DSA Mapper

Once a DSA has been edited and analysed, a translation between the Controller Natural Language (CNL) policies to the executable ones is needed. Indeed, CNL policies are written at a high-level of abstraction. However, in order to be enforceable and executable, policies must be converted into low level ones, as XACML-based policies [17]. The set of policies to be enforced can be extremely rich, including aspects derived from legislation, from business policies and security requirements, all of which have been given without making specific assumptions about the enforcement model. The component in charge of making the passage between the two abstraction levels is the DSA mapper, which translates each CNL statement of the DSA into a XACML based policy. The DSA mapper exposes two main functionalities:

- a mapping of both CNL syntax and semantics;
- a refinement of the terms of the vocabulary in such a way that they result understandable for the enforcement component.

A preliminary idea of a possible mapper function has been presented in [14], in which the translation function maps the CNL constructs into process-algebra-like operators. In the current and newest version, we have simplified the process. CNL has been developed with an eye to XACML constructs, thus it is possible to identify in each CNL statement the main XACML elements:

- A subject element is the entity requesting the access. A subject has one or more attributes.
- The resource element is a data, service or system component. A resource has one or more attributes.
- An action element defines the type of access requested on the resource. Actions have one or more attributes.
- An environment element can optionally provide additional information.

As first action, the DSA mapper considers all the rules into a DSA as policies of a policy set in XACML. Then, the translation algorithm takes each basic fragment {s, a, o}, where s identifies the subject, a the action, and o the object (mainly the data which the DSA is referred to), and puts each of this element into a XACML policy by using the appropriate tag, i.e., <subject> ... <\subject>, <action> ... <\action>, and <resources> ... <\resources>, respectively. These represent the elements of the XACML policy target (<Target>).

All the contextual conditions expressed in CNL are mapped into the tag <Condition>. It is worth noting that even the attributes related to both subject and resources are mapped into the tag <Condition>, in such a way to put all the contextual conditions under the same tag. This choice has been made for three main reasons: (i) the executable policy structure reflects the one of the CNL statement in which the conditions on subject, object, and environment are specified all together into the context; (ii) it allows to consider conditions update during the application of the policy itself, and (iii) it simplifies the translation function because it is not necessary to identify for each property in CNL which is its domain. Such information can be found by interacting with the vocabulary. Indeed, the domain and the range of each property is defined only into the vocabulary and not in the DSA.

Example. Let us consider the following simple CNL policy:

```
IF  hasCategory(data,medical)
AND  isStoredIn(data,Spain)
THEN  can [subject, Read, data]
```

An excerpt of the executable policy related to this CNL statement has the following <Target> definition:

```
<Rule Effect="Deny" RuleId="data\_subject\_authorization\_28">
<Target>
 <AnyOf>
  <AllOf>
  <MatchMatchId="urn:oasis:names:tc:xacml:1.0:function:string-equal">
   <AttributeValue DataType=''http://www.w3.org/2001/XMLSchema#string">
               MEDICAL_DATA
   </AttributeValue>
   <AttributeDesignator
   AttributeId="urn:oasis:names:tc:xacml:3.0:resourceclassification
   Category="urn:oasis:names:tc:xacml:1.0:resource-category"
     DataType="http://www.w3.org/2001/XMLSchema#string"
     MustBePresent="false" />
   </Match>
    ...
   </Match>
  </AllOf>
 </AnyOf>
</Target>
```

and the following <Condition> definition:

```
<Condition>
 <Match MatchId="urn:oasis:names:tc:xacml:1.0:function:string-equal">
  <AttributeValue
  DataType="http://www.w3.org/2001/XMLSchema#string">READ
  </AttributeValue>
  <AttributeDesignator
AttributeId="urn:oasis:names:tc:xacml:3.0:action-id"
Category="urn:oasis:names:tc:xacml:1.0:action-category"
DataType="http://www.w3.org/2001/XMLSchema#string"
MustBePresent="false" />
 </Match>
  ...
 <Match MatchId="urn:oasis:names:tc:xacml:1.0:function:string-equal">
  <AttributeValue DataType="http://www.w3.org/2001/XMLSchema#string">Data
  </AttributeValue>
   ...
 </Match>
 <Match MatchId="urn:oasis:names:tc:xacml:1.0:function:string-equal">
  <AttributeValue
```

```
  DataType="http://www.w3.org/2001/XMLSchema#string">Medical
   </AttributeValue>
  </AttributeValue>
   ...
  </Match>
</Condition>
```

We have defined a proper field where the executable expressions will be saved. The resulting output of the DSA Mapper is a new version of the XML DSA, in which XACML expression fields are automatically filled with the executable expressions automatically generated by the mapping function.

5.4   DSA Lifecycle Manager

The DSA Lifecycle Manager (DSA LM) provides a common infrastructure for the creation, development, analysis and management of the DSA. The framework manages and orchestrates the communications and functionalities of the DSA components presented before. Additionally, it communicates and exchanges information with the DSA Repository by means of the DSA Repository API, which provides DSA and DSA Templates management functionality. Therefore, the DSA LM is the component that guides the management of DSA objects for all the tools and its use in Coco Cloud-aware (and unaware) applications. The DSA LM uses the DSA components described previously as building blocks and implements their communications by doing specific calls or providing APIs (e.g., for communicating with the DSA Repository). These communications are done in a transparent way so the user will not need to interact manually with the individual tools. The DSA LM interacts with the DSA components by calling their operations according to the functionality expected by the user and provides the necessary input (e.g., DSA identifier, role of the user, status of the DSA, etc.). For example, when a Policy Expert wants to modify a DSA, the framework calls the DSAAT with the specific functionality requested by the user and passing a reference to the DSA to be used. Then the DSAAT obtains the DSA from the DSA Repository using its interface,

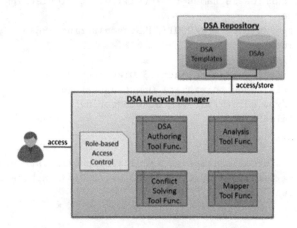

Fig. 5. DSA lifecycle manager structure.

Fig. 6. DSA LM interface for policy expert.

performs the necessary actions, and sends back a confirmation message to the DSALM with the result of the operation. The same holds when users with different roles would like to modify or make other allowed operations on a DSA. This level of modularity allows any CocoCloud application to easily use and/or integrate the DSALM.

Figure 5 shows a high-level diagram of the DSA System tools, their functionalities, input and output. The DSA LM is in charge of orchestrating their functionality, providing an individual application for the management of the DSA. Additionally, the DSA Repository stores the DSA and DSA Templates and provides an API for managing them. That way all the different DSA components can communicate with the DSA Repository and request/store DSA and DSA Templates.

As an example, Fig. 6 shows the interface of the DSA Lifecycle Manager as a Policy Expert role. There we can see some DSA, their names, creator, description and ID (which is used internally for working with them). In the right part of the interface we can see the different options the user can do with the selected DSA: Show DSA, Edit DSA, Analyse DSA and Delete DSA. The other roles have different functionalities in the DSA but, due to pages limits of the paper, we describe the ones of this role:

- Show DSA: it calls the functionality of showing the DSA in a user-friendly way. It is provided by the DSA Authoring Tool. This interface is shown in Fig. 7.
- Edit DSA: it calls the functionality for editing the DSA. It is provided by the DSA Authoring Tool.
- Analyse DSA: it calls the functionality for analyzing if the DSA has any conflict. It is provided by the Analysis and Conflict Solver Tool.

5.5   DSA Repository

The DSA Repository is a component of the DSA System in charge of storing, managing and providing DSAs and DSA Templates. Figure 8 shows a high-level definition of its

Fig. 7. Show DSA functionality of the DSA LM.

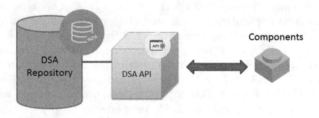

Fig. 8. DSA repository high-level architecture.

architecture. It provides these functionalities through an API (DSA API) that any component can use. The DSA LM, the DSAAT, the Analysis and Conflict Solver Tool and the Mapper Tool use it.

The DSA file storage is managed using state-of-the-art technologies. The DSA files are stored on the OpenStack^{TM} Swift object storage and MySQL relational database tables are used for storing metadata and access control related attributes. The Authentication system for accessing the DSA objects is provided by OpenStack^{TM} Keystone and OpenLDAP. Keystone is used for Authentication service and OpenLDAP provides account backend for the Keystone service. The DSA Repository stores both DSA Templates and DSAs, being the API developed to work transparently with both type of objects as a single one.

6 Conclusions

The paper presents a system for managing the lifecycle of Data Sharing Agreements, electronic documents regulating data access and usage. The DSA system is made up of more components, which implements the phases of a DSA lifecycle: from DSA specification and editing, through DSA validation and analysis, till the refinement to low level policies which are directly enforceable. As future work, we will integrate the DSA system with an enforcement engine, proving their applicability in practical use cases provided by eHealth, Mobile, and e-Governance pilots.

References

1. Arenas, A.E., Aziz, B., Bicarregui, J., Wilson, M.D.: An Event-B approach to data sharing agreements. In: Méry, D., Merz, S. (eds.) IFM 2010. LNCS, vol. 6396, pp. 28–42. Springer, Heidelberg (2010)
2. Feige, U., Arenas, A.E., Aziz, B., Massonet, P., Ponsard, C.: Towards modelling obligations in Event-B. In: Börger, E., Butler, M., Bowen, J.P., Boca, P. (eds.) ABZ 2008. LNCS, vol. 5238, pp. 181–194. Springer, Heidelberg (2008)
3. Brodie, C., et al.: The coalition policy management portal for policy authoring, verification, and deployment. In: POLICY, pp. 247–249 (2008)
4. Casassa Mont, M., Matteucci, I., Petrocchi, M., Sbodio, M.L.: Enabling data sharing in the Cloud. HP Labs Technical report HPL-2012-22 (2012)
5. Craven, R., et al.: Expressive policy analysis with enhanced system dynamicity. In: ASIACCS (2009)
6. Hansen, R.R., Nielson, F., Nielson, H.R., Probst, C.W.: Static validation of licence conformance policies. In: ARES, pp. 1104–1111 (2008)
7. Kaljurand, K.: Attempto Controlled English as a Semantic Web Language. Ph.D. thesis, in Mathematics and Computer Science, Tartu Univ. (2007)
8. Lunardelli, A., Matteucci, I., Mori, P., Petrocchi, M.: A prototype for solving conflicts in XACML-based e-Health policies. In: Proceedings of the 26th IEEE International Symposium on Computer-Based Medical Systems, pp. 449–452 (2013)
9. Lupu, E.C., Sloman, M.: Conflicts in policy-based distributed systems management. IEEE Trans. Softw. Eng. **25**(6), 852–869 (1999)
10. Martinelli, F., Matteucci, I.: Preserving security properties under refinement. In: The 7th International Workshop on Software Engineering for Secure Systems, SESS (2011)
11. Martinelli, F., Matteucci, I., Petrocchi, M., Wiegand, L.: A formal support for collaborative data sharing. In: Quirchmayr, G., Basl, J., You, I., Xu, L., Weippl, E. (eds.) CD-ARES 2012. LNCS, vol. 7465, pp. 547–561. Springer, Heidelberg (2012)
12. Matteucci, I., Mori, P., Petrocchi, M., Wiegand, L.: Controlled data sharing in E-health. In: Socio Technical Aspects in Security and Trust, pp. 17–23. IEEE (2011)
13. Matteucci, I., Mori, P., Petrocchi, M.: Prioritized execution of privacy policies. In: Herranz, J., Damiani, E., State, R., Pietro, R. (eds.) DPM 2012 and SETOP 2012. LNCS, vol. 7731, pp. 133–145. Springer, Heidelberg (2013)
14. Matteucci, I., Petrocchi, M., Sbodio, M.L.: CNL4DSA: a controlled natural language for data sharing agreements. In: SAC Privacy on The Web (2010)

15. Matteucci, I., Petrocchi, M., Sbodio, M.L., Wiegand, L.: A design phase for data sharing agreements. In: Garcia-Alfaro, J., Navarro-Arribas, G., Cuppens-Boulahia, N., de Capitani di Vimercati, S. (eds.) DPM/SETOP 2011. LNCS, vol. 7122, pp. 25–41. Springer, Heidelberg (2012)
16. De Nicola, R., Ferrari, G.-L., Pugliese, R.: Programming access control: the KLAIM experience. In: Palamidessi, C. (ed.) CONCUR 2000. LNCS, vol. 1877, pp. 48–65. Springer, Heidelberg (2000)
17. OASIS, eXtensible Access Control Markup Language (XACML) Ver. 3.0 (2013)
18. Rensink, A., Gorrieri, R.: Vertical implementation. Inf. Comput. **170**(1), 95–133 (2001)
19. Saaty, T.L.: How to make a decision: the analytic hierarchy process. Eur. J. Oper. Res. **48**(1), 9–26 (1990)
20. Scalavino, E., Gowadia, V., Lupu, E.C.: PAES: policy-based authority evaluation scheme. In: Gudes, E., Vaidya, J. (eds.) Data and Applications Security 2009. LNCS, vol. 5645, pp. 268–282. Springer, Heidelberg (2009)
21. Scalavino, E., Russello, G., Ball, R., Gowadia, V., Lupu, E.C.: An opportunistic authority evaluation scheme for data security in crisis management scenarios. In: ASIACCS10
22. Swarup, V., Seligman, L., Rosenthal, A.: A data sharing agreement framework. In: Bagchi, A., Atluri, V. (eds.) ICISS 2006. LNCS, vol. 4332, pp. 22–36. Springer, Heidelberg (2006)
23. Swarup, V., et al.: Specifying data sharing agreements. In: POLICY, pp. 157–162 (2006)
24. Coco Cloud Consortium, Deliverable 4.2 First DSA Management Infrastructure (2015). http://www.coco-cloud.eu/deliverables. Accessed 07 June 2016

A Process for Data Protection Impact Assessment Under the European General Data Protection Regulation

Felix Bieker[1]([⊠]), Michael Friedewald[2], Marit Hansen[1], Hannah Obersteller[1], and Martin Rost[1]

[1] Unabhängiges Landeszentrum für Datenschutz Schleswig-Holstein (Independent Centre for Privacy Protection Schleswig-Holstein), Kiel, Germany
{fbieker,marit.hansen,hobersteller,mrost}@datenschutzzentrum.de
[2] Fraunhofer Institute for Systems and Innovation Research ISI, Karlsruhe, Germany
michael.friedewald@isi.fraunhofer.de

Abstract. With the General Data Protection Regulation there will be a legal obligation for controllers to conduct a Data Protection Impact Assessment for the first time. This paper examines the new provisions in detail and examines ways for their successful implementation. It proposes a process which operationalizes established requirements ensuring the appropriate attention to fundamental rights as warranted by the GDPR, incorporates the legislation's new requirements and can be adapted to suit the controller's needs.

Keywords: Data Protection · Data Protection Impact Assessment · General Data Protection Regulation · Privacy · Privacy Impact Assessment

1 Introduction

While the proliferation of technological innovation has made the processing of personal data by automated means ubiquitous, the enforcement of the individual's rights has not been at the forefront of concern. Although the European Union's (EU) Charter of Fundamental Rights (CFR) is equipped with a new right to the protection of personal data, which accompanies the well-established right to private life, there has been a disconnect between the debate of rights protection and the implementation of new technologies. Carrying out a Data Protection Impact Assessment, while keeping in mind its purpose of ensuring the protection of individual rights, is able to bridge this divide. In order to help organizations and enterprises to assess the data protection impact of their processing of data, the now EU General Data Protection Regulation (GDPR), under the conditions of its Article 35, prescribes the execution of a Data Protection Impact Assessment (DPIA). A DPIA is an instrument to identify and analyze risks for individuals, which exist due to the use of a certain technology or system by an organization in their various roles (as citizens, customers, patients,

S. Schiffner et al. (Eds.): APF 2016, LNCS 9857, pp. 21–37, 2016.
DOI: 10.1007/978-3-319-44760-5_2

etc.). On the basis of the outcome of the analysis, the appropriate measures to remedy the risks should be chosen and implemented. Since the inception of impact assessments there have also been approaches to adapt a model for the area of privacy and data protection. However, as there was no obligation to carry out such an assessment, these attempts had a wide range. This will change once the GDPR comes into force. Data protection authorities are the logical proponents of a comprehensive and operational model for these assessments.

In the following, previous models for Privacy Impact Assessment (PIA) will be briefly introduced (Sect. 2), the legal requirements of the GDPR will be analyzed (Sect. 3) and a methodology, in a broad sense, based on operational models outlined (Sect. 4). It is concluded that the process outlined in this paper realizes the full potential of DPIA with regard to the protection of fundamental rights as envisaged by the GDPR and provides a convenient instrument, built on established for controllers to comply with legal requirements (Sect. 5).

2   Related Work

Even though the current EU data protection regime, the Data Protection Directive 95/46/EC, does not foresee a DPIA, the concept has been discussed within the EU before. In response to recommendations by the European Commission [1,2], the Article 29 Working Party set out general requirements for PIAs [3,4]: any process had to contain provisions on the evaluation of data protection risks and incorporate the concept of data protection targets. In conformity with Article 8 Data Protection Directive 95/46/EC the process had to include requirements for the processing of special kinds of data, such as ethnicity, political or religious beliefs as well as health data. While parts of the concept of risk assessment could be incorporated in a PIA, the Working Party stressed that regarding legal requirements compliance could not be optional and that no discretion could be awarded to the organization under any circumstances. These demands can be seen as minimum requirements.

In parallel, there have been conceptualizations in academia based on methodologies developed inter alia in the UK, Canada, Australia and the USA [5] and industry [6], which follow their own respective methodologies based on the varying interests. Furthermore, the data protection authorities of the UK and France developed their own approaches to PIA. However, as these procedures were developed well before a legal obligation to conduct a DPIA, they are largely phrased as mere recommendations and the UK Information Commissioner's Office (ICO) Code of Practice is explicitly issued in order to promote good practices under Article 51 of the UK Data Protection Act, which does not impose a legal obligation to conduct a PIA. Further, ICO and to some extent also the French Commission Nationale de l'Informatique et des Libertés (CNIL) follow a checklist approach. While this makes it easy for organizations to carry out an assessment, it also entails the risk of overly focusing on the points set out instead of adapting the process to the specific risks and requirements of an individual data processing operation.

2.1   The UK Information Commissioner's Office Privacy Impact Assessment Code of Practice

The generic PIA model [7] developed by ICO defines PIA as a process to assess and reduce the risks of a given project for privacy. In order to systematically assess these risks an organization should apply PIA throughout the entire life-cycle of a project, from development to implementation. It defines six phases for assessment

1. Firstly, the necessity for an assessment and its scope should be examined. This may depend on the sensitivity of the data processed as well as the personnel and resources allocated to the project.
2. An assessment of data flows during all phases of processing, including access rights follows.
3. This information is then used to identify the risks for privacy and possible solutions.
4. The Code of Practice explains that the surveillance of users or loss of data are not only liable to affect users' rights, but also pose financial risks for the organization itself.
5. It refers to data minimization, training of employees in handling personal data and the implementation of technical security measures to protect the data. Although ICO takes a tiered approach to risks – ranking from elimination to acceptance of a risk – it emphasizes that legal obligations have to be fulfilled.
6. Lastly, the results should be secured and implemented in the project plan. During each phase, internal and external consultations should accompany the assessment and involve stakeholders whose rights may be affected.

2.2   The Privacy Impact Assessment Developed by the French Commission Nationale de l'Informatique et des Libertés

The CNIL's [8] methodology was developed to respond to risks for data protection, especially with regard to the rights of the individuals concerned. According to CNIL PIAs are aimed at finding technical and organizational measures to counter risks for rights of the data subjects. It emphasizes that these rights have to be upheld. Therefore, PIA is a continuous cycle, which starts with the definition of the data processed, including particularly the purposes of the processing and the persons concerned as well as the proportionality of the operation. This further extends to existing or planned control mechanisms.

In a further step the data protection risks have to be identified and assessed to ensure they are addressed appropriately. For this, it has to be ascertained how seriously any acts, omissions or circumstances which may occur as well as the use of certain (technical) tools, would interfere with the individuals' rights. These consequences are then ranked depending on their gravity and likeliness of occurrence. Lastly, it has to be decided whether the results of the assessment are satisfactory or whether the assessment has to be repeated. In addition, a report, detailing the assessment of risks and the findings, should be prepared and submitted to the data protection authority by request.

3   Legal Requirements

As it has been published in the EU's Official Journal, the GDPR according to its Articles 88(1) and 91(2) will be applicable from 25 May 2018 and replace the current Data Protection Directive 95/46/EC. It will be directly effective in the Member States as prescribed by Article 288(2) TFEU. The obligation to carry out a DPIA, as well as its minimum requirements are provided in Article 35 GDPR.

3.1   Conducting a Data Protection Impact Assessment

When a high risk for the rights of individual concerned is likely to emanate from the nature, scope, context or purposes of data processing, a DPIA has to be carried out according to Article 35(1) GDPR. Paragraph 3 lists examples of when such a high risk is likely to occur

(a) When data are systematically and extensively evaluated to analyze the personality of a natural person based on automated processing, including profiling, and decisions which have legal or similarly serious consequences for those concerned,
(b) when sensitive data or data on criminal convictions or penalties are processed in large scale, or
(c) when public areas are monitored systematically on a large scale.

With the new provision, the EU legislator demands the identification of risks: The controller has to assess whether there is a risk in order to determine whether a DPIA has to be conducted. However, this approach is not to be confused with the general procedure of risk management. The latter usually addresses risks for an organization and its activities. This is not the case in Article 35(1) GDPR, which concerns the risk for the rights and freedoms of individuals. Thus, unlike in risk management, there is no acceptable residual risk and every processing of personal data is an interference with the individual rights and freedoms and has to be justified.

Where necessary, the controller has to review whether the processing is still compliant with the findings of the DPIA according to Article 35(11) GDPR. According to the provision this is the case at least when there is a change in the risk posed by the processing of data. The European Parliament's proposal included an obligatory biannual review of the compliance with data protection provisions to demonstrate that the processing of personal data is compliant to the DPIA. While this was not adopted in the final version, it is clear that a change in the risk is merely one of the options for a review of the DPIA. Such a necessity however, is also brought about by changes in technology (i.e. when new technologies allowing for data minimization) or when the modes of data processing are changed.

Further, the data protection authorities are authorized to enumerate cases of data processing which do and do not require a DPIA under Article 35(4) and (5) GDPR in specific lists. Even though Article 35(3) GDPR already lists categories where a high risk is likely to occur, it can be useful to enumerate further instances that clearly demonstrate a high level of interference with the rights of individuals, such as big data or processing of any special categories of personal data as enumerated in Article 9(1) GDPR. However, as the compilation of a list under Article 35(5) – cases where the necessity of a DPIA can be rejected under all circumstances – is not obligatory, this should not be pursued by data protection authorities. Article 35(1) GDPR already requires a high risk for the rights of individuals in order to require a DPIA. The high level of protection of fundamental rights such as the right to private life according to Article 7 CFR and data protection under Article 8 CFR envisaged by Recitals 1 through 4 and 10 as well as Article 1(1) and (2) GDPR mandates that any high risk for the rights of an individual be subject to all relevant safeguards, including a DPIA.

According to Article 35(10) GDPR the obligation to conduct a DPIA is limited when it comes to public authorities relying on legal bases of EU or national law, the law regulates the specific processing operations and a DPIA has already been carried out as part of the legislative procedure. However, this incurs a risk with regard to the actual processing of personal data in a specific case. Although the specific processing operations are to be regulated in the relevant law, this has necessarily to be achieved in a general manner and cannot cover the specific setting of data processing in every instance regulated. Thus, risks that are realized at the implementation stage are not assessed. A further concern in this regard is that privacy-enhancing technologies may not yet be available at the time of the legislation. Accordingly, while a general DPIA in the course of the legislative process is welcome, each individual implementation calls for a separate specific DPIA to assess its own specific risks. Of course, these specific assessments can be built on top of the general DPIA and thereby would consume significantly less resources.

3.2   Requirements for a Data Protection Impact Assessment

The GDPR itself merely provides a minimum standard for carrying out a DPIA, as stipulated by Article 35(7) GDPR. The starting point is a systematic description of the envisaged data processing and its purposes, including, where applicable, the legitimate interests of the controller under Article 35(7)(a) GDPR. In order to facilitate the considerations as to the nature, sources and seriousness of the risk, the controller must involve data subjects in the process where appropriate and give the persons concerned a chance to express their views on the intended processing (Article 35(9) GDPR). With this information the necessity and proportionality of the processing in relation to its purposes as well as the risks for the rights of the persons concerned can be assessed according to Article 35(7)(b) and (c) GDPR. Lastly, any DPIA has to contain measures to remedy the risks identified, including safeguards, security mechanisms and measures to protect personal data and to demonstrate compliance with the GDPR as a whole (Article 35(7)(d) GDPR). An example of this last category is the measures to be taken in case of a breach of personal data under Articles 33 and 34 GDPR, i.e. the notification of the data protection authority and – where the breach is likely to result in a high risk for the individuals – a communication to the data subject.

Article 35(8) GDPR provides that compliance with codes of conduct according to Article 40 GDPR is a factor which must be taken into account when assessing the impact of the processing operations. However, this step must also take into consideration the rights and legitimate interests of data subjects and other persons concerned by the processing.

A DPIA report can also be helpful with regard to the certification process as envisaged under Article 42 GDPR. With regard to the certification mechanisms and data protection seals and marks, which are to be developed by the Member States, the data protection authorities and the European Data Protection Board, Article 42(1) GDPR employs the same phrase of demonstrating compliance with this Regulation as Article 35(7)(d) GDPR. A DPIA report may thus facilitate the certification process: It contains several elements, such as data flows or actors and their roles in the processing, which are also of interest for this evaluation. However, in order to realize the common, high standard of protection within the entire EU as set out in the GDPR, the mere compliance with legal obligations should not give way to a guaranteed certification within the sense of Article 42 GDPR. As the GDPR incorporates general data protection principles, for instance data protection by design and default in Article 25 GDPR, an organization striving to be certified should incorporate processes and technologies which further these principles in order to demonstrate full compliance.

Regarding the documentation or presentation of results, the GDPR does not include any explicit provisions. Article 36(1) GDPR requires that the competent data protection authority has to be consulted in cases where the absence of the measures taken by the controller in accordance with the results of the DPIA would lead to a high risk for individual rights. However, as Article 36(3)(e) GDPR merely states that the DPIA is to be provided to the data protection authority by the controller it does not stipulate any further requirements for the DPIA itself.

4 Elements of a Data Protection Impact Assessment

The process outlined below (Fig. 1) is the basis of the suggested DPIA process [9]. It has been derived from the extensive analysis of existing processes [5] and combines procedural as well as evaluation elements, which were tested and approved in practice in the EU projects PIAF and SAPIENT in an extensive empirical assessment of existing PIA schemes that the authors carried out in collaboration with Trilateral Research [10–12]. The process developed ensures that results can be reproduced and verified, enabling inter alia the competent data protection authorities to check whether all legal obligations have been satisfied. The process allows for comparison of different solutions and is technology-neutral.

The process consists of three stages, which are described in the following.

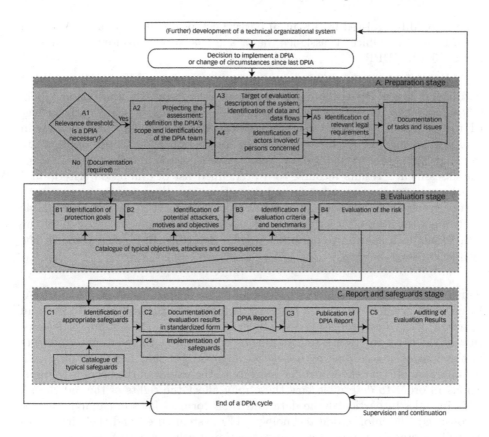

Fig. 1. DPIA process

4.1   Preparation Stage

Firstly, the controller should consider whether there is a legal obligation to carry out a DPIA. As described above, this is the case under the conditions of Article 35(1) GDPR, when a high risk for the rights of individuals is likely, especially in the cases expressly mentioned in Article 35(3) GDPR, i.e. profiling, sensitive data or systematic surveillance of public places are concerned. Further, in order to assess whether a DPIA has to be conducted, the lists concerning cases when a DPIA has to be carried out and which kinds of data processing are exempt, which are to be published by the data protection authorities under Article 35(4) and (5) GDPR have to be consulted.

Projecting the Assessment. If a DPIA is to be carried out, the goals and scope of the assessment should first be laid out. The personnel assigned to carry out the assessment has to have sufficient resources and competence available to achieve an objective analysis. Ideally, the person responsible for the development and implementation should be responsible for carrying out the DPIA.

They should be assisted by a neutral party, such as quality assurance. Where a Data Protection Officer is assigned, he or she has to be consulted according to Article 35(2) GDPR.

Standard Data Protection Model. The Standard Data Protection Model [13] is useful to implement the assessment as envisaged by the European legislator in order to demonstrate that a specific system for data processing is in compliance with the requirements of data protection and identify appropriate safeguards. In order to enable data protection authorities and the public to trace the assessment's results recourse to a predefined list of evaluation criteria and benchmarks, and safeguards can be taken. However, the primary purpose is to ensure transparency as warranted by Article 35(9) GDPR, rather than enable controllers to check off a list instead of assessing the risks for the rights of the individuals in a specific scenario, as will be described in further detail in the evaluation stage below.

Target of Evaluation. The target of evaluation defines the scope of the DPIA. In order to evaluate whether a high risk is likely, the controller has to have an overview of the data processing in question. At this point, the systematic description of the data processing and its purposes, as well as the legitimate interests of the controller according to Article 35(7)(a) GDPR thus has to be prepared. It is paramount that the controller is aware of the extent of the processing operations in order to determine how these may affect the rights of the individual. This includes in particular the data and their formats for storage and transfer (protocols), the information technology (IT) systems used and their interfaces as well as processes, procedures, and functional roles. A DPIA as required by Article 35 GDPR may not be limited to a single component or function, but must describe the predefined object of evaluation in its entirety, including its technical as well as the organizational implementation at the controller level. This concerns any use cases that are to be implemented and should pay particular regard to the purposes of the data processing, Further, it is necessary to comply with data protection principles such as purpose limitation (Article 5(1)(b) GDPR) and data minimization (Article 5(1)(c) GDPR) and, where necessary, competing interests have to be balanced in order to ensure the protection of fundamental rights.

Identification of Actors Involved/Persons Concerned. Equally important as the proper identification of the target of evaluation in this phase is the proper identification of actors involved and persons concerned. Aside from organizations and persons participating in the development or implementation (and thereby potential attackers), all persons affected by the use should be involved, such as

- the manufacturer of the test object,
- operators e.g. as processors (data centers, internet service providers),
- the controller employees,

- the persons concerned in their respective roles as citizens, patients, customers, employees, etc.,
- third parties who take note of personal data, either by chance (persons randomly present) or by intent (security services).

Identification of Relevant Legal Requirements. While the GDPR has a wide scope of application – i.e. whenever an establishment within the EU processes personal data or personal data of data subjects who are in the EU are processed according to Article 3 GDPR – it does not regulate all legal aspects exhaustively. There are provisions which leave the Member States a certain degree of discretion in the implementation of the measures, e.g. for the public sector under Article 2(2) GDPR or the health and social security sector in Article 9(2)(h) GDPR. Furthermore, there may be sector specific national legislation inter alia for the areas of telecommunications, social security, rules on professional secrecy or the protection of minors. However, as a DPIA deals with processes and technical operations, these rules are only of concern if they are implemented directly in the process.

Documentation of Tasks and Issues. The results of the preparation stage have to be documented. This should be done following a standardized procedure in the form of a scoping report.

4.2 Evaluation Stage

Identification of Protection Goals. The requirements of data protection are prescribed by law and can be operationalized as protection goals (as developed in [14–18]) which have proven very effective in IT and information security. This provides a methodology fit to elucidate risks that have to be covered by appropriate measures and safeguards.

Six protection goals have been established (Fig. 2): The classical risks of IT security are incorporated with the first three protection goals (1) availability, (2) integrity and (3) confidentiality.[1] Building on this framework, three additional data protection specific protection goals were formulated: (4) unlinkability, (5) transparency, (6) intervenability.

Availability is the requirement to have data accessible, comprehensible and processable in a timely fashion for authorized entities. Integrity represents the need for reliability and non-repudiation concerning information, i.e. unmodified, authentic and correct data. Confidentiality concerns the need for secrecy, viz. the non-disclosure of certain entities within the IT system in question. Unlinkability ensures data cannot be linked across different domains and/or be used for purposes differing from the original intent. Transparency means that the data

---

[1] Note that Article 32(1)(b) GDPR, in addition to the classical security goals confidentiality, integrity, and availability, also stipulates the resilience of systems and services processing personal data as an objective.

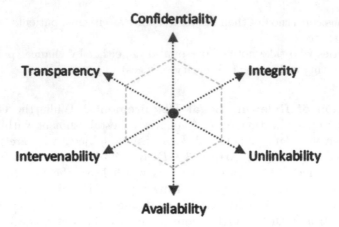

Fig. 2. Protection Goals

subjects have knowledge of all relevant circumstances and factors regarding the processing of their personal data. Lastly, intervenability entails the control of the data subjects, as well as the controller or supervisory authority over the personal data.

Note that the protection goals are meant to represent the perspective of the data subject whose rights are at stake. If, e.g., transparency is violated because the controller does not inform the data subject appropriately as required by law, this has to be tackled in the DPIA: not knowing who processes data for which purpose and being deprived of possibilities to intervene – even if the personal data is kept safe and secure – infringes the data subject's rights and thus constitutes a risk.

Each protection goal incorporates further, derived protection goals, each of which can be deduced from legal provisions in the GDPR. Alternatively the central principles of data protection law can be assigned to a specific protection goal. However, there are certain legal provisions which cannot be accommodated within the concept, especially the check for lawfulness of processing, which has to be done prior to any Data Protection Impact Assessment.

The protection goals are in a state of dual interplay. This leads to a tension, as usually the strengthening of one protection goal leads to the detriment of its counterpart. The evaluation therefore has to achieve the proper balance between the protection goals. For instance, a system that processes highly confidential data will restrict the access to the data as much as possible, thereby limiting the availability. Still authorized entities should be able to access the data, but depending on the implemented safeguards they may need to undergo a cumbersome process, e.g. applying a four-eye principle and demanding necessary paperwork before access is granted, requiring specific hardware for access of the clear text etc.

Identification of Potential Attackers, Motives and Objectives. While in IT security threats are usually assessed from an organizational point of view, in a DPIA the perspective is that of the persons concerned. Consequently, attackers are not limited to third parties, but can also be rule-abiding internal users of the organization itself, e.g. employees or contractors gaining access to personal data. The goal of a DPIA is, correspondingly, not the protection of business processes but of the rights and interests of an organization's customers, employees, etc. Thus, it has to be ascertained whether the following organizations pose a risk to the rights and interests of the individual

- Public authorities, e.g.
  • Security services: Department of State, police, intelligence services, military, etc.
  • Public benefit administration, i.e. social security services
  • Statistics agencies
  • Failing authorities, which open spaces for illegal activities
- Enterprises, e.g.
  • Technology companies, system integrators, IT providers (access, content, etc.)
  • Banks, insurance companies
  • Credit agencies, address and data trading companies
  • Advertising agencies
  • Advocacy groups and lobbyists
  • Employers
- Health care, e.g.
  • Hospitals, doctors
  • Public and private health insurers
- Research, e.g.
  • Medical, social research
  • Universities

There is, of course, a conflict of interest when the organization conducting the DPIA is also seen as a serious risk for data protection. In order to avoid any blind spots in the risk evaluation, there should at least be retroactive external supervision. Further, an organization's data protection officer, where one is appointed, is by definition expected to take the point of view of the persons affected by the processing.

Identification of Evaluation Criteria and Benchmarks. Every processing of data, even if it is entirely in compliance with the legal requirements, is an interference with the individual's rights to private life and data protection as guaranteed by Articles 7 and 8 CFR. Therefore, while the IT-Grundschutz methodology [19] developed by the German Federal Office for Information Security (BSI) has demonstrated its value in practice, the standard of protection cannot be simply measured in severity of damage and likelihood of occurrence categories when it comes to data protection. As every processing interferes with fundamental rights and thus has to be justified and assessed under the conditions of Articles 8(2) and 52(1) CFR in order to be in accordance with the law, it follows that the level of protection has to be normal by default, as detailed below. Due to the pivotal nature of fundamental rights and the fact that their protection is the very basis of data protection law, a lower level must not be considered. However, depending on the use of specific data or kinds of processing, the intensity of interference can rise to a high or very high level. The three protection standards are thus

- Normal: personal data are processed and there are no scenarios in which the nature of the processing shows potential for a high intensity of interference.
- High: special categories of personal data according to Article 9 GDPR are processed and thus require a high protection standard by law and/or the persons concerned depend on the decisions/services of the organization, if
  - the high intensity of interference of the data processing can lead to serious consequences for the persons concerned and/or
  - there are no effective safeguards, methods of intervention for the persons concerned (including the availability of judicial redress).
- Very high: personal data requiring a high protection standard are processed and the person concerned depends on the decisions/services of the organization to an existential level and there are additional risks posed by insufficient data security or illegitimate changes of the purposes of processing, which the persons concerned cannot become aware of and/or correct by themselves.

Additionally, a high protection standard may be required when there is a cumulative effect of various aspects of the data processing, which by themselves do not demand a high level. This may be the case where data from a large group of persons are collected or when data from fewer persons are collected for various purposes and persons concerned are affected in various roles.

Evaluation of the Risk. At the core of the evaluation is the comparison of the controller's envisaged measures or those determined in the course of the assessment with a catalogue of reference measures (Fig. 3). Currently, the technical working group of the conference of German data protection authorities (AK Technik) is developing a catalogue of such data protection measures [20].

Table 1 contains selected measures which – when implemented correctly – can ensure the safeguarding of the protection goals as detailed above in Fig. 2. While this list is generic, the measures taken may have to be updated in line with the advance of the state of the art, as referred to in Recitals 78 and 83 and Articles 25(1) and 32 GDPR. Additionally, due to its generic nature the list cannot be used as a mere checklist. The mere implementation of a listed measure does not satisfy the risk evaluation. For instance, a system, to ensure confidentiality, may implement a rights and roles concept. However, this alone cannot satisfy the requirement of confidentiality. If the rights are granted overly generous and roles are not clearly separated, the concept is not effective. Therefore, the controller will have to explain how the rights and roles concept of the specific system in question ensures confidentiality of the data processed.

Table 1. Examples of generic protection measures

Protection goal	Component	Measure
Ensuring availability	Data, systems, processes	Redundancy, protection, repair strategies
Ensuring integrity	Data	Comparing hash values
	Systems	Limitation of write permissions, regular integrity checks
	Processes	Setting references values (min/max), control of regulation
Ensuring confidentiality	Data, systems	Encryption
	Processes	Rights and roles concepts
Ensuring unlinkability through definitions of purposes	Data	Anonymity, pseudonymity, attribute-based credentials
	Systems	Separation (isolation) of stored data, systems and processes
	Processes	Identity management, anonymity infrastructures, audits
Ensuring unlinkability through definitions of purposes	Data	Documentation, logging
	Systems	System documentation, logging of configuration changes
	Processes	Documentation of procedures, logging
Ensuring intervenability through anchor points	Data	Access of persons concerned to their data (information, rectification, blocking, deletion)
	Systems	Off-switch
	Processes	Helpdesk/single point of contact for modification/deletion, change management

In the course of the risk evaluation any deviances from the reference measures have to be assessed in the light of their gravity and in how far they compromise the protection goals. Turning back to the example of the rights and roles concept, this means that if the controller did not even implement such a basic measure, it is prima facia doubtful whether the system can satisfy the requirement of confidentiality. Where the analysis demonstrates such failures to comply with protection goals, such a finding – from the viewpoint of a data protection authority – leads to an assumption of deficiencies in data protection and has to be redressed. The data protection authority in its consultancy role may provide advice on remedies.

In practice it can easily be ascertained if criteria and benchmarks have not been satisfied through recourse to this model, as the envisaged measures and the quality of the implementation according to the protection standard will be missing. If different measures are chosen, the assessment may be more complex

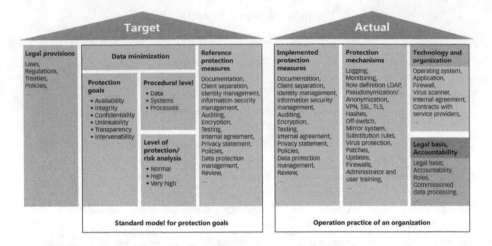

Fig. 3. Risk-assessment through target/actual comparison

and a proof of appropriateness and at least equivalence to the reference measure will have to be provided.

Taking into account the proper measures identified at this stage, the necessity and proportionality of the data processing envisaged by the controller can be assessed, as prescribed by Article 35(7)(b) and (c).

4.3   Report and Safeguards Stage

Identification and Implementation of Appropriate Safeguards. Based on the results of the evaluation, a plan for risk management has to be prepared. According to Article 35(7)(d) GDPR the DPIA must contain measures to remedy the risks identified including safeguards, security mechanisms and measures to protect the personal data, as detailed above with regard to the reference measures, and demonstrate compliance with the GDPR as a whole. Particularly with regard to the rights of individuals it is not acceptable to follow a de minimis approach and rank risks for these rights as acceptable when only few persons are concerned. However, there is the possibility to prioritize risks and take those measures with the highest benefit for the persons concerned in compliance with legal requirements. The action plan should explicitly detail

- which safeguards are taken to reduce the gravity of or avoid interference with fundamental rights or specific harm for the persons concerned,
- who is responsible to implement the safeguards and the persons to be consulted,
- by when these safeguards are to be implemented and which resources are available,
- the criteria to measure the results of the safeguards, and
- who is responsible to evaluate and document these criteria.

The selection of appropriate safeguards is facilitated by the list of generic safeguards as provided above for risk assessment (Sect. 4.2).

Documentation and Publication of a Report on Evaluation Results. In order to achieve the intended effects of a DPIA it is necessary to comprehensively document and publish a report on the findings. Like the scoping report it should follow a standardized form to facilitate evaluation and comparison by data protection authorities, enterprises and the public. For the latter, a special version of the report, excluding any business secrets, may be created. Nonetheless, such a shortened version must not be used to conceal negative findings, but should be subject to legitimate and documented grounds.

Auditing of Evaluation Results. In order to ensure that the DPIA has been duly conducted, the DPIA report should be evaluated by an independent third party – where appropriate also the competent data protection authority. This includes especially an appropriate handling of conflicts of interest, taking due regard of the rights and interests of the persons concerned when selecting safeguards, adequate information of the public and ensuring that the envisaged safeguards are actually implemented.

Supervision and Continuation. A DPIA is not a singular and linear process, but rather has to be repeated to ensure continuous supervision over the lifetime of a project. Accordingly, Article 35(11) GDPR calls for a review at least when there are changes in the risks posed by the processing of data. Such changes may occur whenever organizational or legal conditions change or new risks for data protection in general are identified. It then has to be ensured that the safeguards chosen are able to adapt to these changes.

5 Conclusions

Although DPIA is a relatively new instrument in most of the Member States, it can be extremely helpful to identify risks for the rights of persons concerned by the use of new data processing technology. It can be regarded as an early warning system enabling all actors to systematically address potential deficiencies in a process. Controllers can foresee risks and their causes and are thus enabled to distribute responsibilities and competences accordingly in order to implement data protection at the core of the operations. A DPIA allows for better decision-making at the implementation stage and avoids the need for costly subsequent improvements or potential leaks of personal data. Thus, for controllers it is an important instrument to demonstrate the compliance with legal requirements and can build trust between the controller and its customers, who are empowered to make informed decision when using the controller's services. A standardized DPIA procedure also helps data protection authorities to find weaknesses and legal infringements, but also allows for a better overview on best practices which is important to advise controllers on how to improve their products or processes.

Once the legal obligation to carry out a DPIA comes into force in 2018, a standard will be required to ensure an effective implementation of this legislation. With the interdisciplinary methodology proposed in this paper, which is based on and expands components that have been implemented successfully in practice, the full potential of DPIA can be realized. This is particularly true with regard to the importance of fundamental rights protection as the raison d'être of data protection legislation, as can be seen inter alia from Recitals 1–4, 10, 47, 51–53, 102 and Article 1(2) GDPR, which is achieved by the incorporation of the data protection goals in the process. Through their operationalization with regard to the new data protection framework, this methodology provides a convenient instrument for controllers to assess risks and enables them to offer better services and improves their ability to compete in a market for privacy-friendly solutions, which also incorporates the requirements imposed by the upcoming EU legislation.

Acknowledgement. This paper was partially funded by the European Commission under the 7th Framework Programme, grant agreement no. 261698 (SAPIENT project) and the Bundesministerium für Bildung und Forschung (German Federal Ministry of Education and Research) for the project Forum Privatheit – Selbstbestimmtes Leben in der Digitalen Welt (Privacy-Forum), www.forum-privatheit.de.

References

1. European Commission: Recommendation of 12 May 2009 on the implementation of privacy and data protection principles in applications supported by radio-frequency identification. OJ L 122/47 of 16 May 2009. http://eur-lex.europa.eu/legal-content/EN/TXT/PDF/?uri=CELEX:32009H0387&from=EN
2. European Commission: Recommendation of 9 March 2012 on preparations for the roll-out of smart metering systems. OJ L 73/9 of 13 March 2012. http://eur-lex.europa.eu/legal-content/EN/TXT/PDF/?uri=CELEX:32012H0148&from=EN
3. Article 29 Working Party: Opinion 5/2010 on the Industry Proposal for a Privacy and Data Protection Impact Assessment Framework for RFID Applications. WP 175 (2010). http://ec.europa.eu/justice/data-protection/article-29/documentation/opinion-recommendation/files/2010/wp175_en.pdf
4. Article 29 Working Party: Opinion 07/2013 on the Data Protection Impact Assessment Template for Smart Grid and Smart Metering Systems ('DPIA Template') prepared by Expert Group 2 of the Commission's Smart Grid Task Force. WP 209 (2013). http://ec.europa.eu/justice/data-protection/article-29/documentation/opinion-recommendation/files/2013/wp209_en.pdf
5. Wright, D., De Hert, P. (eds.): Privacy Impact Assessment. Springer, Heidelberg (2012)
6. ISO/IEC 29134: Information technology – Security techniques – Privacy impact assessment – Guidelines. ISO/IEC, International Organization for Standardization (2016)

7. ICO (Information Commissioner's Office): Conducting privacy impact assessments code of practice. ICO (2014). https://ico.org.uk/media/for-organisations/documents/1595/pia-code-of-practice.pdf
8. CNIL (Commission Nationale de l'Informatique et des Libertés): Privacy Impact Assessment: Methodology (how to carry out a PIA). CNIL (2015). http://www.cnil.fr/fileadmin/documents/en/CNIL-PIA-1-Methodology.pdf
9. Friedewald, M., Bieker, F., Nebel, M., Obersteller, H., Rost, M.: Datenschutz-Folgenabschätzung - Ein Werkzeug für einen besseren Datenschutz. Forum Privatheit und selbstbestimmtes Leben in der digitalen Welt, Karlsruhe (2016). https://www.forum-privatheit.de
10. Wright, D., Gellert, R., Bellanova, R., Gutwirth, S., Langheinrich, M., Friedewald, M., Hallinan, D., Venier, S., Mordini, E.: Privacy Impact Assessment and Smart Surveillance: A State of the Art Report, Deliverable 3.1 SAPIENT Project (2013). http://www.sapient-project.eu
11. Wadhwa, K., Rodrigues, R.: Evaluating privacy impact assessments. Innov. Eur. J. Soc. Sci. Res. 26(1–2), 161–180 (2013)
12. Wright, D., Friedewald, M., Gellert, R.: Developing and testing a surveillance impact assessment methodology. Int. Data Priv. Law 5(1), 40–53 (2015)
13. AK Technik der Konferenz der Datenschutzbeauftragten des Bundes und der Länder, Schulz, G., Rost, M.: Das Standard-Datenschutzmodell – der Weg vom Recht zur Technik: Ein Datenschutzwerkzeug für Aufsichtsbehörden und verantwortliche Stellen (2015). https://www.datenschutzzentrum.de/uploads/sdm/SDM_Tagungsband2015_Hannover.pdf
14. Hansen, M., Jensen, M., Rost, M.: Protection goals for privacy engineering. In: 2015 International Workshop on Privacy Engineering (IWPE), Security and Privacy Workshops (SPW), pp. 159–166. IEEE (2015)
15. Rost, M., Pfitzmann, A.: Datenschutz-Schutzziele - revisited. DuD - Datenschutz und Datensicherheit 33, 353–358 (2009)
16. Rost, M., Bock, K.: Privacy by Design and the New Protection Goals, EuroPriSe Whitepaper (2011). https://www.european-privacy-seal.eu/AppFile/GetFile/ca6cdc46-d4dd-477d-9172-48ed5f54a99c
17. Hansen, M.: Top 10 mistakes in system design from a privacy perspective and privacy protection goals. In: Camenisch, J., Crispo, B., Fischer-Hübner, S., Leenes, R., Russello, G. (eds.) Privacy and Identity 2011. IFIP AICT, vol. 375, pp. 14–31. Springer, Heidelberg (2012)
18. Danezis, G., Domingo-Ferrer, J., Hansen, M., Hoepman, J.H., Le Métayer, D., Tirtea, R., Schiffner, S.: Privacy and Data Protection by Design - from policy to engineering, ENISA (2014). https://www.enisa.europa.eu/activities/identity-and-trust/library/deliverables/privacy-and-data-protection-by-design/at_download/fullReport
19. Bundesamt für Sicherheit in der Informationstechnik (Federal Office for Information Security): BSI-Standard 100-2, IT-Grundschutz Methodology (2008). https://www.bsi.bund.de/SharedDocs/Downloads/EN/BSI/Publications/BSIStandards/standard_100-2_e_pdf.pdf
20. Probst, T.: Generische Schutzmaßnahmen für Datenschutz-Schutzziele. DuD - Datenschutz und Datensicherheit 36, 439–444 (2012)

Bring Your Own Identity - Case Study from the Swiss Government

Gion Sialm[1] and Silvia Knittl[2(✉)]

[1] Federal Office of Information Technology,
Systems and Telecommunication FOITT, Bern, Switzerland
[2] CSC Deutschland Consulting GmbH, Wiesbaden, Germany
sknittl@csc.com

Abstract. Imagine that you are a citizen or a company and you are able to file your tax declaration or exchange governmental information by using your favourite existing electronic identity (eID), such as your bank or consumer account. At present, citizens and companies quite often have to create an individual account for almost every government application to share or exchange information. Enabling "bring your own identity" (ByoID) for eGovernment means that access management (AM) will gradually converge to create a single, user-friendly approach in the future. From a technical point of view, many of the necessary features and protocols already exist but have not yet been widely implemented in eGovernment environments. This poses a very complex challenge, both from an operational point of view and from an IT governance and compliance perspective. The only way to solve this is close collaboration among citizens, the private sector and the government. The basis will be an identity and access management (IAM) system that can be adapted to the comprehensive requirements resulting from the aforementioned collaboration. In this article, we describe the path the Swiss government has taken for establishing such a flexible IAM system from the IT providers' perspective while respecting security and privacy requirements.

1 IAM and Data Protection

The process of digitisation makes daily work easier by providing the possibility to do things such as shopping at any time from home or elsewhere in the world. The result for the user is a list with dozens of accounts and passwords. Hence, the efficient use of digital offerings still lacks an uniform identity and access management (IAM). People are very understanding when it comes to log-in to different companies' applications. However, when it comes to interactions with the government, people are not as understanding as with the private sector, since they see the government as one single "company". Therefore, they want to be able to log-in to all eGovernment applications with a single account or even reuse an existing account. Moreover, governments increasingly want to motivate people to use their electronic offerings in order to save money, as banks are doing with online banking. This means that such a transformation will have an impact on all levels, such as social, economic and political. On the governmental level, the government will gradually become an IT service provider. According to the

© Springer International Publishing Switzerland 2016
S. Schiffner et al. (Eds.): APF 2016, LNCS 9857, pp. 38–47, 2016.
DOI: 10.1007/978-3-319-44760-5_3

study prepared for the European Commission in [17], the prerequisites for the increased future use of eGovernment services are both trust and accessibility.

IAM is the core building block to implement trust and accessibility and to enable "bring your own identity" (ByoID). Holistic IAM provides the technical means to ensure protection against unauthorised processing while providing good usability for users. The basic function blocks of IAM are identity management (IM), access management (AM) and access governance (AG). IM covers the tasks involved with creating and maintaining an (electronic) identity. AM relies on IM and deals with authentication and authorization of electronic identities. This sounds very easy. But establishing an electronic identity (eID) that is accepted both by the government and the private sector is a huge challenge. However, this means that the IAM building block has to be very flexible while also providing high security. That is why strong AG will be essential in the future. AG is the functionality within the IAM discipline that is responsible for ensuring, inter alia, that:

- Policies and regulations are applied correctly
- Access to IT resources is managed according to their risk profile
- User access is documented for valid reasons and separation-of-duty conflicts are prevented
- Accountability, manageability and reporting to both business and IT owners is deployed

Figure 1 illustrates a simplified view of IAM from an IT-provider perspective. Depending on the type of data the IT resources are processing (personal data, health records, critical business information, etc.), they are subject to different kinds of compliance requirements. Examples are the Information Protection Ordinance [9], Data Protection Law [8] or Electronic Health Record Law [3]. One aspect of ensuring the data's privacy is to control who has access to the IT resources. The Swiss Data Protection Law states that "personal data must be protected against unauthorised processing through adequate technical and organisational measures" (Art. 7 in [8]). We will outline the complexity of this task from an IT provider's perspective and introduce the necessary IT components, such as a broker infrastructure in the following.

Switzerland is a federal republic, and the federal administration consists of seven federal departments and the Federal Chancellery. Each department consists of several federal offices or agencies (approximately 90) and about 40,000 employees. We will focus here mainly on IAM for the Swiss federal administration's applications as described in [12]. Outcomes of the Identity Network Switzerland [20] programme - which takes into account the confederation, the cantons, and the communes - will be considered where appropriate. A thorough analysis of the establishment of an eID that could be used nationally and internationally is part of a strategic project [14] and summarised in [22].

In the following, we delineate on the basis of the development steps, starting from an isolated approach in Sect. 2.1 and moving on to a modern microservice architecture in Sect. 2.4, how loosely coupled IAM microservices better support the implementation of legal requirements imposed by data privacy and other

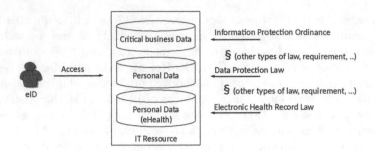

Fig. 1. Controlled access to IT resources

laws. Further, we outline in Sect. 2.3 that the need for delivering eGovernment services, beside legal requirements, was an additional strong driver for this development. While we demonstrate from the technical perspective that IAM could be implemented to address the various compliance aspects, we describe in Sect. 2.4 the challenges from the IT governance and management point of view.

2   IAM - from Silo to Services

2.1   Past IAM - Monolithic Şilos

In the past, direct interactions, such as business-to-business, were the core business of most companies. Client-server architectures helped to address this business. In this architecture, IAM was directly integrated into each application, because at that time each application provided mostly only name and password as an authentication method. Moreover, the application was usually connected to an identity directory such as the Active directory[1] from Microsoft. The separation of applications was even seen as a unique selling proposition against competitors, because separation provided high security.

A simplified outline of our environment following this architecture pattern is illustrated in Fig. 2. The Swiss government consists of seven departments, which are further divided into agencies. Every agency is supposed to serve its dedicated mission according its legislative basis. In order to fulfil their mission, purposive applications, such as tax processing applications for the tax office or data warehouse applications for the statistical office, had to be developed, installed and operated for the agencies. Every application had its own inbuilt IAM functionality.

Users, such as internal staff, staff from other agencies, citizens or people at companies needed to be registered and maintained on an individual application basis. Application owners were responsible for both administration and governance. Hence, every application owner was responsible for addressing compliance issues, such as identifying the laws and legal requirements that had to be followed according to the federal administration's IT processes [13]. From an IT

---

[1] https://msdn.microsoft.com/en-us/library/bb742424.aspx.

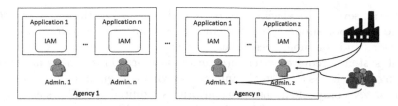

Fig. 2. IAM integrated in each application

governance perspective, the main drawbacks of this monolithic IAM set-up were poor scalability, high maintenance costs and a lack of a comprehensive overview concerning compliance. Questions, such as "who has access to what" or "what kind of access" individuals have at agency, department or even government level could only be answered by asking every application owner separately.

As consumer orientation (business-to-customer) became the main driver for business, Web application became the main key architecture. However, as the number of Web applications grew, users started to complain about the fact that they had to maintain a list of passwords to access applications. Therefore, organisations started to integrate all of their applications into a single personalised portal. This approach was tedious and expensive. For that reason, other solutions were required. By this time, a new approach for IAM appeared.

2.2 Near Past IAM - Service Orientation

A few years ago, IAM solutions were developed that were still monolithic but could be separated completely from Web applications. The advantages of this approach are obvious. There was no need to introduce a separate identity directory for each Web application. As a result IAM governance became easier by centralising the AM infrastructure while still giving the full freedom of AM to the agencies. Figure 3 shows the fact that IAM is provided as a dedicated service for the agencies. The increasing level of centralisation induced the necessity of having a formalised legal basis for providing IAM and other IT services by dedicated IT providers. Therefore, the relevant enactments came into effect delivering clear guidance on the roles and responsibilities of IT governance and management, such as [4,5]. IT management functions were partly consolidated and transformed to one dedicated agency.

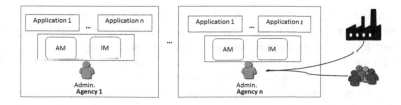

Fig. 3. IAM as a Service per Agency

But still, several drawbacks have to be tackled, such as the focus on internal staff and the poor support of governance requirements [16]. Externally hosted applications and commonly used platforms, such as Sharepoint or content management systems, require better integration support. This can be achieved by managing each site as a "normal" application within a tenant of an agency. This saves money, as only one license per platform is required and allows each agency to manage one or more sites. There is a strong need for supporting a centralised IM with decentralised AM structures. This enables citizens to register themselves just once for all Swiss government applications while allowing AM to remain on the agency side. Quite often, users already have (external) eIDs. Therefore, they demand to re-use these to simplify log-in and AM. This requires the possibility of linking different identities. In the next section, we describe how additional eGovernment requirements foster the need for a new approach to IAM.

2.3   eGovernment: New Requirements for IAM

As competition grew increasingly fierce on the market, close collaboration between companies became more and more important. Centralised AM was no longer an appropriate solution, as each company or organisational unit, rather than a centralised AM department, knew better who should have access to an application. Moreover, centralised AM also required centralised IM. As a consequence, sharing applications among different companies meant that employees again had to manage a list of passwords. A similar development could be observed in government infrastructures.

To cope with this, an IAM programme was launched [12], and requirements for future IAM were broadly gathered from the relevant stakeholders. An initial overview of the results is shown in [15]. The structuring of the requirements was aligned with the business attribute taxonomy according to the SABSA framework [18]. Of course, the attributes "access control" and "accessible" were requested most frequently by the interview partners, both from the technical as well as business side, in the context of an IAM programme. But "business enabled", "continuous" and "compliant" were also concerns voiced by many of the stakeholders.

The meaning of every illustrated business attribute is derived directly from the SABSA framework and adapted to the own context as needed. For example, in our context the requirement "business enabled" means support for seamless and smart eGovernment as defined in [17] and includes, inter alia, the following aspects:

- Government-to-government: support secure interactions between government agencies on the same federal level, but also between government agencies on different levels (international, national, federal, community)
- Government-to-business: support secure interactions of people at companies that have to interact with government agencies, e.g. for tax affairs, social security aspects, and many other government-to-business applications
- Government-to-citizens: support secure interactions between citizens and government agencies

The attribute "compliant" comprises both the needs to define the adequate legal foundations for IAM in the context of eGovernment and to ensure compliance of the IAM solution with the relevant laws. The requirement "continuous" includes the continuity of the technical systems and the related business processes. The more eGovernment applications are operational and accessible, the higher the need for the operation of the IAM solution around the clock. This is even more important for critical infrastructures, such as police applications, road control systems, etc. - and impacts the IT organisation of the provider for running IAM. Finally, easy-to-use interfaces and applications are a feature most stakeholders are asking for in their interaction with online government services. In the next section, we will outline our architecture to implement these requirements.

2.4   Present and Future IAM - Microservice Architecture

Figure 4 shows the current IAM architecture. It is a microservice architecture consisting of small decoupled services such as a reverse proxy, trust broker, identity provider, IM system and identity directories (for details, see also [19]). This architecture offers standardised application programming interfaces (APIs), meaning that the integration of all existing IAM components with the IAM broker could be accomplished quite easily. The usage of a dedicated API component makes it possible both to integrate existing directories and to seamlessly migrate from old applications on the mainframe to modern architectures such as Web applications and, ultimately, the commonly used SuisseID for citizens [21]. This broker architecture relies heavily on trust. Hence, a thorough IT governance is needed to maintain a high level of security. Explicitly managing trust is therefore essential in such a system.

Federation and ID Linking Services. In future, the IAM system will be even more strictly developed according to the standards defined for the so called SuisseTrustIAM (STIAM [7]). The STIAM-related standards are designed to provide generic IAM services for eGovernment, eHealth, eEducation and eEconomy in a standardised way across Switzerland. The most important service will be a broker infrastructure that allows the verification of attributes derived

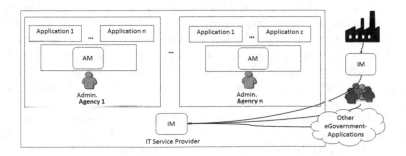

Fig. 4. IAM as a modular Service Application

from registers or directories for any subject that has been authenticated via its eID. Traceability to support compliance will also be a part of the STIAM functionality.

Subjects are able to re-use their already issued eID in the sense of ByoID. The issuers of such IDs need to be assigned an appropriate trust level according to the related eCH-standard (see eCH-0170: eID Qualitätsmodell). The criteria for defining the trust level are the identification procedure (physical presence, quality and validation of assertions), the credential-issuing process or the security of the authentication mechanism. The Swiss standardisation working group developed the STIAM standards with an eye to being compliant with the relevant European and international standards.

By implementing this modular IAM, the following improvements are achieved: easier access via a self-service portal for all types of users; users are able to customise individual configurations for fine granular access as requested in [3] and link their existing external accounts (e.g. bank account) to agencies' accounts and vice versa. Additionally, the administrators' work is also simplified by linking accounts and by managing internal staff and external users in the same way. Moreover, it is even possible to integrate applications from the private sector into government processes or vice-versa, resulting in lower costs for the government and the private sector.

IAM: Future Work. In the sections above, we described how the functional development of IAM has evolved from a silo approach to modular open architecture. Widespread technical standards are available and have been the main drivers of this development. The ongoing concentration, consolidation and migration of the former IAM silos to open architecture on the one hand, while opening interactions for eGovernment across the boundaries of own organisations on the other hand, imposes new challenges on the steering and management of IAM services.

The implementation of such trust and federation services is supported by technical standards that are already in place and incorporated in many off-the-shelf products. Further, the Swiss government funded participation in the pilot environments of the STORK project [1]. The aim of this project was to establish an European eID interoperability platform that will allow citizens to establish new e-relations across borders, just by presenting their national eIDs. One of this project's outcomes was an essential contribution to the eIDAS Regulation [6]. A statement in the final report, "STORK 2.0 für die Schweiz", is the recommendation of Swiss participation in mutual eID recognition as part of the eIDAS regulation. Therefore, a process has to be started that is estimated to last about two years. There will be a need of interim arrangements until this process is implemented

Having the legal enactments in place is a vital premise for such eGovernment services. In the initiation phase of a project, the mandatory project management method HERMES prescribes that risks and the operational risks have to be determined and the legal framework and the protection needs have to be analysed [10]. This method covers various scenarios, such as procurement of standard software or dedicated software development, but not IT operation. Therefore, the legal basis for providing and operating the described STIAM services has to be adjusted, and a dedicated IAM enactment is already under development. The continuity of centrally provided IAM services was named frequently in the above cited requirements from the stakeholders interviewed. To build the legal foundation, the Swiss Federal Council has opened the consultation phase for what will be known as the Informationssicherheitsgesetz (Information Assurance Law [2]).

Besides legal considerations, it is also fundamental to have the organisational structures aligned. To do so, the current design of boards, responsibilities and processes in the management and steering domain will be reconsidered. The Swiss government is responsible for granting what is known as the "Marktmodell" [5] for all services that are operated as standardised services for the federal administration. This model contains the future IAM service model, including the required resources for its operation and future development. The revised Marktmodell is an outcome of the IAM programme [12] and will be presented to the Swiss government in the near future.

3 Conclusion - IAM as a Service is by Far More Flexible but also Needs More Governance

In recent decades, the in-house production depth within manufacturing has decreased gradually by focusing on assembly. The same development can be seen in IT environments. Compared to the highly integrated IT systems of the past, functional decomposition is now considered state of the art. In this paper, we have illustrated this aspect of the IAM function and showed the development from monolithic IAM to loosely coupled IAM consisting of microservices, where users are able to bring their own identity (ByoID). ByoID can help to overcome inhibitions related to eGovernment and may promote the collaboration between the government and the private sector. This development will make easier some aspects of IAM governance, such as AM, as stated in various laws. On the other hand, ByoID is a challenging task for IAM governance in its mission to maintain the same security as in the past. To master these challenges, the Swiss government recently published specific actions in its IT strategy for the years 2016 to 2019 as:

- Strengthening the IT management system of the federal administration with concise assignments of tasks, competences and responsibilities
- Regularisation of the governance of IT architecture
- Further developing strategic IT controlling
- Consolidating the IT default documents across all levels

The goals of these strategic aims are to steadily strengthen IT steering, to reliably deliver a sound basis for decisions and to gradually increase the maturity of the IT [11]. The next big challenge in IAM is to consider and integrate the identity of things as the Internet of things grows. Governments' IAM will have to follow this development, and policy makers will have to address this issue by providing the relevant legal framework.

References

1. Bern University of Applied Science: STORK 2.0 für die Schweiz. Projektabschlussbericht, State Secretariat for Economic Affairs (SECO) (2016). http://www.seco.admin.ch/themen/05116/05118/05315/05329
2. Bundesversammlung der Schweizerischen Eidgenossenschaft: Bundesgesetz über die Informationssicherheit (ISG). Web, March 2014. http://www.news.admin.ch/NSBSubscriber/message/attachments/34224.pdf, draft. Accessed 25 May 2016
3. Bundesversammlung der Schweizerischen Eidgenossenschaft: 2011 - Bundesgesetz über das elektronische Patientendossier (EPDG). Web (2016). http://www.bag.admin.ch/themen/gesundheitspolitik/10357/index.html?lang=de. Accessed 9 Mar 2016
4. Der Schweizerische Bundesrat: Verordnung über die vom BIT betriebenen Verzeichnisdienste des Bundes. Web (2014). https://www.admin.ch/opc/de/classified-compilation/20132589/index.html. Accessed 6 Mar 2016
5. Der Schweizerische Bundesrat: Verordnung über die Informatik und Telekommunikation in der Bundesverwaltung. Web (2016). https://www.admin.ch/opc/de/classified-compilation/20081009/index.html. Accessed 6 Mar 2016
6. European Commission: Trust Services and eID. Web (2015), https://ec.europa.eu/digital-single-market/trust-services-and-eid. Accessed 10 Mar 2016
7. Fachgruppe Identity und Access Management: SuisseTrustIAM Rahmenkonzept. Standard eCH-0167, Verein eCH - E-Government-Standards, June 2014. http://www.ech.ch/
8. Federal Assembly of the Swiss Confederation: Federal Act on Data Protection (FADP). Web (2014). https://www.admin.ch/opc/en/classified-compilation/19920153/index.html. Accessed 9 Mar 2016
9. Federal Assembly of the Swiss Confederation: Ordinance on the Protection of Federal Information (Information Protection Ordinance, IPO). Web (2015). https://www.admin.ch/opc/en/classified-compilation/20070574/index.html. Accessed 9 Mar 2016
10. Federal IT Steering Unit: HERMES 5.1. Federal IT Steering Uni, 5.1 edn. (2015). http://www.hermes.admin.ch/onlinepublikation/index.xhtml
11. Federal IT Steering Unit: IKT-Strategie des Bundes 2016–2019. Web, December 2015. https://www.isb.admin.ch/isb/de/home/ikt-vorgaben/strategien-teilstrategien/sb000-ikt-strategie-des-bundes.html. Accessed 20 May 2016
12. Federal IT Steering Unit: Programme IAM of the confederation. Web (2015). https://www.isb.admin.ch/isb/de/home/themen/programme_projekte.html. Accessed 25 May 2016
13. Federal IT Steering Unit (FITSU): P000 - federal administration's IT processes. Web, September 2015. https://www.isb.admin.ch/isb/en/home/ikt-vorgaben/prozesse-methoden/p000-informatikprozesse_in_der_bundesverwaltung.html. Accessed 25 May 2016
14. Federal Office of Police (fedpol): Establishment of an electronic identity (eid) that is valid nationally and internationally. Web (2016). https://www.egovernment.ch/en/umsetzung/schwerpunktplan/elektronische-identitat/. Accessed 25 May 2016

15. Hoernes, P.: Ein IAM Grossprojekt aus der Perspektive des Enterprise Architekten - Erfahrungen aus der Schweizer Bundesverwaltung. Web (2014). https://rg-muenchen.gi.de/node/1291, presentation at the EAM working group of the Gesellschaft für Informatik. Accessed 8 Mar 2016
16. Knittl, S., Wiedmer, H.U.: Dienste und IT-Governance in der Bundesverwaltung - Bedarf, Nutzen und Potenzial. eGov Präsenz (2015)
17. Lörincz, B., Tinholt, D., van der Linden, N., Oudmaijer, S., Jacquet, L., Kerschot, H., Steyaert, J., Cattaneo, G., Lifonti, R., Schindler, R., Millard, J., Carpenter, G.: eGovernment Benchmark Framework 2012–2015. Web (2012). http://ec.europa.eu/newsroom/dae/document.cfm?doc_id=1929. Accessed 9 Mar 2016
18. Open Group TOGAF-SABSA Integration Working Group: TOGAF-SABSA Integration WG: TOGAF and SABSA Integration. Whitepaper, The Open Group and The SABSA Institute (2011)
19. Sialm, G.: eIAM: Neue Möglichkeiten dank offener Architektur. Eisbrecher (54), June 2014. http://www.bit.admin.ch/dokumentation/00090/00156/index.html?lang=de
20. State Secretariat for Economic Affairs SECO: Identity network Switzerland. Web (2016). https://www.egovernment.ch/en/umsetzung/schwerpunktplan/identitatsverbund-schweiz/. Accessed 25 May 2016
21. Trägerverein SuisseID: SuisseID - Die SuisseID ist der Schweizer Standard für sichere Authentifikation und elektronische Signatur. Web (2016). http://suisseid.ch/de. Accessed 30 May 2016
22. Weber, C., Bernold, R., Brian, O., Brugger, J., Dungga Winterleitner, A., Fraefel, M., Hosang, R., Riedl, R., Selzam, T., Walser, K., Weissenfeld, K.: eID-Ökosystem Modell. Technical report Version 1.1, Fachhochschule Bern, June 2015. https://www.wirtschaft.bfh.ch/uploads/tx_frppublikationen/eID-OEkosystem_V1_2.pdf

The E-Waste-Privacy Challenge
A Grounded Theory Approach

Barbara Krumay(⊠)

WU Vienna University of Economics and Business, Vienna, Austria
bkrumay@wu.ac.at
http://www.wu.ac.at

Abstract. Hardware is replaced with increasing frequency, whether it is broken or not. The constantly increasing pile of e-waste contains hardware that has been used for producing, processing, and storing data. Although mechanisms exist to erase data before disposal, it is unclear how companies apply them to different types of hardware. In this exploratory research based on a grounded theory approach, we developed a framework showing relationships between privacy awareness, hardware types, end-of-life handling, and data protection measures. Based on the sample data, we identified types of hardware that are experienced as being critical storage devices, whereas the storage capacity of others is not perceived as being critical. Based on the framework, research could begin to further elaborate solutions to this problem. This work also recommends the development of guidelines that integrate e-waste and privacy or data protection.

Keywords: Privacy · E-waste · Data protection · Awareness · ICT products

1 Introduction

As modern society depends on information, threats evolve from creating, collecting, and processing information as well as from the information and communication technology (ICT) that fulfills this task. After having reached its end-of-life (EoL), ICT devices become electronic waste (e-waste), which seems to be the curse of the information society [1,2]. Besides the environmental impacts of e-waste, information stored on it also becomes an issue for society. Of course, deleting data and formatting hard drives are widely applied measures to erase data from storage media [3]. Nevertheless, some examples showed how alarmingly easy it is to recover data from ICT devices in landfills or from secondhand hardware [4–6]. Consequently, research and practice alike are seeking data deletion methods at the EoL of hardware that will make recovery impossible [7]. But the technological measures are only one side of the coin. The other is a socio-organizational aspect based on companies' awareness of privacy issues and data protection beyond technological measures [3]. As we have seen in other

© Springer International Publishing Switzerland 2016
S. Schiffner et al. (Eds.): APF 2016, LNCS 9857, pp. 48–68, 2016.
DOI: 10.1007/978-3-319-44760-5_4

areas, including e-waste and privacy, awareness and responsibility are preconditions for the successful avoidance of unintended misbehaviour [8,9]. Research on the socio-organizational aspect is scarce; hence, the main research question of our exploratory study is: what are the influencing factors for handling data on devices at their end-of-life? Accordingly, our aim is to identify and further explore these factors and their relationships. Based on interviews with executives responsible for e-waste handling, we developed a framework illustrating the different concepts to protect data on discarded devices. We focus on people responsible for e-waste, to extend the research beyond data protection specialists and hence gain a better understanding concerning the awareness of data protection at EoL.

The remainder of the paper is structured as follows: First, we provide a short introduction to the current state of the field with specific focus on privacy, data protection, and EoL of devices with respect to e-waste. Second, we describe our methodological approach. Third, the resulting framework grounded in data is presented, followed by an in-depth discussion of the results. We finish the paper with a conclusion, consideration of limitations, and an outlook on future research.

2   State of the Field

2.1   Privacy and Data Protection

In 1890, Warren and Brandeis had already discussed privacy as the 'right to be let alone', when the then new technology of photography seemed to intrude into the private sphere of human beings [10]. In the following decades and even ages, privacy has been widely discussed in various ways by research, business, and policy makers. There is a common understanding of privacy as a 'claim of individuals, groups and institutions to determine for themselves, when, how and to what extent information about them is communicated to others' [11]. Individuals have to decide which data should be provided when and how, and reluctance to data provision has been evidenced [12]. However, research has revealed that individuals intend to provide only a minimum of information, but in reality disclose more private information. This is the so-called privacy paradox [13], which has lately been investigated from different points of view [12,14]. It has been stated that privacy awareness may help to close this gap as it 'enables people to make informed decisions and should lead to less unintentional privacy-invasive behaviour' [15].

However, businesses collect, store, and process data as a means to stay competitive [16]. This sensitive or personal data (termed Personally Identifiable Information - PII) of an individual [17] is the most precious and challenging form of information to manage. Customer data plays an important role for marketing, enabling companies to reach their target audiences directly and in a personalized way [18–20]. In the early years of e-commerce, privacy and security concerns of potential buyers were seen as major barriers [21]. Companies consequently implemented various data protection measures to overcome customers' reluctance to provide information, with the aim to establish or retain the trust and loyalty of their customers [22]. Hence, data protection has been identified as a measure to operationalize privacy [23]. Technological data protection approaches (e.g. encryption, anonymization, and pseudonymization) mainly target towards securing data on operating hardware. At the EoL, measures to fully erase data on hardware have yet to be established. Typical commands provided by operating systems to delete data are available. However, this does actually not erase the data; rather, it only marks the space where the data is stored on the hardware as 'being free'. A more reliable measure is high-level formatting, which means setting up the file system from scratch and removing file-location information. Low-level formatting, by contrast, resets values per bit to zero and re-initializes the hard drive. An even more reliable way to erase data is degaussing, which randomizes the magnetic domains, but often makes the hard drive unusable. In addition, overwriting meaningful data with senseless data has been mentioned as a useful method. Finally, by physically destroying the drive, data recovery becomes almost impossible [3,6,7]. Those general approaches vary by device types, since data on mobile devices, for example, can sometimes be securely deleted via factory reset. Of course, technological measures have to be supported by organizational measures and policies, to raise awareness and avoid unintended leaking of data [24].

Lately it has been demonstrated that data can be restored easily from EoL hardware in landfills or purchased in the secondhand market [4–6]. This is surprising, since privacy and data protection responsibilities of companies are widely regulated by laws. For example, the European Commission published in May 2016 new legislation with regard to the processing of personal data and the free movement of such data [25]. It requires that 'Personal data should be processed in a manner that ensures appropriate security and confidentiality of the personal data, including for preventing unauthorised access to or use of personal data and the equipment used for the processing' [25]. In the US, the Federal Trade Commission's Fair Information Practice Principles (FIPs) [26] are applicable. Due to differences between regulations and global trade relationships, inter-governmental agreements like the Safe Harbor Privacy Principles (Safe Harbor PP) [27], issued in 2000, have been established [28] (However, this agreement was declared invalid in 2015 [29]). Other frameworks like the Online Privacy Alliance (OPA) [30], Network Advertising Initiative (NAI) [31], Global Business Dialogue on e-Society (GBDe) [32], or the AICPA/CICA Privacy Frameworks [33] are mainly self-regulating agreements binding for participating companies. In these regulations, the borders between privacy, data protection, and security are often blurry. This is also reflected by different approaches to data security, such as the ISO/IEC 27002 [34], which names privacy goals as part of security goals. Furthermore, the BSI IT-Grundschutz defines procedures on how to handle data and how to securely delete or destroy it [35]. The vague definition of privacy as a basis for lawmaking [36], the different laws and regulations, as well as unclear definitions of what 'delete' means further increase the complexity in this area.

2.2   E-Waste

The term 'e-waste' is closely related to the EoL of computers. In general, this term refers to waste evolving from electrical and electronic equipment (WEEE), including ICT products and also white goods [37]. In a common understanding, the term e-waste is specifically connected to ICT products, referring to goods including microchips. The advent of the Internet of Things (in the form of smart and small devices integrated into non-ICT products [e.g. cars, refrigerators] [38], able to store and process data), shortening life cycles of products, as well as the lifestyle-based fast replacement of products [1,2] increase the amount of e-waste. Having reached EoL, ICT products are replaced. Besides technological and business reasons for EoL (e.g. broken hardware, better and faster technologies, deterioration, or incompatibility with current software) [39–41], psychological reasons may play a role. This lifestyle-indicated rebuy or psychological obsolescence – the perceived need of users to replace a device due to non-technical reasons (e.g. colours) - further increases the number of discarded ICT hardware devices [40,42]. As long as ICT products are usable and reused by others, they do not become e-waste in the classical meaning [43]. By contrast, when the technological EoL has been reached, electronic devices still can be refurbished or recycled [44]. Clearly, on each and every device having reached EoL, data has been stored when it was used. Quite often, it still is available on the storage media at EoL. Regardless of whether the devices are resold in the secondhand market or disposed in landfills, the data has to be carefully deleted to prevent unauthorized recovery of data [4–6] to avoid severe consequences for the company. Besides legal issues, leakage of sensitive or private data leads to loss of reputation and trust [24]. Surprisingly, 'data waste' or 'D-waste' and challenges evolving from it [45,46] have rarely been addressed in research. Jones [47], for example, claims that he was able to recover personal and organizational data from more than 50 % of storage media disposed and that 'Only 31 % of the disks had had all of the data removed to a standard where it could not easily be recovered' [47]. The reasons for this unintended disclosure of data on disposed devices are various, including low awareness of data protection of e-waste for those who are responsible for waste management. As EoL handling of hardware due to high costs and required know-how is too challenging for many companies, they often rely on the support from specialists. As these tasks require specific technological knowledge and expertise concerning specific regulations, an 'end-of-life industry' has evolved [48]. This industry covers both the secure deletion of data before selling the hardware in the secondhand market or disposing of it in landfills as well as correct disposal. Currently, reliable results are lacking regarding whether the EoL industry will change the situation for the better or the worse.

2.3   Research Question

As the state of the field summary above has shown, there has been some research conducted on e-waste, privacy issues, and data protection. Few researchers have addressed so-called data waste or D-waste [45,46], especially from a socio-organizational point of view. It has been discussed how this issue can be integrated via privacy by design considerations [49] or extended producer responsibility [50]. However, research concerning factors influencing data protection measures at the EoL of hardware and the awareness for this issue is missing. Accordingly, the main research question of our exploratory study is: what are the influencing factors for handling data on devices at their end-of-life? Consequently, our aim is to identify and further explore these factors and the relationships between them. This also contributes to knowledge concerning the awareness of people who handle hardware at EoL in companies.

3   Methodological Approach

Initiating a new research topic often relies on qualitative, exploratory approaches. Consequently, we applied a grounded theory approach for developing a basic understanding grounded in data [51]. Grounded theory as an iterative, creative, and interpretive process provides 'procedures to develop an inductively derived grounded theory about a phenomenon' systematically [52]. The researchers are required to dive deeply into the data for identifying 'meanings and connotations that may not be apparent from a mere superficial reading of denotative content' [53]. In grounded theory, data collection and analysis are performed in parallel [52–54]. From the first notion of grounded theory by Glaser and Strauss [55], different streams evolved. Our research is mainly based on the ideas of Strauss and Corbin [51], but integrates ideas from other streams (e.g. [56,57]). We apply theoretical sampling and variations of coding in iterations to follow the grounded theory approach in a rigorous and systematic way [52]. As is common in qualitative research, we use interviews as one of the main sources [53]. Interviews provide exclusive insights into the interviewee's perspective of a topic and very much depend on the flexibility of the interviewers [58,59]. Hence, in grounded theory approaches, additional sources are often used to enrich the sample data and overcome pure individual assessments. These approaches also serve to balance possible misunderstandings that may occur in the spoken language, or interference evolving from the interview situation [59].

Coding of data and making sense of it are important components of this approach. According to Corbin and Strauss, 'open coding and axial coding go hand in hand' [57], which is different from other streams of grounded theory, in which those coding techniques were separated. The idea is to generate concepts from the qualitative data, find relationships between the concepts, and develop categories concerning the object of interest. Concepts are short terms reflecting ideas that exist in the data. They also reflect the context and conditions of the concepts found in terms of properties (characteristics) and dimensions (variations) of concepts [53]. Whereas initially, analysis of the data is somehow similar to brainstorming about the data, later on the data is more condensed to make the concepts easier to grasp. All incidents are constantly compared to each other to identify similarities and differences. Similar concepts are collected under the same term or code, enriching it by properties and dimensions. This has to be done until conceptual saturation has been reached, which means that no new properties or dimensions seem to evolve. Throughout the entire process, memos are used to document all considerations of the researchers while coding [53]. Concepts are aggregated in the form of categories (or themes) on a higher level, which may or may not have lower-level sub-categories. This process lasts until theoretical saturation has been reached. This means that 'all categories are well developed', hence adding more data would not change the categories, but could lead to context-dependent variations. The development of the framework integrating all concepts and categories and their relationships is the final step. While developing it, the researchers have to check for logical inconsistencies or gaps and correct them. This requires returning to the data, especially the memos, and identifying the sources from where the inconsistencies stem. In this step, we integrated feedback from another researcher and two privacy experts from business. We exposed them to the then-current versions of the framework, discussed unclear parts, and addressed the relationships between categories. We critically compared this external feedback with the data for refining the framework. The final framework depicts relationships among the concepts and categories, which proved to be steady in the data [53].

Although grounded theory requires parallel collection and analysis of data, we describe the research process by reporting data collection and analysis separated from each other. We conducted semi-structured topical interviews with eight managers from seven different companies. All interviews were conducted within a short period of time, in spring and summer 2015. The main purpose of the interviews was to gain knowledge about the perceptions, concerns, and observations of the interviewees regarding privacy issues evolving from e-waste. We deliberately did not focus on experts in data protection, since this is not the idea of this study. Hence, we designed a rough interview guideline with pre-defined topics. In this way, we were able to cover the entire subject area in accordance with the research question [60]. Moreover, the interviewers attempted to keep the interviews open by encouraging the interviewees to further explain their thoughts [58].

The data was collected and analyzed based on the idea of theoretical sampling [54]. We selected 25 companies from different industries (see Appendix), but excluded micro-companies (fewer than 10 employees) and ICT-manufacturing companies, which we suppose would have very different approaches. We refer to company size in terms of the number of employees, as this seems to be an accurate estimator of e-waste created by the company. We started the series of interviews with two companies (Interviews 1 and 2). Based on the categories developed from the first interviews, we felt the need to further analyze them with companies from the ICT service industry (Interviews 3–5), since the information and data seem to be of high importance in this sector. In a third iteration, we interviewed representatives from multinational companies (Interviews 6 and 7), as we wanted to strengthen the categories. Table 1 summarizes the interviewees' characteristics. Concerning position in the company, all interviewees were at least at the middle management level, but with different functions. All interviewees had been at their companies for several years and in their current position for at least three years. Interviews were conducted on the phone and face-to-face (see Table 2). Interview length was between approx. 20 and 66 min. In general, the interviews were audio-recorded, transcribed, and analyzed. Due to technical problems, Interview 3 was only partly audio-taped. Thus, the missing parts were reconstructed from memory and notes taken. All interviews were held in the native language of the interviewees and interviewers.

Table 1. Interviewees

No.	Position	Years/ Company	Years/ Position	Industry	No. of Empl.
I1	Technical Manager	12	7	Media	400
I2	CIO & CFO	10	5	Pharmaceutical	110
I3	CSM (two participants)	7/10	5/3	DCP	1 200
I4	CIO & CTO	10	10	ISP	25
I5	Sustainability Officer	7	5	Telco	8 600
I6	Chief Buyer	3	3	Insurance	2 700
I7	CSR Manager	5	4	Consulting	190 000

Legend: Years/Company: years at the company; Years/Position = years in the current position; No. of Empl. = number of employees of the company; CSM = Change & Supply Management; DCP = Data Center Provider; ISP = Internet Service Provider; Telco = Telecommunication Provider.

Table 2. Interview situation

No.	Duration (min.)	Type	No. of participants	Additional sources
I1	32:50	Phone	1	E-waste guidelines
I2	47:57	Face-to-face	1	Disposal process including data protection measures
I3	55:06	Face-to-face	2	E-waste guidelines
				Disposal process
				Data protection guidelines
I4	20:31	Phone	1	Press releases
I5	33:00	Phone	1	-
I6	50:31	Face-to-face	1	Annual report
I7	45:15	Phone	1	-

4   Research Results

By analyzing the interviews, we were able to identify important topics concerning privacy issues evolving from e-waste handling, especially awareness and data protection measures. Hardware life cycles and handling at and after the business end-of-life (e.g. recycling, refurbishment, and reuse) are also important influencers of privacy issues. Overall, assessment of the storage device - whether it is critical, non-critical, or has not been indentified as such - is important. In addition, the perceived responsibility for the data influences companies' approach to handle data on e-waste. In the following section, we describe the information gained from the interviews. We first describe the framework developed and explain the categories and concepts. Whenever we refer to the data used for analysis, we use the term 'sample data' to avoid misunderstandings with the data stored on hardware.

4.1   E-Waste Privacy Awareness Framework

We identified privacy awareness to be the main category, and six other categories were established (device assessment, hardware types, reasons for segregation, data protection measures, end-of-life handling, and perceived responsibility) (see Fig. 1). Interestingly, data protection regulations were not salient in the sample data. The relationships between the categories are labelled with capitalized letters for better orientation. Concepts in a category are shown in the same box, and properties are in italics.

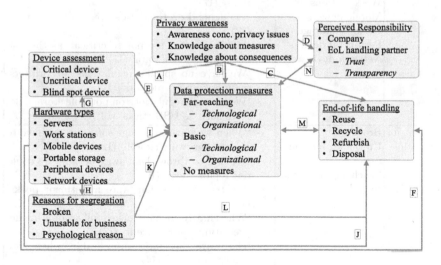

Fig. 1. E-waste privacy awareness framework

Table 3. Categories, concepts, and data

Categories	Concepts	Data
Privacy Awareness	Awareness concerning privacy issues Knowledge about measures Knowledge about consequences	− 'It could ruin the company if data from inside the company became available outside' (I2). − 'Our reputation is in danger when hard drives with customer data are accessible' (I7). − 'Protection of customer data is our main concern' (I3). − 'The private data of users can be used to harm them, e.g. when passwords or account data is stored on it' (I1).
Device Assessment	Critical device Uncritical device Blind spot device	− 'We differentiate between hardware able to store data and hardware without data' (I3). − 'We have no regulations on portable storage devices such as USB sticks' (2). − 'All parts holding data have to be handled separately' (I4). − 'Mobile devices are not so critical, as they do not store a lot of data' (I7). − 'We have no specific regulations for printers, scanners and projectors' (I7). − 'The network devices such as hubs, routers and firewalls are uncritical' (I2). − 'We do not store data on peripheral devices' (I5).
Hardware Types	Servers Work stations Mobile devices Portable storage Peripheral devices Network devices	− 'Data is mainly stored on servers and workstations' (I7). − 'We depend on the data stored on our servers' (I2). − 'Mobile devices are not so critical, as they do not store a lot of data' (I7). − 'We have no specific regulations for printers, scanners, and projectors' (I7). − 'We have no regulations on portable storage devices such as USB sticks' (I2).
Reasons for Segregation	Broken Unusable for business Psychological reasons	− 'When we have to change software, we have to change hardware as well' (I2). − 'We had to throw them away because we could not repair them' (I6). − 'We try to avoid hardware investment peaks' (I2). − 'When hardware has reached full accounting depreciation, we replace it' (I7). − 'Hardware becomes unprofitable when you can't manage it' (I4). − 'We discard hardware as long as it has some value on the market' (I5).

(*Continued*)

Table 3. (*Continued*)

Data Protection Measures	Far-reaching – *Technical* – *Organizational* Basic – *Technical* – *Organizational* No measures	– 'We take out hard drives, disks, and all parts capable of storing data before disposing hardware' (I6). – 'We have strict policies on how to store data and how to erase it' (I4). – 'We apply all commonly used measures to erase data from hard drives, such as delete and format' (I2). – 'We have a very strict procedure on how to erase data from hard drives, such as degauss, overwriting 30 – 50 times' (I4). – 'Devices with very sensitive customer data are destroyed' (I5). – 'There is a person responsible for reminding employees to delete all data when buying a phone from the company' (I5). – 'We have boxes where employees can dispose their phones' (I2). – 'We rely on our employees that they reset phones to factory settings when they buy them for private use from the company' (I3). – 'We have no specific regulations for printers, scanners and projectors' (I7). – 'Data on mobile devices should not be an issue' (I6). – 'We have very strict policies on how and where data is stored' (I4). – 'We have no regulations on portable storage devices such as USB sticks' (I2).
End-of-Life Handling	Reuse Recycle Refurbish Disposal	– 'We can sell our hardware on the market almost to no costs' (I5). – 'Employees can buy their own mobile phone for private use' (I7).
Perceived Responsibility	Company EoL handling partner – *Trust* – *Transparency*	– 'We erase data on hard drives before handing them over to our EoL partners' (I1). – 'No data leaves the company, when our EoL partner collects all devices from us' (I3). – 'Based on contracts, our EoL partners are responsible for fully erasing data on the devices' (I4). – 'Our partners are responsible for erasing data on printers and scanners' (I7). 'We trust our partners, that they take full responsibility for the devices they receive from us' (I5).

(*Continued*)

Table 3. (*Continued*)

		— 'We expect from our EoL partners that they fully report what happens with the devices after collecting it from us' (I4). — 'When hardware leaves our doors we are not responsible anymore' (I2). — 'We have found a responsible solution on different levels' (I1). — 'It is a perfect solution since they provide full transparency in their processes' (I1). — 'We receive full access to all documents: where our hardware is, how it has been used or destroyed, how hazardous substances have been disposed' (I6).

4.2   Privacy Awareness

As it has been stated in the literature, 'Privacy awareness enables people to make informed decisions' [15]. Although this statement targets users and their knowledge about the sensitive or personal data they provide, we adopt the term and use it for our framework. In our framework, privacy awareness is seen as companies' awareness of privacy issues, knowledge about measures to protect data and privacy, and the consequences evolving from sensitive or personal data being unintentionally provided to the public. This idea refers to the underlying concepts found in the sample data, which have been clearly expressed by the interviewees (see Table 3).

4.3   Device Assessment

The category 'Device Assessment' refers to the differentiation between critical and non-critical data. This has been specifically addressed by the interviewees and in the documents. Thus, a differentiation between customer data, user data, and company data, all of which must be protected when the hardware leaves the company, seems logical. However, in terms of e-waste, the interesting concept is not this qualification of data, but the knowledge concerning where the data has been stored. In the sample data, this has often referred to storage media in terms of a single component (e.g. hard drive) or a whole system (e.g. server, work station). Besides the differentiation between critical devices (that are storing sensitive or personal data) and non-critical devices (not storing sensitive or personal data), we found a rather blind spot for some devices. The blind spot covers devices where the storage is not perceived as part of the functionality (e.g. printers, scanners) or perceived as having a very limited storage capacity (e.g. mobile phones, network devices such as routers). Some of them are perceived as being not under control of the company or as unimportant (e.g. direct attached storage like USB sticks).

4.4   Hardware Types

In general, the concept of e-waste has been described as waste evolving from the end-of-life of ICT hardware, depending on different types of hardware. Distinguished concepts are servers, work stations, mobile devices, network (e.g. routers, switches, hubs), and peripheral (printers, displays, input devices, projectors) components. The interviewees explicitly excluded other technical equipment used in the production (I2) and household machines (I1, I2) used in the office (e.g. coffee machines, refrigerators, microwave ovens). This differentiation is important, since life spans are very different. The shorter the life span, the more often privacy issues evolve from e-waste. According to numbers estimated by the interviewees, the life span of ICT products is very different. Mobile devices (smart and mobile phones, tablets) are used for between two to three years. Notebooks, personal computers, and associated peripheral devices (e.g. monitors) stay in the companies between four to six years. Servers as well as network equipment and printers range between five and ten years. There has been no information about direct attached storage or portable storage, especially USB sticks and external hard drives. The significance of hardware types was salient for most of the interviewees. Policies, data protection measurement, assessment of criticality, and end-of-life handling are directly influenced by hardware types. We will further elaborate on this when we explain these relationships.

4.5   Reasons for Segregation

The interviewees clearly differentiated between unusable (broken) hardware and hardware that is usable but does not fulfill business requirements. The most obvious technical reason is that hardware becomes unusable - i.e. it breaks. The root causes of problems are sometimes very difficult to find, making repairs and also basic data protection measures (e.g. delete) almost impossible. In addition, technology that is no longer fulfilling performance requirements must be replaced by 'current but approved technology' (I2). Furthermore, new software may require high-performance hardware. Other reasons for discarding usable hardware are due to the end of maintenance contracts, investment cycles, or accounting depreciation. In addition, the value of hardware on the resale market may play an important role when discarded. Another reason for discarding hardware is based on the perceived need of employees to receive new hardware. This has been referred to as lifestyle-indicated end-of-life of hardware and mainly applies to mobile devices (smartphones, tablets, laptops) and monitors. Interestingly, psychological reasons have been related primarily to powerful people in the company - i.e. those in the higher management levels or in sales. Consequently, discarding hardware is clearly connected to the hardware lifecycle, since hardware reaches its end-of-life in a company as soon as it ceases to fulfill the company's requirements.

4.6 Data Protection Measures

In general, measures to protect data can already be applied when the hardware is in use. In our framework, we exclusively concentrate on measures at the end-of-life of hardware within companies. The measures can be far-reaching, on a basic level, or may not exist, mainly depending on hardware type and device assessment. Far-reaching technological (e.g. deleting, burning, degaussing, formatting, overwriting data multiple times, restoring to factory settings) and organizational measures (policies, agreements, confidentiality undertaking, and contracts) are applied when the discarded device is assessed as being critical. For example, servers are centrally handled to ensure that the data or even hard drives are fully destroyed. Basic measures often refer to data on personal computers, notebooks, and mobile devices. Data protection measures are often managed by the user or employee herself. For some devices (printers, scanners, mobile phones, projectors), measures have rarely been found in the sample data. For network components, technological measures are mainly found to be on a very basic level (e.g. reset).

4.7 End-of-Life Handling

The processes at the EoL of devices described in the interviews are quite similar. In general, devices having reached EoL from the company's point of view (unusable for business) are prepared for discard by removing parts able to store data and collected at a specific storage site or location. Preparing for discard means applying the above-mentioned data protection measures. Concepts include reuse (e.g. sell devices for reuse on the market or to employees; use as spares) and transfer to partner companies for recycling and/or refurbishment. Devices are sold either to an intermediary (third party) or to employees. The intermediary purchases the hardware from the company and sells it on the market. Some devices are stored as spares. When transferring hardware to EoL handling partners, the sending company decides whether the hardware should be recycled, refurbished, or disposed, depending on hardware type, criticality of device, and reason for segregation.

4.8 Perceived Responsibility

The perceived responsibility describes whether the company adopts data protection as their responsibility or shifts it to the EoL handling partner. Trust in the partner and transparency of partners' processes are main properties of this concept. However, the selection of these partners is one of companies' responsibilities, as has been expressed by all interviewees. The additional available documents revealed clear guidelines for selecting partners, and interviewees addressed that having insights into the processes of EoL handling partners is a precondition.

4.9   Relationships

Although already partially reported in the description of the categories, we provide here an overview of the relationships between privacy awareness, hardware types, end-of-life handling, and data protection measures. Examples of the relationships refer to the sample data (interviewee data and information gained from the provided documents).

A   Privacy awareness influences the assessment of devices. Example: awareness of privacy issues influences the assessed criticality of devices.

B   Privacy awareness influences data protection measures. Example: knowledge about consequences influences the level of data protection measures.

C   Privacy awareness influences end-of-life handling. Example: awareness of privacy issues influences whether a device will be reused.

D   Privacy awareness influences the perceived responsibility for data protection. Example: awareness of consequences influences a shift of responsibility to the EoL handling partner.

E   Device assessment influences data protection measures. Example: blind spot devices have no measures.

F   Device assessment influences end-of-life handling. Example: critical devices are rarely subject to reuse.

G   Hardware types influence device assessment. Example: peripheral devices are often blind spot devices.

H   Hardware types influence reasons for segregation. Example: mobile devices are often segregated due to psychological reasons.

I   Hardware types influence data protection measures. Example: on network devices, basic data protection measures are applied.

J   Hardware types influence EoL handling. Example: mobile devices are often sold for reuse.

K   Reasons for segregation influence data protection measures. Example: Broken hardware often allows new measures.

L   Reasons for segregation influence EoL handling: Unusable for business devices can be reused.

M   Data protection measures influence EoL handling. Example: physically destroyed hardware is disposed; EoL handling influences data protection measures. Example: devices for reuse require far-reaching data protection measures.

N   Data protection measures influence perceived responsibility; perceived responsibility influences data protection measures. Example: Responsibility within the company evolves far-reaching data protection measures. Basic data protection measures are applied when trust in the EoL partner is high.

Interestingly, some relationships between categories, which may have been expected, did not evolve from the sample data. First, regarding the relationship between perceived responsibility and EoL handling: although there is a logical link between the construct (EoL handling partner is processing EoL handling), the sample data did not reveal this relationship. In addition, an influence of privacy awareness on reasons for segregation (e.g. on psychological reasons for segregation) has not been found.

5   Discussion

Our goal was to explore which factors influence companies' approaches to privacy when hardware has reached EoL. Based on the sample data obtained from interviews and documents, we were able to identify seven factors and their relationships. Together with the underlying concepts, we developed our grounded theoretical framework. Although it has been created inductively, based on a small sample of eight interviewees and seven additional documents, we attempt to link it back to literature for enhancing 'internal validity, generalizability, and theoretical level of theory building from case study research' [61]. In this discussion, we will primarily focus on the socio-organizational categories of our framework, which are awareness and responsibility, as they have not previously been extensively addressed in this context.

The sample data revealed that privacy awareness influences how information stored on hardware is handled at EoL. The influence of awareness has already been addressed in other research fields. In the Human Resources context, for example, it has been investigated how moral awareness influences judgement, intent, and activities [62]. Other studies revealed that situational awareness influences decision-making [63,64]. This is in accordance with privacy awareness in our framework, which also influences decisions, especially the assessment of criticality of devices. Another category is the responsibility of companies. First, companies' responsibility for their impacts is a widely discussed topic in research [65] and on the policy level [66]. Research on corporate social responsibility (CSR) is comprehensive. In general, CSR has often been seen as adopting responsibility beyond economic and legal responsibilities [65]. Economic responsibilities are reflecting business' goal of being profitable to sustain workplaces and contribute to welfare [65]. Legal responsibilities – for e-waste and data protection – evolve from regulations and laws [66–70]. Beyond these two, ethical and philanthropic responsibilities have been named [65]. We argue that this applies to privacy and e-waste alike. Privacy has often been seen as an ethical issue [71] related to human rights [72]. Therefore, a moral responsibility of companies to protect the privacy in terms of protecting sensitive or personal data can be hypothesized. This is also reflected by the sample data, as data protection was not related to regulations and laws, but to the perceived responsibility. Knowledge about the laws and regulations, however, can be seen as a precondition. The sample data also revealed that companies share their responsibility for data protection with the EoL partners. The concept of shared responsibility has hardly been investigated concerning data stored, but has been studied along the supply chain of ICT products, especially concerning resources and energy use [73]. Shared responsibility requires that participants in the supply chain have an interest to enter into a dialogue, since all share responsibilities and consequences [73]. As the analysis of the sample data has shown, trust and transparency are important parts of the relationship with the EoL partners.

We link these requirements back to the idea that reputation loss due to leaking of sensitive or personal data is among the feared scenarios. Transparency, on the other hand, is often connected to accountability, which has also found attention in privacy research [74]. 'Information accountability means the use of information should be transparent so it is possible to determine whether a particular use is appropriate under a given set of rules and that the system enables individuals and institutions to be held accountable for misuse' [75]. This idea can be further expanded in two ways: First, to provide transparency on data handling at EoL of hardware. Second, to extend transparency between companies and EoL handling partners, reporting which measures both sides apply to fully erase data on the segregated (or reused) devices.

This research may serve various target groups. On one hand, the framework allows further investigation of the topic by evaluating it against quantitative data. Thus, the framework contributes to research in being a starting point for further investigation. On the other hand, for business, we provide a basic framework upon which companies may build their measures, especially in identifying their blind spot devices and setting up measures for them. In addition, it can be used as a guideline for assessing awareness of privacy issues at EoL among people responsible for e-waste handling in companies. For the EoL industry, it supports their understanding of what to integrate into their services in terms of further expanding their business by integrating data protection measures. Finally, as the sample data reveals a relationship between e-waste and privacy, future regulations may integrate both topics to support companies in their efforts to tackle both. A general guideline integrating environmental issues of hardware as well as privacy issues could be the next step.

6   Conclusion, Limitations, and Further Research

Environmental and societal impacts of e-waste are challenging business and society. It is important that companies develop awareness of both impact areas. The relationship between the seven categories identified shows that awareness plays an essential role. Further investigating shared responsibility for EoL of hardware thus should integrate privacy. The limitations of this qualitative, inductive research mainly involve the small sample. As already mentioned, evaluation of the framework is required. This will be the next step in our research, planned for late summer 2016.

Acknowledgments. I would like to thank Roman Brandtweiner for supporting me with feedback and re-evaluating previous versions of the framework.

Appendix

Table 4. Pool of companies

Company	Employees	Size	Operating	Industry	Status
C1	400	Large	National	Media	I1
C2	110	Medium	National	Pharmaceutical	I2
C3	1 200	Large	National	Data center provider	I3
C4	25	Small	National	Internet service provider	I4
C5	8 600	Large	National	Telecommunication provider	I5
C6	2 700	Large	Multinational	Insurance	I6
C7	190 000	Large	Multinational	Management consultancy	I7
C8	1 500	Large	National	Transportation	Canceled
C9	45	Small	Multinational	Furniture	Canceled
C10	25 000	Large	Multinational	Manufacture of glass and glass products	Decl.
C11	104	Medium	Multinational	Financial	Decl.
C12	179	Medium	National	Food and beverages	Decl.
C13	700	Large	Multinational	Food and beverages	Decl.
C14	36 000	Large	Multinational	Automotive	Decl.
C15	11 600	Large	Multinational	Construction	No funct.
C16	1 200	Large	Multinational	Financial	No funct.
C17	120 000	Large	Multinational	ICT consultancy	No funct.
C18	7 700	Large	National	Retail	No resp.
C19	35	Small	National	Food and beverages	No resp.
C20	5 484	Large	Multinational	ICT – software	No resp.
C21	76 100	Large	Multinational	Construction	No resp.
C22	7 982	Large	National	Food and beverages	No resp.
C23	1 215	Large	Multinational	Sports equipment	No resp.
C24	130	Medium	Multinational	Healthcare	No resp.
C25	37	Small	National	Sports and leisure equipment	No resp.

References

1. Baldé, C.P., Wang, F., Kuehr, R., Huisman, J.: The global e-waste monitor - 2014. United Nations University (2015)
2. European commission. Directive 2012/19/EU of the European parliament and ofthe council of 4 July 2012 on waste electrical and electronic equipment (WEEE), vol. 2012/19, Brussels (2012)
3. Bennison, P.F., Lasher, P.J.: Data security issues relating to end of life equipment. In: 2004 IEEE International Symposium on Electronics and the Environment, Conference Record, pp. 317–320. IEEE (2004)

4. Sutherland, I., Davies, G., Jones, A., Blyth, A.J.: Zombie hard disks - data from the living dead. In: 8th Australian Digital Forensics Conference, Perth, Western Australia, pp. 156–161 (2010)
5. Pope, J.: Discarded Computer Hard Drives Prove a Trove of Personal Info, vol. 1. Associated Press (2003). http://www.securityfocus.com/news/2055. Accessed 15 Oct 2015
6. Garfinkel, S.L., Shelat, A.: Remembrance of data passed: a study of disk sanitization practices. IEEE Secur. Priv. 1, 17–27 (2003)
7. Diesburg, S.M., Wang, A.-I.A.: A survey of confidential data storage and deletion methods. ACM Comput. Surv. (CSUR) 43, 1–38 (2010)
8. Langheinrich, M.: A privacy awareness system for ubiquitous computing environments. In: Borriello, G., Holmquist, L.E. (eds.) UbiComp 2002. LNCS, vol. 2498, p. 237. Springer, Heidelberg (2002)
9. Khetriwal, D.S., Kraeuchi, P., Widmer, R.: Producer responsibility for e-waste management: key issues for consideration-learning from the Swiss experience. J. Environ. Manage. 90, 153–165 (2009)
10. Warren, S.D., Brandeis, L.D.: The right to privacy. Harv. Law Rev. 4, 193–220 (1890)
11. Westin, A.F.: Privacy and freedom. Wash. Lee Law Rev. 25(1), 166 (1968)
12. Acquisti, A., Brandimarte, L., Loewenstein, G.: Privacy and human behavior in the age of information. Science 347, 509–514 (2015)
13. Norberg, P.A., Horne, D.R., Horne, D.A.: The privacy paradox: personal information disclosure intentions versus behaviors. J. Consum. Aff. 41, 100–126 (2007)
14. Bauer, C., Schiffinger, M.: Self-disclosure in online interaction: a meta-analysis. In: 48th Hawaii International Conference on System Sciences (HICSS), pp. 3621–3630. IEEE, Hawaii (2015)
15. Pötzsch, S.: Privacy awareness: a means to solve the privacy paradox? In: Matyáš, V., Fischer-Hübner, S., Cvrček, D., Švenda, P. (eds.) The Future of Identity. IFIP AICT, vol. 298, pp. 226–236. Springer, Heidelberg (2009)
16. Castells, M.: The Rise of the Network Society: The Information Age: Economy, Society, and Culture. Wiley, New York (2009)
17. Bélanger, F., Crossler, R.E.: Privacy in the digital age: a review of information privacy research in information systems. MIS Q. 35, 1017–1042 (2011)
18. Goldfarb, A., Tucker, C.E.: Privacy regulation and online advertising. Manage. Sci. 57, 57–71 (2011)
19. Charters, D.: Electronic monitoring and privacy issues in business-marketing: the ethics of the double click experience. J. Bus. Ethics 35, 243–254 (2002)
20. Awad, N.F., Krishnan, M.: The personalization privacy paradox: an empirical evaluation of information transparency and the willingness to be profiled online for personalization. MIS Q. 30, 13–28 (2006)
21. Udo, G.J.: Privacy and security concerns as major barriers for e-commerce: a survey study. Inf. Manage. Comput. Secur. 9, 165–174 (2001)
22. Flavian, C., Guinaliu, M.: Consumer trust, perceived security and privacy policy: three basic elements of loyalty to a web site. Ind. Manage. Data Syst. 106, 601–620 (2006)
23. Fischer-Hübner, S.: IT-Security and Privacy: Design and Use of Privacy-Enhancing Security Mechanisms, p. 358. Springer, Heidelberg (2001)
24. Andrade, E.B., Kaltcheva, V., Weitz, B.: Self-disclosure on the web: the impact of privacy policy, reward, and company reputation. Adv. Consum. Res. 29, 350–353 (2002)

25. European parliament and the council of the European union: regulation (EU) 2016/679 of the european parliament and of the council of 27, vol. 2016/679 official journal of the European union, April 2016
26. FTC: Fair Information Practice Principles. Federal Trade Commission (FTC) (1998)
27. U.S. Department of Commerce: The U.S.–EU Safe Harbor Framework. A Guideto Self-Certification, U.S. (2009)
28. Solove, D.J., Schwartz, P.M.: Privacy law fundamentals. International Association of Privacy Professionals (IAPP) (2015)
29. Court of Justice of the European Union (CJEU): Judgment of the Court (Grand-Chamber) of October 2015. Maximilian Schrems v Data Protection Commissioner, vol. Case C-362/14, Luxembourg (2015)
30. PrivacyAlliance.org (2015). http://www.privacyalliance.org/. Accessed 10 Feb 2015
31. Network advertising initiative (2015). http://www.networkadvertising.org/. Accessed 10 Feb 2015
32. Global business dialogue on e-society (2015). http://www.gbd-e.org/. Accessed 10 Feb 2015
33. American institute of CPAs (2015). http://www.aicpa.org/InterestAreas/ InformationTechnology/Resources/Privacy/Pages/default.aspx. Accessed 10 Feb 2015
34. International organization for standardization: ISO/IEC 27002 information technology – security techniques – code of practice for information security management. International Organization for Standardization (ISO) (2008)
35. Bundesamt für Sicherheit in der Informationstechnik (BSI): IT-Grundschutz Catalogues, Bonn (2013)
36. Solove, D.J.: A taxonomy of privacy. Univ. PA Law Rev. **154**, 477–560 (2006)
37. European Parliament: directive 2012/19/eu of the European parliamentand of the council of 4 July 2012 on waste electrical and electronicequipment (WEEE) (2012)
38. Weiser, M.: Ubiquitous computing. In: ACM Conference on Computer Science, p. 418(1994)
39. Van den Ende, J., Dolfsma, W.: Technology-push, demand-pull and the shaping of technological paradigms – patterns in the development of computing technology. J. Evol. Econ. **15**, 83–99 (2005)
40. Slade, G.: Made to Break: Technology and Obsolescence in America. Harvard University Press, Cambridge (2009)
41. Prasad, P.J.: Information communication technology (ICT) – its waste and consequences. Int. J. Environ. Technol. Manage. **15**, 363–376 (2012)
42. Cooper, T.: Inadequate life? Evidence of consumer attitudes to product obsolescence. J. Consum. Policy **27**, 421–449 (2004)
43. Widmer, R., Oswald-Krapf, H., Sinha-Khetriwal, D., Schnellmann, M., Böni, H.: Global perspectives on e-waste. Environ. Impact Assess. Rev. **25**, 436–458 (2005)
44. Cairns, C.N.: E-waste and the consumer: improving options to reduce, reuse and recycle. In: Proceedings of the 2005 IEEE International Symposium on Electronics and the Environment, pp. 237–242. IEEE (2005)
45. Schafer, B.: D-waste: data disposal as challenge for waste management in the Internet of Things. Ethics for the Internet of Things 22, 100 p. (2014)
46. Patrignani, N.: Computer ethics 2013: from policy vacuum to slow-tech. Mondo Digitale **13**, 1–4 (2014)
47. Jones, A.: Lessons not learned on data disposal. Digit. Invest. **6**, 3–7 (2009)

48. Wakolbinger, T., Toyasaki, F., Nowak, T., Nagurney, A.: When and for whom would e-waste be a treasure trove? Insights from a network equilibrium model of e-waste flows. Int. J. Prod. Econ. **154**, 263–273 (2014)
49. Shapiro, S.S.: Privacy by design: moving from art to practice. Commun. ACM **53**, 27–29 (2010)
50. Schnoor, J.L.: Extended producer responsibility for e-waste. Environ. Sci. Technol. **46**, 7927–7927 (2012)
51. Strauss, A., Corbin, J.M.: Basics of Qualitative Research: Techniques and Procedures for Developing Grounded Theory. Sage Publications, Inc., Thousand Oaks (2008)
52. Strauss, A., Corbin, J.: Grounded theory methodology. In: Handbook of Qualitative Research, pp. 273–285 (1994)
53. Suddaby, R.: From the editors: what grounded theory is not. Acad. Manage. J. Arch. **49**, 633–642 (2006)
54. Corbin, J.M., Strauss, A.: Grounded theory research: procedures, canons, and evaluative criteria. Qual. Soc. **13**, 3–21 (1990)
55. Glaser, B.G., Strauss, A.L.: The Discovery of Grounded Theory: Strategies for Qualitative Research. Aldine Publishing, New York (1967)
56. Charmaz, K.: Constructing Grounded Theory. Sage, London (2014)
57. Glaser, B.G.: Theoretical Sensitivity: Advances in the Methodology of Grounded Theory. Sociology Press, Mill Valley (1978)
58. Charmaz, K., Belgrave, L.: Qualitative interviewing and grounded theory analysis. In: The SAGE Handbook of Interview Research: The Complexity of the Craft, vol. 2 (2002)
59. Myers, M.D., Newman, M.: The qualitative interview in IS research: examining the craft. Inf. Organ. **17**, 2–26 (2007)
60. Rubin, H.J., Rubin, I.S.: Qualitative Interviewing: The Art of Hearing Data. Sage, Thousand Oaks (2011)
61. Eisenhardt, K.M., Graebner, M.E.: Theory building from cases: opportunities and challenges. Acad. Manage. J. **50**, 25–32 (2007)
62. Butterfield, K.D., Trevin, L.K., Weaver, G.R.: Moral awareness in business organizations: influences of issue-related and social context factors. Human Relat. **53**, 981–1018 (2000)
63. Reynolds, S.J.: Moral awareness and ethical predispositions: investigating the role of individual differences in the recognition of moral issues. J. Appl. Psychol. **91**, 233 (2006)
64. Endsley, M.R.: Toward a theory of situation awareness in dynamic systems. Hum. Factors J. Hum. Factors Ergon. Soc. **37**, 32–64 (1995)
65. Carroll, A.B.: Corporate social responsibility. Bus. Soc. **38**, 268 (1999)
66. European commission: a renewed EU strategy 2011-14 for corporate social responsibility (2011)
67. Miller, A.R.: Personal privacy in the computer age: the challenge of a new technology in an information-oriented society. Mich. Law Rev. **67**, 1089–1246 (1969)
68. Solove, D.J., Rotenberg, M., Schwartz, P.M.: Information Privacy Law. Aspen Publisher, New York (2005)
69. The commission of the European community: commission recommendation onthe implementation of privacy and data protection principles in applications supportedby radio-frequency identification, Brussels (2009)
70. Culnan, M.J., Bies, R.J.: Consumer privacy: balancing economic and justice considerations. J. Soc. Issues **59**, 323–342 (2003)

71. Moor, J.H.: Towards a theory of privacy in the information age. Comput. Soc. **27**, 27–32 (1997)
72. Stahl, B.C.: Responsibility for information assurance and privacy: a problem of individual ethics? In: Advanced Topics in End User Computing, p. 186 (2005)
73. Lenzen, M., Murray, J., Sack, F., Wiedmann, T.: Shared producer and consumer responsibility–theory and practice. Ecol. Econ. **61**, 27–42 (2007)
74. Pearson, S., Charlesworth, A.: Accountability as a way forward for privacy protection in the cloud. In: Jaatun, M.G., Zhao, G., Rong, C. (eds.) Cloud Computing. LNCS, vol. 5931, pp. 131–144. Springer, Heidelberg (2009)
75. Weitzner, D.J., Abelson, H., Berners-Lee, T., Hanson, C., Hendler, J., Kagal, L., McGuinness, D.L., Sussman, G.J., Waterman, K.K.: Transparent accountable data mining: new strategies for privacy protection (2006)

IoT and Public Clouds

Challenges of the Internet of Things: Possible Solutions from Data Protecy and 3D Privacy

Luca Bolognini[✉] and Camilla Bistolfi

Istituto Italiano per la Privacy (Italian Institute for Privacy), Rome, Italy
`luca@lucabolognini.it`

Abstract. In the course of this brief work we have tried to provide answers to questions that have arisen concerning some of the most critical aspects of IoT, in terms of individuals' fundamental rights safeguard, especially concerning the emerging complexities with respect to the protection of the personal sphere and the information of the data subject. We attempted to re-read the right to privacy, recombining it with data protection and giving life to what we have called "*data protecy*", a merger of safeguards which should be always considered in IoT. Hence, we focused on the new concept of "3D Privacy", as a consequence of the *data protecy* approach, that consists in adopting also physical security measures, empowering users and non-users as data subjects with material tools in order to self-control over their information and to self-defend from data collection in IoT open environments. This new approach has shown that it should be now necessary not only to appeal to abstract rules or policies, but also to find concrete, material instruments, ranging from the "off" button until very "personal anti-radar gadgets" or other sensors misleading devices, however limiting their use only to strictly private contexts.

1 Introduction: IoT Complexity and the Challenge of Balancing Technology, Privacy and Data Protection

Internet of Things can normally complicate the "legal chain" of accountability in data controlling and processing, as well as it could imply several, brand new risks for individuals and their fundamental rights, if means are misused. This brief study, however, aims not so much to make a general analysis of the legal issues raised by IoT–for which one can see, among others, the vast amount of work elaborated by the Article 29 Working Party and the European Commission, a number of which are cited here in the footnotes–but rather to detect possible concrete solutions, from a juridical point of view, that could be adoptable within the existing legal framework with regards to the relationship between intelligent objects, privacy and data protection. We will focus, particularly, on the conceivable capability of data subjects to "self-control" over their data and to directly protect themselves–their own personal sphere–without requesting for data controllers' and processors' actions, simply by-passing the difficult (and often almost unattainable for a simple user or even "non-user") attempt to retrace the interconnections of legal responsibilities in IoT.

Firstly, it is clear that the Internet of Things is able to produce such incredible quantities of information from more or less raw data so that it is impossible not to bring the

© Springer International Publishing Switzerland 2016
S. Schiffner et al. (Eds.): APF 2016, LNCS 9857, pp. 71–80, 2016.
DOI: 10.1007/978-3-319-44760-5_5

processing operations of personal data, carried out by objects, into the context of so-called "Big Data" and related profiling. In fact, even if different objects acquire data in an isolated fashion, they can process the same with algorithms and/or interact with other objects in order to analyze information and generate profiles related to the subject they belong to. Therefore, even if a given piece of data is anonymized by a device, it is not certain that the above data does not become part of a functional process to (re)identify the data subject. This is possible, in some cases, starting from the unique identifier assigned to the object; in others, however, thanks to the combination of information made possible through interconnection with other devices or sensors that do not use anonymous data.

Secondly, it is worth considering the risk of the subject losing control of the personal data belonging to him/her since most of the IoT communicate with other objects, creating data streams that can hardly be dealt with by oneself. Interactions between "things", however, normally take place in a "silent" manner, not manifested in any way, making it difficult for the user to control the streams of data.

Moreover, there may no longer be a single data controller and it may not necessarily be located in the European Union or anyway close to the data subject, since the entities involved are indeed many: the developer of the object and the developer of the third-party applications installed on the object, the cloud service provider that provides space on the servers in which the information is transferred and stored, the developer of a third object which interacts with the primary device, the social platform where the information acquired from the object are shared–just to name a few. These are actors which are not always found in the same figure, and therefore require a more effective identification of controllership of the acquired personal information, not only to determine the powers of the supervisory authority but also to guarantee the data subject his/her ability to exercise their rights.

Also the aspect relating to the relationship between IoT and privacy protection, that is of personal sphere, is key. In this sense, given their pervasiveness with respect to daily life, the IoT should require reconsideration of the concept of privacy and data protection, as the continuous processing of personal data is also accompanied by the invasion of what, according to art. 7 of the Charter of Fundamental Rights of the European Union (hereinafter, "CFREU") [1] we will define as private and family life. In this sense, it is interesting–and useful–to try to understand what the tools possibly available to the data subjects, users, and citizens are to directly defend their own space and their own person from the invasion of smart objects. These should be tools that, in hindsight, are not just immaterial, such as the withdrawal of consent or the exercise of a right (i.e. to data portability or to be forgotten), but are gradually turning into objects/physical shields, too, whose materiality allows one to contrast the ethereal dimension of data streams and the ever-more concrete intelligent "things" that surround us. These could be objects that protect or shield the person from the activity of other objects, giving three-dimensionality to privacy and data protection, transforming them also into material bulwarks.

Smart technologies forge ahead in the direction of 3D, forcing (or enabling) the world of privacy and data protection to re-work and re-think the forms of self-protection to ensure a subject that is not only the user, but also the citizen who lives in a Smart City, the housekeeper who turned on the oven and the lights from the same control panel or the passer-by who, unaware, is photographed by his neighbor's drone.

Finally, the aspect of security is not to be underestimated. When you consider that the IoT sensors are connected to the Internet and that they are also located inside homes, it is clear that the violation of the home gives way to cracking. Imagine, for example, the possibility that a thief accesses the data collected by the device sensors and discovers the times when the lights are used, deducing when the house is uninhabited. Or, through illegal access to the Smart Grid, the thief might be able to disable the home alarm, or to turn off the electricity and illegally enter the home. This is also relevant in case of a car where, through data collected from GPS sensors, the places where the car is parked unattended for an extended period of time could be known, maybe also combining the data with those collected by the Smart Watch connected via Bluetooth to the car's system. Data protection and privacy then become safeguards that also encompass aspects of cyber security, not only in order to prevent unauthorized access to data (data breach), but also to avoid intrusions aimed at the remote management of IoT devices.

2   Data Protection or Privacy? The New Concept of "Data Protecy"

Privacy and data protection are still two separate fundamental rights according to the European normative approach, which represented, indeed, an innovative intuition at the end of XXth Century but, now, could risk to turn itself in an obstacle for IoT. Article 8 of the CFREU, dedicated to the Protection of Personal Data, is bound to a set of principles that data processing must comply with (identification of specific purposes, consent from the data subject or grounded on other bases of legitimacy) and a set of rights (access and rectification) regardless of whether the processing is carried out in the public or private sector.

From a data protection perspective therefore, the provisions of Art. 8 guarantee not only a fundamental right, but are also aimed at ensuring that the right to the free flow of information is not impeded by way of the legal certainty provided to the data subject for the protection of his/her personal data. Similarly, the CFREU also guarantees the "Respect for private and family life" [2], more specifically the right to privacy or the possibility for the individual to enjoy his personal space (private and family life, home and communications) [2], without interference from the "public". In this sense both article 7 of the CFREU and article 8 of the European Convention on Human Rights (hereinafter "ECHR") protect the "private sphere".

While the privacy of personal space includes the protection of an individual, such as the home, communications and family life, the protection of data has to do with privacy, but its purpose is not only to protect the privacy/confidentiality of data, preventing illicit spread. It also wants to ensure that the individual is able to check the information concerning him/her, guaranteeing the respect of other complementary rights such as the freedom of access, correction or modification of data, but also the erasure of the data or knowledge of who the data controller is and the information he possesses.

In 2009 the European Commission, in its Communication on the internet of Things, stated that IoT *"should not be seen as a mere extension of today's Internet but rather as a number of new independent systems that operate with their own infrastructures (and partly rely on existing Internet infrastructures)"* [3]. Taking into account this relevant precision concerning the exceptional features of the IoT, the above-mentioned definitions of privacy and data protection can (and should) be reinterpreted and redesigned in order to increase their margins under which the IoT could be placed.

The use of smart "things" seems to require an extension of the negative right to privacy for two reasons. First, the concept of "personal sphere" has changed. It has lost its classic features, opening its doors to the first inanimate objects which now are able to act independently in terms of the information they reveal and can even talk to each other, exchange data that they have acquired. Secondly, smart "things" are objects which are precisely part of the "personal sphere" which carry risks of "interference" with respect to the individual's privacy–it's no longer just the "public authority" referred to in Article 7 of the CFREU. The IoT is located inside homes, it's worn on our wrists, installed in our cars and often shared with the whole family: this makes "private life" increasingly "public", placing intelligent objects in dimensions thought of as inviolable (or almost) until now.

Hence, given that privacy should be (re)designed as a negative right (and not only with respect to the public authority, but also with respect to smart objects to tackle the possible invasion of the personal sphere), what about the data protection? What is the relationship established with the new concept of privacy?

It was said, in fact, that to date, the two rights were designed in a disconnected manner, admitting, at most, that the two guarantees ended where it was believed that the personal data deserve the same privacy attributed to private life. In this sense, thanks to the intrinsic characteristics of the IoT, we have witnessed the reunification of the rights that Articles 7 and 8 of the CFREU had divided: the Internet of things requires that data protection and privacy are fused together in order to protect the individual from the activities of connected and interconnected intelligent objects that invade the private sphere while processing personal data. The result is an entirely new concept that, playing with syncretic neologisms and proposing the merger of the two rights demanded by IoT, we define as *"data protecy"*.

3   IoT "Smart" Rights Protection: Possible *Data Protecy* Safeguards

The aforementioned complexity requires the formulation of brand new mechanisms for the data subject's empowerment and, in general, for ensuring safety and respect of fundamental rights in IoT.

3.1   Objects "Without Eyes": Non-Users, Social Awareness and Empowerment of Users

End-users awareness, knowledge of the users, must (still) be built and diffused, both with reference to the knowledge of the protection of personal data and privacy in the Internet of Things, as well as with regards to the perception of the connected (and interconnected) environment that surrounds them.

In the 2013 Fact-sheet published by the European Commission following the public consultation and the work of several groups of IoT experts [4], the concept of transparency is linked to that of trust and understanding by users of the smart object's operation, offering a certification system that will further help them to understand what type of objects they are [5]. The latter, in fact, may often seem to be ordinary objects, hiding their intelligence.

First, there is the question of the information notice and then there are questions that arise thinking of the many types of smart objects on the market today: where is the information notice? In what way is it provided? What should its content be?

It cannot not appear each time the object is being used and, though in some cases it is provided in print with the product, in the other cases it is made available on-line. This observation already poses a first problem, as the product information is likely to be disconnected from the product itself.

Furthermore, IoT devices are often "without eyes", lacking visual interfaces, dashboards or screens, considering also that most IoT technologies entirely resemble "classic" objects, apparently ordinary and not connected, without the awareness of the individual who uses them. The lack of informed consent–as it has been understood until now as a result of the nature of computers and mobile phones (with appropriate information notices followed by a tick-flag, electronic signature, click, etc.)–is derived not only from the concrete impossibility for certain devices to provide an information notice following which consent could be collected, but also by way of the lack of the information notice and, therefore, the eventual consent, both in the case of automatic and "silent" interconnection with other devices with which the data is exchanged as well as when the object interacts with the surrounding environment without being immediately visible.

Then, it is important to consider that there are "non-users" whose personal data may be captured from the interactions they have with the owner of the object (e.g. "Smart Glass" which also captures images of the environment, registering the faces of those who interact with the owner of the glasses). In this sense, the restoration of the asymmetry of power between man and object in terms of data management gives particular importance to the concepts of privacy-by-default and privacy-by-design, which reduce user exposure thanks to what the European Commission has defined privacy enhancing technologies [6].

As has been highlighted, respect of the principles governing the processing of personal data is a necessary condition for the IoT to cohabitate with what has been defined as *data protecy*. Considering that the first of those principles requires that data be treated *"in a lawful, fair and transparent"* [7] manner with respect to the data subject, one cannot consider that *"the number of connected devices is increasing, while their size is reduced below the threshold of visibility to the human eye"* [3]. This means that data subjects are no longer only those who make a conscious decision to use smart objects, but also those who are in the sphere of action of the device and, therefore, legality, fairness and transparency in the processing are principles that also extend to non-users whose data, more or less consciously, are acquired.

For this reason, the Article 29 Working Party emphasizes the need for positive action on the part of data controllers [8], who must notify all individuals who are in close proximity (geographic or digital) to intelligent devices, of the fact that their data, in form more or less crude form, are acquired. However, it is not easy to imagine this to be possible.

It should be pointed out here that–only in the case of users of specific and limited services (while it seems unattainable for non-users)–a possible solution to the transparency challenges posed by IoT is elaborated in the so-called sticky policy, overturning the information factors and enabling users to set their bottom-up notices. There are systems similar to digital right management which allow to attribute "Terms of use" to the personal data of the user that travel together with the data when it is transferred from one device to another. In this sense, the personal data is processed maintaining the consent granted (or not) by the user.

A positive aspect of the sticky policy system is the potential capacity for the data subject to "virtually" regain control over their personal data, where the IoT may threaten certainty about the use of such data by different controllers and despite the lack of their transparency. This particularly applies to those objects that collect sensitive data or information aimed at generating sensitive data using deductive algorithms for processing of which requires the consent of the data subject [9]–see next paragraph.

Also crowd/social dynamics could help data subjects in self-organising protection and in sharing knowledge in order to defend themselves from IoT risks. In this sense we look at the European Privacy Flag project–supported by Horizon 2020 program funds–whose purpose is to create tools based on users' self-assessment and crowdsourcing awareness mechanisms to disclose each other the privacy-data protection risk levels in apps and websites, but even in the IoT world.

3.2   *Data Protecy*-by-Design and by-Default

"The controller shall implement appropriate technical and organisational measures for ensuring that, by default, only personal data which are necessary for each specific purpose of the processing are processed. That obligation applies to the amount of personal data collected, the extent of their processing, the period of their storage and their accessibility. In particular, such measures shall ensure that by default personal data are not made accessible without the individual's intervention to an indefinite number of natural persons." Article 25(2) of the General Data Protection Regulation thereby imposes, *a priori*, the maximum protection of data aiming for minimal processing.

IoT devices are often designed to directly access the web without the user having to configure them. This implies a possible loss of user control over the data that concern him, in the sense that he may not know how (or be able) to manage the flow of data that the device exchanges with the net. In this respect it is crucial that the factory settings–default settings–are as near as possible to the purpose for which the object was conceived.

In the case of domotics, for instance, it could be questioned whether or not the device could be used for the basic functions only. In general, it would be interesting to understand whether there is an option, implemented in the object "by design", making it possible to turn off its intelligence, restoring privacy of the personal sphere as well as establishing the right to privacy [2, 10] and preventing the collection of personal data. The nature of the IoT strongly lends itself to privacy enhancing technologies (hereinafter "PET"), defined as a *"system of ICT measures that protects privacy by eliminating or reducing personal data or by preventing unnecessary and/or undesired processing of personal data, all without losing the functionality of the information system* [6].

These measures can be part of what we might call *data protecy*-by-design, i.e. the implementation, from the design stage, of the *"appropriate technical and organizational measures and procedures in such a way that the processing will meet the requirements of this Regulation and ensure the protection of the rights of the data subject"* [11] and also to restore the privacy of the personal sphere. In other words, it is the commitment of the data controller to take account of data protection rules–and of privacy in the cast of IoT–from the technical design of products and services.

This means, for example, designing the object in a way that does not allow it to automatically connect to other devices, making that the decision of the user, as well as carrying out personal data processing operations of that are closely linked to its primary purposes. Furthermore, if in the example of home automation the answer to the question about the possibility of blocking "smart" functions could have been "yes" and rather immediate, the degree of certainty could change with reference to other technologies, such as in the aforementioned case of cars or the Smart Watch and other IoT objects. What if the user does not want his watch to count his steps or monitor his pulse, limiting the function of the watch to only tell time? And the GPS in the car, can it be turned off? Even the existence of an "off" button on "connected" smart objects embodies data protecy-by-default.similar solutions are incorporated within the objects themselves in the design phase allowing for the restoration of the protection of privacy with respect to the pervasiveness the IoT, a version of privacy which also extends to the personal data that are silently acquired by the "things".

Returning to the dimension of *data protecy,* Article 29 Working Party Opinion 8/2014 reflects on the relationship between private life and the massive collection of information, noting a particular that is quite reminiscent of Orwellian Big Brother scenarios. In fact, the simultaneous illumination of several sensors that collect data can affect the spontaneity of the data subject [12] who feels observed and monitored, losing the right established in art. 7 of the CFREU and processing operations in art. 8 CFREU. The function should be similar to "do not disturb" - which in the case of data protection we could translate into "do not collect" – which would serve to turn off the collection of data to restore privacy for individuals. Here, again, we return to the concept of *data protecy*: in the IoT, data protection is "protection of the personal sphere" and the protection of the personal sphere is possible through data protection.

It seems appropriate to conclude the paragraph with a fitting and very current quote, even if dating back to 2004, taken from the speech given by Stefano Rodotà during the twenty-sixth International Conference on Privacy and Personal Data Protection, *"'We shall not lay hand upon thee', This was the promise made in the Magna Charta–to respect the body in its entirety: Habeas Corpus. This promise has survived technological developments. Each processing operation concerning individual data is to be regarded as related to the body as a whole, to an individual that has to be respected in its physical and mental integrity. This is a new all-round concept of individual, and its translation into the real world entails the right to full respect for a body that is nowadays both 'physical' and 'electronic'. In this new world, data protection fulfills the task of ensuring the 'habeas data' required by the changed circumstances–and thereby becomes an ineliminable component of civilisation, as has been in the history for the habeas corpus"* [13].

4   3D Privacy: Things that Protect from Things, in Data Subjects' Hands

As briefly analysed so far, it seems that often one cannot choose to not be a data subject and to remain invisible to sensors: it happens all time we are non-users and the data controllers and/or technology designers have not implemented robust by default measures in order to avoid data collection. This is the reason why we should also, gradually, find solutions in defense of *data protecy* that are no longer based on by-design approaches - as the aforementioned case of a possible "off" button - but on material objects and tools in the hands of subjects. The protection of the personal sphere and its data is becoming three-dimensional and lies in what might be called "3D privacy". That is, the use of other objects or other physical elements in order to not collect personal information but to cloak or shield the individual from such collection, restoring the privacy of the individual sphere.

Importantly, we could even partially leave digital logic behind. The encryption of the transmissions does not eliminate the risk of security breaches of the IoT system because the violation may consist either in the viewing of the personal data and in mere access to the data from which inferences can be made by combining the vast amount of information the sensors collect. It seems that we are not so far from using tools that were designed with combat functions, as in the case of steel, which could be used to isolate environments and IoT sensors from electromagnetic waves.

In short, it is no longer the invisible ink or applications that automatically delete chats and images, but real objects, material elements, which allow one to go "unnoticed" by IoT sensors. The scenario seems to be taken from a James Bond movie, but, anyway, isn't shielding oneself from smart objects an anti-spying measures itself?

We will probably wear accessories that can reveal the presence of sensors that are not immediately visible. Looking to the future, it does not seem unrealistic to imagine that search engines will soon no longer serve only to provide access to information, but also to locate smart objects. In fact, taking into account the possibility of identifying the IoT through their unique identifiers, the "IoT search" feature of search engines could be directly based on the location of the above-mentioned identifiers. This would allow users to know not only the location of the sensors, but also to obtain news about their possible interconnection with other IoT objects. This would be a noteworthy form of user empowerment for two reasons that involve data protection understood both as the exercise of rights and in terms of re-acquisition of control over data flows themselves. First of all, smart objects could be traced and located through the search engine, returning the rights belonging to the data subject also to non-users (and even the users themselves). In fact - and this is the second reason why a similar search function constitutes a form of empowerment - the data subject may proactively access the privacy policies of different connected and interconnected objects through the unique identifier, being able to obtain information concerning the data controller and allowing for the exercise of his/ her rights to be informed of the data flow regardless of whether or not he/she is a user that has requested the service. The use of small area geolocation applied IoT and the crossing of this information with the functions of search engines could become the digital evolution of the aforementioned three-dimensional device that intercepts and indicates the presence of sensors. The new search feature would reduce the risks linked to the fact that "the number of connected devices is increasing, while their size is reduced below the threshold of visibility to the human eye" [3] and the hypothesis that by way of the aforementioned function, in some cases the data subject (user or non-user) will have the possibility to disable the smart features and therefore assert his/her right to *data protecy* according to the logic of the off button.

Those which until today have been bugging detectors, GPS signals or micro cameras soon become wearable/portable items for detecting IoT sensors. Once enabled to detect sensors, consequently and more effectively, data subjects can be empowered to use inhibitors of the sensors themselves. In this way, the lack of the "off" button would no longer be a problem, and at the same time the age-old dilemma of the way in which the data controller can inform the non-user of the collection of data concerning him through sensors of the device would be solved.

An example: glasses invented in Japan that make the wearer "invisible": the National Institute of Informatics decided to counter the technology for facial recognition through special lenses that do not allow the photo/video cameras to focus on the face, reflecting, refracting and absorbing light. The utility is pretty obvious, especially considering that, at the same time in the United States symmetrical and antithetical *Smart Glass* was developed and in Italy was designed a software for the biometric identification of individuals aimed at profiling for marketing purposes. In practice, entering a store equipped with such a system, the software identifies the subject in real time, analyzing their characteristics and consumer choices by means of proximity sensors. It's here that the Japanese glasses are the ideal instrument to avoid the acquisition of one's raw data (man, over 50, Caucasian, above five foot-eight) which is then processed by the software to obtain the consumption profile.

We could even expect something more, somehow analog and derived from military and national security practices (e.g. TEMPEST technology), such as portable radio/ electromagnetic mini-devices working as "personal anti-radar gadgets".

Of course, these 3D Privacy cloaking or misleading tools should be considered as double-edged swords: they could be used in the wrong way, sometimes impeding legal controls and reducing, *de facto*, the level of public security. Such instruments could contrast with specific regulations (i.e. in case of permitting burdens and public licenses required for radio equipments, or in case of particular prohibitions to wear masks and disguise). For this reason, it seems in general reasonable to set limits of their usability outside any strictly private area.

In the meantime, however, while we wait for further developments in 3D privacy, a Danish company has decided to train eagles to capture drones that fly over unauthorized areas or invade the privacy of the underlying subjects. This is a definitely three-dimensional solution.

References

1. Charter of fundamental rights of the European Union, 2012/C 326/02. eur-lex.europa.eu
2. Art. 7, European Union, *Charter of Fundamental Rights of the European Union*, 26 October 2012, 2012/C 326/02. http://www.europarl.europa.eu/charter/pdf/text_en.pdf
3. European Commission, COM(2009) 278, Internet of Things – An action plan for Europe. eur-lex.europa.eu
4. Ethics Subgroup IoT, Internet of Things Fact-sheet Ethics. ec.europa.eu
5. Ethics Subgroup IoT, Internet of Things Fact-sheet Ethics, pp. 17–18. ec.europa.eu
6. Communication from the Commission to the European Parliament and the Council on Promoting Data Protection by Privacy Enhancing Technologies (PETs), COM/2007/0228. http://eur-lex.europa.eu/legal-content/EN/TXT/?uri=celex:52007DC0228
7. Art. 5(1)(a), Regulation (EU) 2016/679 of the European Parliament and of the Council of 27 April 2016 on the Protection of natural persons with regard to the processing of personal data and on the free movement of such data, and repealing Directive 95/46/EC (General Data Protection Regulation), http://eur-lex.europa.eu/legal-content/EN/TXT/HTML/?uri=CELEX:32016R0679&from=IT
8. Article 29 Working Party, Opinion 8/2014 on Recent developments on the Internet of Things, p. 16. ec.europa.eu
9. Art. 8, Directive 95/46/EC of the European Parliament and of the Council of 24 October 1995 on the protection of individuals with regard to the processing of personal data and on the free movement of such data and Art. 9, Regulation (EU) 2016/679 of the European Parliament and of the Council of 27 April 2016 on the Protection of natural persons with regard to the processing of personal data and on the free movement of such data, and repealing Directive 95/46/EC (General Data Protection Regulation). http://eur-lex.europa.eu/legal-content/EN/TXT/HTML/?uri=CELEX:32016R0679&from=IT
10. Art. 8, Council of Europe, European Convention for the Protection of Human Rights and Fundamental Freedoms, as amended by Protocols Nos. 11 and 14, 4 November 1950, ETS 5. http://www.echr.coe.int/Documents/Convention_ENG.pdf
11. Art. 23(1), GDPR
12. Article 29 Working Party, Opinion 8/2014 on Recent developments on the Internet of Things, p. 8. ec.europa.eu
13. Stefano Rodotà, Privacy, Freedom, and Dignity Conclusive Remarks at the 26th International Conference on Privacy and Personal Data Protection, 16 September 2004. www.garanteprivacy.it

Smart Meters as Non-purpose Built Surveillance Tools

Jonida Milaj[(✉)] and Jeanne Pia Mifsud Bonnici

Department of European and Economic Law, Faculty of Law,
University of Groningen, Groningen, The Netherlands
{j.milaj-weishaar,g.p.mifsud.bonnici}@stop-rug.nl

Abstract. This paper analysis the potential use of smart meters as surveillance tools by law enforcement authorities. In assessing the challenges that the introduction of smart meters in the European Union creates for the right to privacy and data protection of individuals the paper takes a fundamental rights approach based on the existing European legal framework, case law and doctrine. The legal analysis is augmented by technical/engineering studies that show the interest that smart meter data has for law enforcement authorities. It is argued that the current EU legal framework is not adequate for addressing the challenges that surveillance via smart meter data creates for the rights of the individuals and that the existing legal gap must be taken into account and used in favour of the protection of the fundamental rights of the individuals.

1 Introduction[1]

Smart meters are introduced in the European Union because of the contributions they are expected to make towards the energy saving targets adopted by the Member States [20, art. 13]. A key feature of smart meters is the collection of data for energy usage[2] and their almost real time communication between the meter and service providers.[3] The detailed data collection and their communication is said to benefit not only the service providers (learning about the specific energy demand and enabling energy companies to enhance the accuracy of their long term predictions which would impact their production and purchasing strategy) but also the consumers (allowing them to have an accurate overview on their consumption which might impact their consumption behavior in accordance with electricity fees) [28].

The European legislator has set the target of substituting at least 80 % of the electricity meters in the EU with smart ones by the year 2020 [21, annex I, para. 2]. After a high speed start in some countries (e.g. Sweden, Finland and Italy) [14, 40] the

---

[1] See Ref. [45] for earlier version of this paper.

[2] For the scope of this paper we consider only smart meters that measure the consumption of electricity and not of water or gas. In addition, also our usage of the term "energy" is limited to electric energy and does not cover gas or other forms of energy.

[3] With this term in this paper are understood distribution system operators, transmission system operators, electricity supply undertakings or other parties that receive the data directly from the meter in accordance with the electricity distribution system.

© Springer International Publishing Switzerland 2016
S. Schiffner et al. (Eds.): APF 2016, LNCS 9857, pp. 81–95, 2016.
DOI: 10.1007/978-3-319-44760-5_6

introduction of smart meters has faced in other countries (e.g. the Netherlands and Germany) concerns that were not considered before, among which privacy and data protection challenges [15, 47].

A number of studies have shown the interest of actors other than energy suppliers for accessing smart meter data [53, 38, 48, 41, 39, 7, 1, 6, 30, 42]. Law enforcement authorities are among them.

The use of data from electricity measuring devices for law enforcement purposes is not a new phenomenon. The so-called "dumb" meters[4] give information on the total consumption of energy in the households and the possibility for readings of the data in monthly or longer time intervals. Law enforcement authorities have been using these data and regarded very high electricity consumptions as an indicator that certain illegal activities (e.g. cultivation of illegal narcotic plants) are performed in the household. Smart meters, in contrast, transfer not only final energy consumption data but also detailed data related with the specific use of the electricity in a household. These data might give the possibility to law enforcement authorities to check electric devices, their times of use and other activities taking place within the walls of a private residence [45].

The communication of the energy consumption related data from smart meters is said to create accurate maps of the activities taking place within a household. As stated by Martin Pollock[5] from Siemens Energy: *"We, Siemens, have the technology to record it (energy consumption) every minute, second, microsecond, more or less live.... From that we can infer how many people are in the house, what they do, whether they're upstairs, downstairs, do you have a dog, when do you habitually get up, when did you get up this morning, when do you have a shower: masses of private data"* [57].

This paper contributes to the literature developed on privacy and data protection issues of smart meters [36, 51, 58] by focusing on the challenges that their use for surveillance purposes by law enforcement authorities creates for safeguarding the rights to privacy and data protection of individuals in the current European legal framework. After this short introduction Sect. 2 analyses the nature of smart meters as non-purpose built surveillance tools and qualifies the collected data within the framework of data protection and privacy rules in Europe. Section 3 identifies potential uses of smart meter data by law enforcement authorities. Section 4 discusses the challenges to the protection of the rights to privacy and data protection that are created by surveillance with smart meter data. In Sect. 5 are presented the concluding remarks together with suggestions on the interpretation of the new Data Protection Directive for safeguarding the rights of individuals in case law enforcement authorities plan to use smart meters for surveillance purposes.

---

[4] Analog meters that are still present in those households that have not yet installed smart ones.

[5] Director of metering services at Siemens Energy.

2   Smart Meters as Non-purpose Build Surveillance Tools and the Nature of the Data Collected

This section starts by giving a qualification of smart meters as non-purpose built surveillance tools (Subsect. 2.1). To assess the effects that surveillance via smart meters has for the right to privacy and data protection of individuals it elaborates on the nature of smart meter data and their qualification under the applicable European rules (Subsect. 2.1).

2.1   Smart Meters as Non-purpose Built Surveillance Tools

The term surveillance derives from the French language and literally refers to a close watch kept over someone or something.[6] For Wigan and Clarke [56] the origin of 'surveillance' derives from the times of the French revolution. The term is related with the systematic investigation or monitoring of the actions or communications of one or more persons [4]. In contemporary social and political sciences, surveillance refers to the *"process of watching, monitoring, recording, and processing the behavior of people, objects and events in order to govern activity"* [31].

Surveillance can be physical or performed with the aid of surveillance tools. Development of technology has, however, created the possibility that also devices that are not originally built for the purpose of surveillance are used for this purpose. Some examples of these non-purpose built devices are: smart phones, GPS navigation systems, smart television, etc.

To say that a device has not been originally built for the purpose of surveillance might be a bit speculative especially since we cannot assure the existence of cases in which the design and development of a certain technology or device might have been supported by underlying interests of intelligence and law enforcement bodies. That is why we limit the definition of devices non-built for the purpose of surveillance for this study to those devices that are introduced in the markets mainly for the performance of another activity. For this study it is the combination of the ability and of the official accreditation that determines the qualification of a device as not built for the purpose of surveillance. Smart meters are certainly not built for the purpose of surveillance, but as it will be argued in Sect. 3 they present possibilities and potential to be used for such a purpose.

Surveillance with non-purpose built devices is more intrusive into the life of the individuals than traditional surveillance [43] and risks to turn surveillance into an ubiquitous activity. The choice for the use of traditional surveillance or surveillance with non-purpose built tools is of course left with the law enforcement authorities. These must take into account the risks created to the fundamental rights of the individuals before taking their decisions.

---

[6] As defined by the Merriam-Webster Online Dictionary.

2.2   Smart Meter Data as Personal Data

The current EU legal framework for smart meters is composed of Directive 2009/72/EC [21] (Energy Internal Market Directive), and Directive 2004/22/EC [18] (Measuring Instrument Directive). These directives focus on the operation of the system and do not regulate privacy and personal data issues. Other provisions in the field have the form of soft law, recommending rather than requiring the application of safeguards for the protection of the rights to privacy and data protection [10, para. 4-9,11]. The provisions suggest, however, the respect of the general legal regime in the field.

Smart meter data give information that is not limited to energy consumption but reveal also domestic activities on the basis of the usage of electric appliances in a household [55]. Electricity consumption might give also more direct information on the habits of the members of the household - when they are at home, if they have healthy habits (e.g. cooking regularly or using largely the microwave for convenience food), if they spend time together or in separate rooms, the activities they perform, and even sensitive information (e.g. the use of medical devices) [33].

There has been no reluctance to qualify smart meter data as personal data [24, 15] even though different ideas have been presented as to whom these data belong. Since personal data are defined as data linked to an identified or identifiable person [22, art. 2 (a)], as potential data subjects have been targeted: (a) the member of the household that is the signatory of the electricity supply contract; (b) all the members of the household as a group; or (c) each individual member of the household.

For the Article 29 Working Party [2] a domestic consumer of energy is associated with unique identifiers that are inextricably linked with the member of the household who is responsible for the account. The data would therefore belong to him. This qualification would, however, attribute to one member of the household all the generated electricity data, even in periods of time when it is clear that he is not present at the location.

In contrast, Knyrim and Trieb [36] suggest that the definition of personal data should be interpreted broadly in line with some national data protection laws. They present the example of the Austrian law that refers to personal data as belonging not only to a single person but also to a 'community of persons' [16, para. 4(3)]. With this broad interpretation smart meter data would qualify as personal data belonging to all the inhabitants of the household as a community. This idea is supported also by King and Jessen [35] that plead for the adoption of a more inclusive definition of the data subject which would cover a group of natural persons living together in a household, including temporary guests.

It is easy and automatic to link smart meter data to the person that has signed the contract with the electricity supply company or to refer to a community of persons instead, even though the latter might create problems with regards to the consent needed for the use of the data by third parties. But as stated by the European Data Protection Supervisor [24] the long period of retention and the possibility of profiling while linking different databases gives the possibility to separate the data and link them to the right identified or identifiable members of the household: "*Profiles can thus be developed, and then applied back to individual households and individual members of these households*". We would agree with this view and consider smart meter data as personal data belonging to individual household members.

Qualifying smart meter data as personal data brings them into the realm of application of the European data protection legislation. As already seen in the Data Retention Directive case,[7] the collected and processed personal data create the possibility to interfere at the same time also with the private sphere of the individuals concerned [51]. Just from the few examples mentioned above smart meter data give information on different aspects of the private life of the citizens as for example: privacy of behaviour, privacy of data, privacy of association (learning about the presence of guests and how often) and even privacy of the individuals´ body (since it is possible to detect sensitive information as for example medical appliances at home and how often they are used). Thus surveillance of individuals via smart meters creates challenges for the protection of their right to privacy and to the right to data protection at the same time.

3 Smart Meter Data for Law Enforcement Authorities

As already stated, smart meter data present interest for different actors, law enforcement authorities being one of these. They can have direct access to the data, via the smart meter device, or receive the information from the service providers or other parties that have access to the data. The aim of this section is to present a number of possibilities that smart meters offer for collecting data and information on the activities that individuals perform within the privacy of their homes and not only, as well as on the relevance that these data might have for law enforcement authorities.

Smart meters collect detailed data on activities that take place within a household. These data are linked with the usage of different (identifiable) devices and give the possibility to draw accurate maps of the activities that take place within an household. The possibilities of smart meters for collecting data on what happens within the walls of a household, detecting activities and disclosing them to the outside world are, therefore, broad and accurate [32, 26]. These devices give the possibility for detecting illegal activities, for collecting evidence, for verifying defendants' claims [39], suspects' claims and even for creating and verifying profiles of certain criminals.

The frequency of the communicated data discloses not only the presence of electric devices and their on/off status but shows also activities that members of a household do within the privacy of their home. The analyses of energy usage over long periods of time may show also patterns of use and even distinguish situations that are outside the normal every day routine, as for example the presence of guests [34]. Data can assess sleeping times, working times, if someone is at home, when the family goes on holidays, etc.

Some studies present the possibility to use smart meter data for disclosing the television programmes that one watches [46]. Apparently, *"the amount of light and dark emitted on the display for individual frames is unique for each TV program and movie"* and gives the possibility to identify the watched program at any particular point in time. Studies show that also the copyright protection or its absence of a DVD that is played can be detected [25]. In addition data from charging of electric cars would give

---

[7] Joint cases C-293/12 and C-594/12 Digital Rights Ireland and Seitlinger and others [2014] nyr, para. 27.

information on the kilometers traveled and, combined with other information, might validate also other information on the destinations reached and thus on activities taking place outside the walls of a house [52].

From the above possibilities that smart meter data create, one might imagine all the interesting information and evidence that law enforcement authorities would be able to access by using these devices and the data they collect for surveillance. This information would facilitate the creation of detailed profiles of the members of a household and especially of suspected individuals, under formal investigation or not, since the data show patterns of their routine life, behavior and preferences.

The frequent communication between the smart meter and the service provider in short time intervals of 15 min (even though shorter time intervals are not excluded) would also give the possibility to use this feature of the system for direct surveillance of individual members of the household. One can learn about their presence at home, their TV preferences (that might reveal interesting information in cases of, for example, pedophiles or other sexual offenders), if they use the electricity for illegal activities (e.g. cultivation of narcotic plants, unlicensed commercial activities, sweatshops, etc.).

The problem that the frequent access to energy consumption data creates for the right to privacy and data protection is recognized also in the Member States as it is the case of the Privacy Impact Assessment on smart metering done in the UK. On the basis of this assessment, for privacy reasons and also in compliance with the proportionality principle suppliers of energy are allowed to access the data on daily frequency and not with the half-hourly intervals, with the exception of the cases in which they receive explicit consent from the customer [54]. The daily access of the suppliers to the data does not mean, however, that the system is also collecting the data at such an interval. This is also because for the consumers to benefit from the system there is the need to have a more frequent access to their energy consumption data. Law enforcement authorities have thus the possibility to access the generated data more frequently.

Mass surveillance might be yet another possibility for the use of smart meter data from law enforcement authorities. This might be the case when the authorities will target an illegal activity (e.g. cultivation of narcotic plants) and check all smart meter data from households for identifying cases of unlawful behaviour.

4   Challenges that Surveillance with Smart Meters Presents to the Rights to Privacy and Data Protection in the Current EU Legal Framework

Surveillance activities by law enforcement authorities are thus far mainly regulated at Member State level. The absence of harmonised rules on surveillance at EU level is linked to the limited competence of the European institutions in the area of the former third pillar (Judicial and Police Cooperation in Criminal Matters). The EU legislation has thus far focused exclusively on data exchange, as well as on coordination and cooperation between law enforcement agencies of the Member States. Framework Decision 2008/977/JHA [13] on police and judicial cooperation in criminal matters, even if introduced the data protection principles in the field, did not harmonise these sector-specific provisions and applies only in cases of exchange of data between the Member States.

Apart the EU legislation, for activities within the area of police and judicial cooperation all Member States are part of the Council of Europe Recommendation R (87)15 [49], which sets out the principles of Convention 108 [12] for the police sector and has become the effective standard on these issues [37, 113]. This Recommendation is not, however, a legally binding instrument.

In April 2016 the new Data Protection package was adopted. Especially relevant for the work of law enforcement authorities is Directive 2016/680/EU [23] (new Data Protection Directive) on the protection of the personal data of individuals when these are processed by competent authorities for the purposes of prevention, investigation, detection or prosecution of criminal penalties. As the title suggests though, the package focuses on the right to data protection leaving other aspects of the right to privacy uncovered. Member States are required to implement the provisions of this directive by the 6th of May 2018. From that date also Framework Decision 2008/977/JHA is repealed [13].

The directive aims to introduce an equivalent level of protection of personal data within the Member States when these are processed for the purposes mentioned above as well as to facilitate the exchange of data between the Member States. As defined in Article 3(2), processing of data includes also their collection. The technology neutral nature of the directive makes also collection of data (surveillance) with non-purpose built technology fall within its field of application. Though judicial authorities are in general covered by the directive, their acting within the powers of their judicial capability is excluded. The effects that the implementation of the directive will potentially have for the protection of the right of data protection of the individuals while surveilled via smart meters are suggested further in this paper.

Surveillance via smart meter data can be performed by law enforcement authorities themselves, or via service providers that are under a duty to refer suspicious situations and therefore operate as an arm of the State [8, 312].[8] The very detailed and timely way smart meters transfer the data might give the possibility for direct surveillance as well as for dataveillance [9]. In addition, even though there is not yet any legislation requiring smart meter data retention for law enforcement purposes, service providers might keep data for long periods of time for other reasons than surveillance. The Measuring Instruments Directive (Annex MI-003, para. 5(3)), for example, establishes that smart meter data shall remain available for reading for a period of at least 4 months. These period of retention might change from one Member State to another in relation with the electricity payment intervals. In UK for example the customer is sent a bill every 1 to 3 months, but this might be an estimate bill while an accurate bill is sent every two years. In Poland the system is similar but the invoice is issued every 6 months [26, para. 100]. Meter data, even if not detailed, may be retained also for other purposes as for example taxation (3 years in the UK, 5 years in Poland, 7 years in the

---

[8] C-180/04 Vassallo v. Azienda Ospedaliera Ospedale San Martino di Genova e Cliniche Universitarie Convenzionate [2006] ECR I-7251, para. 26; M.M. v. The Netherlands, ECHR application no. 39339/98, 8 April 2003, para. 42; A. v. France, ECHR application no. 14838/89, 23 November 1993, paras. 38–39.

Netherlands, 10 years in France) [26, para. 105]. The data might be retained also from the electricity companies for ensuring an accurate forecasting of energy use.

Apart the retention of data and the possibility thereof to access them at a different moment in time, smart meters are designed to send the information in short time intervals creating a possibility for direct surveillance. When deciding on surveillance with smart meters one has to keep in mind the level of intrusion of this device that has a 24 h presence within the household. That is tantamount to 24 h surveillance of activities that take place in the privacy of one's home and it is also the reason why the need for a warrant similar with the one needed for searching a home has been advised, when smart meter data is asked for [24]. In the following sub-sections the effects that surveillance via smart meter data has for the rights to privacy and data protection in cases of individual surveillance (Subsect. 4.1) and mass surveillance (Subsect. 4.2) are discussed.

4.1   Individual Surveillance

With individual surveillance is understood the surveillance of targeted individuals from law enforcement authorities. As seen in Sect. 3, in the case of use of smart meter data for such a purpose the level of intrusion into the individual's private life might be quite high. Besides the level of intrusiveness, there are other important elements that the authorities issuing the surveillance warrant for the use of smart meters have to keep in mind. These elements are incidental surveillance, accuracy of the data and retroactive surveillance. Each element is discussed in turn below.

a. *Incidental surveillance*

Incidental surveillance is the accidental collection of data from individuals that are not the target of the surveillance activity [29]. As a result of the surveillance activity their private life is interfered. Thus far, there are no proper safeguards of the rights to privacy and data protection of individuals that find themselves in situations of incidental surveillance in the European Union. The legislation does not regulate such situations while in the case law of the European Court of Human Rights this form of surveillance is considered as being compatible with the rules, even though it is done without assessing the standards set in article 8 ECHR.[9]

Essentially two possibilities for an *ex post* remedy of the infringed right exist for an incidentally surveilled individual. The first possibility is to challenge the validity of the surveillance mandate as if it was directed to the incidentally surveilled individual, and the second consists in asking the deletion of the incidentally collected data.

The first possibility applies when the incidentally surveilled individual faces as a consequence of the surveillance activity a case before a court. A similar situation was discussed in *Lambert* where the European Court of Human Rights[10] gave the incidentally surveilled individual the possibility to challenge the validity of the surveillance

---

[9] Kruslin v. France, ECHR application no. 11801/85, 24 April 1990, para. 28.
[10] Lambert v. France, ECHR application no. 23618/94, 24 August 1998, para. 40.

mandate as if he was in person addressed by it.[11] The possibility for "effective remedy" is an *ex post* adjustment and improves only partially the situation of the incidentally surveilled person. In issuing the surveillance mandate the authorities have not been considering the need of such an interference with the incidentally surveilled life and therefore it would be difficult to successfully challenge the surveillance mandate on its merits.

The second possibility is to delete the incidentally collected data once these do not have any more relevance for the investigation or, in alternative, to notify the concerned individual, as stated in Recommendation R(87)15 [49] of the Council of Europe. Such an *ex post* notification has a specific importance for the protection of individuals in cases of incidental recording of data since it is an essential safeguard against abuse of monitoring powers and it is an important part of the right to an effective remedy. However, Recommendation R(87)15 [49] does not have binding effect and has not been incorporated so far in most of the national legislation of the Member States [17]. The European Court of Human Rights has applied the 'notification' principle in a number of cases.[12] The most significant decision is *Ekimdzhiev* were the Court clearly established that omission of notification of surveillance measures, once it does not risk to jeopardize the inquiry, amounts to violation of article 8 ECHR.[13]

Also the new Data Protection Directive does not address situations of incidental surveillance. Even though it introduces a right to information on the individuals whose personal data are processed for the purpose of prevention, detection, investigation and prosecution of crime, this is done on the basis of a request from the data subject [23, arts. 12–14]. Since, if not informed, it is difficult for a data subject to know that their data have been incidentally collected, the exercise of the right to information is most likely not going to be effective.

From the above elaboration it is clear that the right to privacy of individuals that find themselves in situations of incidental surveillance is not properly protected. This important conclusion has to be taken into account when deciding on the use for surveillance of smart meters that per design collect data from all the members (and temporary guests) of a household and not from targeted individuals.

b. *Accuracy of the data for profiling*

Closely linked with the possibility for incidental surveillance is the element of the accuracy of the data used for profiling. As already seen, smart meters refer the energy consumption and activities of a household and not of targeted individuals. As stated earlier, processing of data and linking them with other sources gives the possibility to single out and distinguish the activities of specific individuals. This process, however, has a possibility for errors and for creating false profiles which cannot be ignored [3]. This can be for example in those cases in which one member of the household engages

---

[11] Ibidem para. 38.

[12] Klass v. Germany, ECHR application no. 5029/71, 6 September 1978, para. 50; Weber and Saravia v. Germany, ECHR application no. 54934/00, 29 June 2006, para. 114.

[13] Association for European Integration and Human Rights and Ekimdzhiev v. Bulgaria, ECHR application no. 62540/00, 28 June 2007, para. 91.

in an activity that is normally attributed to another member (e.g. daughter watches football match while the father is not at home). The accuracy of the data for profiling should be taken into account when deciding on the employment of smart meter data for surveillance.

c. *Retroactive surveillance*

As seen above, smart meter data might be retained by service providers for different periods of time, for reasons required by national laws or for their own purposes. Data retention gives the possibility to law enforcement authorities to access data belonging to past activities of targeted individuals. The data create the possibility to scrutinize past activities, belonging to a time that the individual was not under suspicion and no mandate for his surveillance was issued. Surveillance into the past might be easy due to the technology but, apart problems to the right to privacy it creates problems also for the right to presumption of innocence of the individual [44]. The problems created for the rights of the individuals must be taken into account by the national authorities issuing a surveillance mandate.

4.2 Mass Surveillance

Mass surveillance is a measure of preventive nature that, as the name states, is not directed at targeted individuals but at entire categories of them. There is evidence that mass surveillance programmes are used extensively in some Member States of the EU [5, 27, paras. 26–29] and they enable intelligence services and law enforcement authorities to access, without an individual warrant, personal data on a large scale. Mass surveillance targets the use of certain technologies or the presence at certain locations. Smart meter data can be a source of mass surveillance.

The European Court of Human Rights extended the application of article 8 ECHR and of the test it has established for cases of individual surveillance also to cases of mass surveillance. For the Court there are no grounds to apply different principles concerning the accessibility and clarity of the rules governing the interception of individual communications, on the one hand, and more general programs of surveillance, on the other.[14] The effective remedy that individuals have in such situations is the possibility to challenge the mass surveillance programs as such, without the need to prove that they have been individually suffering from these programs.[15]

Apart special mass surveillance programmes that are operational in different Member States, this form of surveillance was introduced also in the EU with the (now invalidated) Data Retention Directive (2006/24/EC) [19]. The Directive essentially introduced a form of mass surveillance [50] via the retention of metadata from electronic communications for periods of time between six months and 2 years (art. 6). This was based on the ability of service providers to collect and retain a number of personal data for different purposes (as for example billing details) and then use these data for

---

[14] Liberty and Others v. The United Kingdom, ECHR application no. 58243/00, 1 July 2008, para. 63.
[15] Weber and Saravia (n 13) para. 78.

other purposes, in our case for mass surveillance of the users of electronic communications. Advancement in technology makes it easier in the future to use the same scheme as under the Data Retention Directive for the massive accessing of personal data collected for other purposes.

Even if there is not yet any evidence of the employment of smart meter data for mass surveillance purposes, this might be a possibility. In the invalidation of the Data Retention Directive the Court of Justice of the EU did not close the door to this form of surveillance and found data retention to be an appropriate method for attaining the objective of fighting serious crime. It was already seen that smart meters have a possibility to detect illegal activities that might take place within a household as for example the cultivation of illegal plants or broadcasting of copyright protected materials, etc. Thus, a routine control by the law enforcement authorities of smart meter data for detecting special crimes is therefore not to be excluded.

With all the activities it might detect, a routine control of retained smart meter data is tantamount to a routine control inside a house and this goes against the right to inviolability of the home. That is why we argue and advice, in line also with the EDPS [24] recommendation, against such uses of smart meters without a specific mandate. The proportionality of the level of intrusiveness into the private life of the citizens of this method of surveillance is to be taken into account when discussing on mass surveillance of smart meter data.

5 Concluding Remarks

Technology developments have created the possibility for law enforcement authorities to use for surveillance purposes many devices that have not been originally designed for such a purpose. Smart meters are an example of these devices. The aim of this paper was not to lobby for prohibiting law enforcement from using non-purpose built devices and smart meters for surveillance purposes, but to alert for the legal shortcomings that might result in infringement of the rights to privacy and data protection of the individuals. Thus legal and technical controls must be imposed to ensure that their use is appropriate and accountable.

The involvement of smart meters in surveillance activities might be the result not only of the amount and detail of the collected data and of the easiness in accessing them but also of economic conveniences. With regards to the latest, one must bear in mind that smart meters are installed in the European households as part of a general European energy saving project. Collection and communication of data is a feature of these devices without requiring any investment from law enforcement authorities. Also retention of data, even if not yet required by the laws for law enforcement purposes, is already present in the system for other purposes than surveillance and for relatively long periods of time. Economic and technical conveniences should, however, not turn to a burden for individuals and the protection of fundamental rights.

Surveillance via smart meters mainly captures activities that take place within the sanctity of the home, with a continuous 24 h duration. Because of the high level of interference with the private life of the individuals, surveillance with such a technology must require a legal warrant. We thus argue for the illegitimacy of the use of smart meters for mass surveillance since this is tantamount to a continuous physical presence in the households of all citizens that are benefiting of this technology.

In cases of individual surveillance the challenges that this form of surveillance creates for the protection of the rights to privacy and data protection of the individuals, especially with regards to cases of incidental surveillance, retroactive surveillance, and to the accuracy of the data must be taken into account. The new Data Protection Directive presents two safeguards that, in line with a fundamental rights approach, we argue can be used in this regards.

The first one is linked with the duty for the controller to introduce appropriate technical and organizational measures ensuring that, by default, only personal data which are necessary for each specific purpose of the processing are processed [23, art. 20]. Interpreted strictly, since processing of data includes explicitly also their collection [23, art. 3(2)], such a provision must have the result that smart meters are not used at all for surveillance purposes since, because of their design and the way of operation, it is impossible to limit their collection of the data to only the ones necessary for the purpose of collection.

The second safeguard is linked with the introduction of a data protection impact assessment in those cases in which the processing of the data is likely to result in a high risk to the rights and freedoms of natural persons [23, art. 27]. The outcome of such an impact assessment does, however, not solve completely the problem of surveillance via smart meters because it focuses only on data protection without covering all the aspects of the right to privacy and it is done for the technology in general, and not for its use in specific cases. To give an example, the problem of incidental surveillance has a different dimension in a household inhabited from a single individual than in a household inhabited from more individuals. The results of a data protection impact assessment are, however, important. They must be integrated in a larger evaluation of the impact that surveillance with smart meters will have in a concrete individual surveillance case.

Apart the coverage of all the aspects of the right to privacy and data protection, such an evaluation must carefully assess also the necessity and the proportionality of the use of smart meters for surveillance purposes in specific cases. Only an assessment of the effects of surveillance for a specific case would be able to safeguard the fundamental rights of individuals at a time in which technology allows for more devices to be used for surveillance and the laws are not able to keep up to these speedy developments.

References

1. Anderson, R., Fuloria, S.: On the security economics of electricity metering. In: Proceedings of the Ninth Workshop on the Economics of Information Security (WEIS 2010), vol. 18 (2010)
2. Article 29 Data Protection Working Party (2011) Opinion 12/2011 on Smart Metering, 4 April 2011
3. Beckel, C., et al.: Revealing household characteristics from smart meter data. Energy **78**, 397–410 (2014)

4. Bennett, C.: The public surveillance of personal data: A cross-national analyses. In: Lyon, D., Zureik, E. (eds.) Computers, surveillance, and privacy, pp. 237–259. University of Minessota Press, Minnesota (1996)
5. Bigo, D. et al.: National programmes for mass surveillance of personal data in EU Member States and their compatibility with EU law, Study submitted to the European Parliament's Committee on Civil Liberties, Justice and Home Affairs (2013). http://www.europarl.europa. eu/RegData/etudes/etudes/join/2013/493032/IPOL-LIBE_ET(2013)493032_EN.pdf. Accessed 1 Nov 2013
6. Bohli, J., Sorge, C., Ugus, O.: On the security economics of the electricity metering. In: Proceedings of 2010 IEEE International Conference on Communications Workshops, vol. 10 (2010)
7. Cavoukian, A., Polonetsky, J., Wolf, C.: Smart privacy for the smart grid: embedding privacy into the design of electricity conservation (2010). https://www.privacybydesign.ca/ index.php/paper/smartprivacy-for-the-smart-grid-embedding-privacy-into-the-design-of-electricity-conservation/. Accessed 15 Apr 2015
8. Chalmers, D., Davies, G., Monti, G.: European Union Law, 3rd edn. Cambridge University Press, Cambridge (2014)
9. Clarke, R.: Introduction to Dataveillance and Information Privacy, and Definitions of Terms (1997). http://www.rogerclarke.com/DV/Intro.html. Accessed 22 May 2014
10. Commission Recommendation 2012/148/EU of 9 March 2012 on preparations for the roll-out of smart metering systems, OJ L 73, 13 March 2012
11. Commission Recommendation 2014/724/EU of 10 October 2014 on the Data Protection Impact Assessment Template for Smart Grid and Smart Metering Systems, OJ L 300, 18 October 2014
12. Convention 108 for the protection of individuals with regard to automatic processing of personal data, 28 January 1981
13. Council Framework Decision 2008/977/JHA of 27 November 2008 on the protection of personal data processed in the framework of police and judicial cooperation in criminal matters, OJ L 350, 30 December 2008
14. Covrig, C.F. et al.: Smart Grids Projects Outlook (2014). http://cencenelec.eu/EN/European Standardization/HotTopics/SmartGrids/SGCG_SGIS_Report.pdf. Accessed 29 Apr 2015
15. Cuijpers, C., Koops, B.-J.: Smart metering and privacy in Europe: Lessons from the Dutch case. In: Gutwirth, S., Leenes, R., de Hert, P., Poullet, Y. (eds.) European Data Protection: Coming of Age, pp. 269–293. Springer, Dordrecht (2012)
16. Datenschutzgesetz 2000, Bundesgesetz über den Schutz personenbezogener Daten (2000)
17. De Hert, P., Boehm, F.: The rights of notification after surveillance is over: ready for recognition? In: Bus, J., et al. (eds.) Digital Enlightment Year Book 2012, vol. 19. IOS Press, Amsterdam (2012)
18. Directive 2004/22/EC of the European Parliament and of the Council of 31 March 2004 on Measuring Instruments, OJ L 135, 30 April 2004
19. Directive 2006/24/EC of the European Parliament and of the Council of 15 March 2006 on the retention of data generated or processed in connection with the provision of publicly available electronic communications services or of public communications networks and amending Directive 2002/58/EC, OJ L 105, 13 April 2006
20. Directive 2006/32/EC of the European Parliament and of the Council of 5 April 2006 on energy end-use efficiency and energy services and repealing Council Directive 93/76/EEC, OJ L 114, 27 April 2006
21. Directive 2009/72/EC of the European Parliament and of the Council of 13 July 2009 concerning common rules for the internal market in electricity and repealing Directive 2003/54/EC, OJ L 211, 14 August 2009

22. Directive 95/46/EC of the European Parliament and of the Council of 24 October 1995 on the protection of individuals with regard to the processing of personal data and on the free movement of such data, OJ L 281, 23 November 1995
23. Directive 2016/680 of the European Parliament and of the Council of 27 April 2016 on the protection of natural persons with regard to the processing of personal data by competent authorities for the purposes of the prevention, investigation, detection or prosecution of criminal offences or the execution of criminal penalties, and on the free movement of such data, and repealing Council Framework Decision 2008/977/JHA
24. EDPS. Opinion of the European Data Protection Supervisor on the Commission Recommendation on preparations for the roll-out of smart metering systems (2012)
25. Enev, M., Gupta, S., Kohno, T., Patel, S.: Televisions, video privacy, and powerline electromagnetic interference. In: Proceedings of the 18th ACM Conference on computers and communications security, pp. 537–550 (2011)
26. Essential regulatory requirements and recommendations for data handling December 2011. data safety, and consumer protection. Recommendation to the European Commission, 5 December 2011
27. Explanatory memorandum on the Parliamentary Assembly of the Council of Europe draft Resolution and draft Report on Mass Surveillance prepared by Mr. Pieter Omtzigt, rapporteur. http://assembly.coe.int/nw/xml/XRef/X2H-Xref-ViewPDF.asp?FileID=21583& lang=en. Accessed 28 Apr 2015
28. Faraqui, A., Harris, D., Hledik, R.: Unlocking the €53 billion savings from smart meters in the EU: How increasing the adoption of dynamic tariffs could make or break the EU's smart grid investment. Energy Policy 38(10), 6222–6231 (2010)
29. Guiding document to the UK Regulation of Investigatory Powers Acts 2000 by the Leeds City Council Legal Services (2013). http://www.leeds.gov.uk/docs/RIPA%20Guidance% 20and%20Procedure%20-%20May%202013.pdf. Accessed 30 Mar 2015
30. Hargreaves, T., Nye, M., Burgess, J.: Making energy visible: a quantitative field study of how households interact with energy from smart energy monitors. Energy Policy 38, 6111–6119 (2010)
31. Jenness, V., Smith, D.A., Stepan-Norris, J.: Taking a look at surveillance studies. Contemp. Sociol. J. Rev. 36(2), vii–viii (2007)
32. Jones, K.B., Zoppo, D.: A Smarter, Greener Grid. Praeger, Santa Barbara (2014)
33. Kalogridis, G., Denic, S.: Data mining and privacy of personal behavior types in smart grid. In: Proceedings of the 11th IEEE International Conference on Data Mining Workshops, pp. 636–642 (2011)
34. Kim, Y., Schmid, T., Srivastava, M., Wang, Y.: Challenges in resource monitoring for residential spaces. In: Proceedings of the first ACM Workshop on Embeded Sensing Systems for Energy-Efficiency in Buildings, pp. 1–6 (2009)
35. King, N.J., Jessen, P.W.: Smart metering systems and data sharing: why getting a smart meter should also mean getting strong information privacy controls to manage data sharing. Int. J. Law Inf. Technol. 22, 1–39 (2014)
36. Knyrim, R., Trieb, G.: Smart metering under EU data protection law. Int. Data Priv. Law 1 (2), 121–128 (2011)
37. Korff, D.: The rule of law on the internet and in the wider world, Issue Paper published by the Council of Europe Commissioner for Human Rights (2014). https://wcd.coe.int/ ViewDoc.jsp?id=2268589. Accessed 1 May 2015
38. Lerner, J.I., Mulligan, D.K.: Taking the long view on the fourth amendment: stored records and the sanctity of the home. Stanford Technol. Law Rev. 3, 13 (2008)
39. Lisovich, M., Mulligan, D., Wicker, S.: Inferring personal information from demand-response systems. IEEE Secur. Priv. 8, 11–20 (2010)

40. Lo Schiavo, L., Fumagalli, E., Olivieri, V.: Changing the regulation for regulating the change - innovation-driven regulatory developments in Italy: smart grids, smart metering and e-mobility. IEFE Working Paper Series, vol. 46, p. 40 (2011)
41. McDaniel, P.: Security and privacy challenges in the smart grid. IEEE Secur. Priv. **7**, 75–77 (2009)
42. McKenna, E., Richardson, I., Thomson, M.: Smart meter data: balancing consumer privacy concerns with legitimate applications. Energy Policy **41**, 807–814 (2012)
43. Milaj, J.: Invalidation of the data retention directive – extending the proportionality test. Comput. Law Secur. Rev. **31**(5), 604–617 (2015)
44. Milaj, J., Mifsud Bonnici, J.P.: Unwitting subjects of surveillance and the presumption of innocence. Comput. Law Secur. Rev. **30**(4), 419–428 (2014)
45. Milaj, J., Mifsud Bonnici, J.P.: Privacy issues in the use of smart meters—law enforcement use of smart meter data. In: Beaulieu, A., De Wilde, J., Scherpen, J.M.A. (eds.) Smart Grids from a Global Perspective, pp. 179–196. Springer, Dordrecht (2016)
46. Mills, E.: Researchers find smart meters could reveal favorite TV shows, CNet News (2012). http://news.cnet.com/8301–27080_3-57364883-245/researchers-find-smart-meters-could-reveal-favorite-tv-shows/. Accessed 27 Apr 2013
47. Pallas, F.: Beyond gut level – some critical remarks on the German privacy approach to smart metering. In: Gutwirth, S., Leenes, R., de Hert, P., Poullet, Y. (eds.) European Data Protection: Coming of Age, pp. 313–345. Springer, Dordrecht (2013)
48. Quinn, E.L.: Privacy and the new energy infrastructure, CEES Working Paper no. 09-0001, vol. 41 (2008)
49. Recommendation no. R(87)15 of the Committee of Ministers regulating the use of personal data in the police sector
50. Roberts, H., Palfrey, J.: The EU data retention directive in an era of internet surveillance. In: Deibert, R., et al. (eds.) Access Controlled: The Shaping of Power, Rights, and Rule in Cyberspace, pp. 35–53. MIT Press, Cambridge (2010)
51. Savirimuthu, J.: Smart meters and the information panopticon: beyond the rhetoric of compliance. Int. Rev. Law Comput. Technol. **27**(1–2), 161–186 (2013)
52. Smart Grid Coordination Group. Document for the M/490 Mandate Smart Grid Information society (2014). http://cencenelec.eu/EN/EuropeanStandardization/HotTopics/SmartGrids/SGCG_SGIS_Report.pdf. Accessed 29 Apr 2015
53. Subrahmanyan, P.A.: Network security architecture for demand response/sensor networks, report for the California Energy Commission, Public Interest Energy Research Group (2005). http://www.law.berkeley.edu/files/demand_response_CEC.pdf. Accessed 15 Apr 2015
54. UK Smart metering implementation programme PIA 2012 (2012). https://www.gov.uk/government/uploads/system/uploads/attachment_data/file/43044/7226-sm-privacy-ia.pdf. Accessed 4 Jan 2016
55. Weiss, M., Helfenstein, A., Mattern, F., Staake, T.: Leveraging smart meter data to recognize home appliances. In: Proceedings of IEEE Pervasive Computing and Communication PerCom, vol. 8 (2012)
56. Wigan, M., Clarke, R.: Social impacts of transport surveillance. In: Prometheus: Critical studies in Innovation, vol. 24, no. 4, pp. 389–403 (2006)
57. Wynn, G.: Privacy concerns challenge smart grid rollout, Reuters 25 June 2010. http://www.reuters.com/article/2010/06/25/energy-smart-idUSLDE65N2CI20100625. Accessed 13 May 2015
58. Zeadalli, S., Pathan, A.-S., Alcaraz, C., Badra, M.: Towards privacy protection in smart grid. Wireless Pers. Commun. **73**, 23–50 (2013)

Consumer Privacy on Distributed Energy Markets

Niklas Büscher[1]([⊠]), Stefan Schiffner[2], and Mathias Fischer[3]

[1] Technische Universität Darmstadt, Darmstadt, Germany
buescher@seceng.informatik.tu-darmstadt.de
[2] ENISA, Athens, Greece
[3] Westfälische Wilhelms-Universität Münster, Münster, Germany

Abstract. Recently, several privacy-enhancing technologies for smart grids have been proposed. However, most of these solutions presume the cooperation of all smart grid participants. Hence, the privacy protection of consumers depends on the willingness of the suppliers to deploy privacy-enhancing technologies. Since electrical energy is essential for our modern life, it is impossible for consumers to opt out. We propose a novel consumer-only (do-it-yourself) privacy-enhancing approach under the assumption that users can obtain their energy from multiple suppliers on a distributed market. By splitting the demand over multiple suppliers, the information each of them can collect about a single consumer is reduced. In this context, we suggest two different buying strategies: a time and a sample diversification strategy. To measure their provided level of privacy protection, we introduce a new indistinguishability metric λ-Indistinguishability (λ-IND) that measures how relative consumption changes can be hidden in the total consumption. We evaluate the presented strategies with λ-IND and derive first privacy boundaries. The evaluation of our buying strategies on real-world energy data sets indicates their ability to hide load profiles of privacy sensitive appliances at low communication and computational overhead.

1 Introduction

Currently, users of the electrical grid are facing the risk of privacy breaches through the upcoming smart grid technology. The idea of the *smart* grid is to modernize the traditional electricity grid by establishing a communication infrastructure in parallel to the energy delivery network. This results in a constant flow of fine-grained consumption information from individual consumers to the energy suppliers. Furthermore, this data enables automatic billing, prediction and stabilizing tasks for suppliers. However, as research has shown, this data can also be used to infer detailed user profiles. Even further, Non-Intrusive Load Monitoring (NILM), the technique to disaggregate energy consumption, is still developing. Recent progress shows that given high resolution load profiles, content displayed on a larger LCD can be identified [12] as well as rendered web pages [5]. Thus, reporting the consumption information is bearing a risk for the

© Springer International Publishing Switzerland 2016
S. Schiffner et al. (Eds.): APF 2016, LNCS 9857, pp. 96–114, 2016.
DOI: 10.1007/978-3-319-44760-5_7

individuals privacy. This is especially the case in a scenario where 'opt out' is not an option, as is the participation in the electricity grid.

Previous presented solutions, which fulfill the suppliers' functional requirements and protect the privacy of users, depend on either the electricity suppliers voluntary commitment to complex cryptographic protocols or on the deployment of physical batteries. Cryptographic protocols are challenging in the correct implementation and require the willingness of the supplier to invest in the necessary hardware and software to run these protocols. Physical batteries require a huge investment in batteries for the consumer. From the individual's point of view, it would be preferable to be protected with less supplier dependency and without costly investments.

Based on these observations, we present a novel privacy enhancing approach that enables the clients to protect their consumption data without the need of involving suppliers. We discuss our solution in the context of smart grids, though it can be generalized for privacy protection on distributed markets. Our main contributions can be structured according to the following two research questions:

How can the consumer's privacy on distributed markets be protected without the technical involvement of suppliers? We answer this question by presenting a novel data perturbation based approach. The idea is to utilize the distributed market by randomly splitting the consumer's demand onto multiple suppliers. Thus, only a fraction of the total demand is observed by each supplier. This approach does not presume any further technical requirements while still guaranteeing accurate trades.

To which degree can privacy be protected and how can this protection be measured? On distributed markets, multiple parties usually trade a good directly and hence need to have knowledge of each other, which turns privacy definitions based on anonymity inapplicable. Furthermore, we show that that our buying strategies can hide only relative changes in the power consumption. As a consequence, the prerequisites of differential privacy or plain indistinguishability are too demanding. Therefore, we introduce a new privacy notion that uses strong formal guarantees to measure the protection of relative changes in the power consumption.

The paper is structured as follows. We discuss the related work in Sect. 2, before introducing our formal model and privacy metric in Sect. 3. Moreover, in Sect. 4 two novel buying strategies are presented and analyzed. Then, the strategies are evaluated on real world data sets in Sect. 5. Finally, we conclude our work in Sect. 6.

2 Related Work

In this section we discuss the state of the art in privacy protection mechanism for the smart grid. Furthermore, we discuss relevant statistical privacy metrics used to measure privacy in the smart grid.

Privacy Mechanisms. According Jawurek et al. [14] Privacy-enhancing technologies (PETs) for the smart grid can be classified into the following categories:

Data perturbation based protection mechanisms enable privacy friendly live monitoring by adding random noise to every raw reading, e.g., Bohli et al. [4] and Shuang et al. [26]. Hence, the actual reported readings are noisy. However, given a sufficiently large number of smart meters, the noise cancels out and thus, the supplier's aggregate becomes accurate. More sophisticated approaches for data perturbation are presented by Acs and Castelluccia [1] and Lin et al. [18] that combine data perturbation and additive blinding. All of these approaches either require a second protocol to allow accurate billing, an infeasible large number of smart meters, or an implementation of the encryption protocol at supplier side.

Batteries can reduce the entropy of the readings by flattening the actual electricity consumption [2,15,24]. Depending on the capacity and throughput of the battery, different privacy goals can be realized. However, it turns out that adequately sized batteries are expensive.

Furthermore, Trusted-Third-Parties (TTPs) have been utilized as PETs in smart grids, e.g., [4,10]. While TTPs can fulfill any privacy definition, they bear two risks: first, any trusted third party can also be compromised and represents a single point of failure; and second, deploying a TTP requires infrastructure and protocol changes at smart meters and suppliers.

One of the most promising solutions are aggregation protocols, which enable accurate live monitoring. Based on various cryptographic primitives, multiple variants have been presented. For example, Garcia et al. [11] and Kursawe et al. [17] presented protocols using either additive secret sharing or homomorphic cryptosystems. These protocols guarantee anonymity on a group level. However, they all make use of expensive computation or require bidirectional communication between groups of smart meters. Moreover, the proposed protocols have an inherent complexity and need to be implemented on the supplier side. Hence, they disqualify as consumer-only approaches.

Lastly, commitment schemes and zero knowledge proofs have been proposed to offload the bill calculation onto the consumers [7,20,23]. Here verifiable computation guarantees the correct calculation of the overall bill without revealing individual readings. This approach requires a protocol implementation on the supplier side and is incompatible to live monitoring, as only the smart meters sum is computed and verified.

Privacy Metrics. We focus on privacy metrics for smart grids that measure the protection level of approaches based on data perturbation.

Quantitative metrics based on statistical and information theoretic measures have been presented. Shuang et al. [26] use the F-Test measure to compare raw and noisy load profiles. Kalogridis et al. [15] measured this relationship using relative entropy and correlation metrics. Furthermore, the authors suggest to use the accuracy of clustering algorithms as a privacy measures. All these metrics are useful when comparing different privacy mechanisms. However, they have the drawback that a measurable threshold for a desired privacy level cannot be given.

To evaluate a battery based approach, Backes et al. [2] developed a metric based on differential privacy for streams, which ensures event-level privacy. The authors make use of the probabilistic variant of differential privacy, i.e., with a small probability δ the definition of differential privacy does not need to be met. Even so, this metric is based on the well defined grounds of differential privacy, it suffers practicability, as the authors note. This is because load signatures of appliances are typically characterized by more than one event, which are not necessarily covered by the presented definition.

Yet, a metric that shows the protection of multiple events is desirable. Bohli et al. present such a metric in [4], which is based on a cryptographic game of the type right-or-left. In this game, an adversary is challenged to identify the originating scenario from a transcript. A scenario consists of load profiles, i.e., load samples in a defined time span from multiple smart meters. We build on this idea in the reminder of this paper.

3 A Formal Smart Grid Model

In this section, we present the *distributed market model*. First, we define the major actors and actions. Then, we introduce the attacker model and the notion of λ-IND.

3.1 Energy Market Model

We define a distributed market as a virtual place where consumers purchase goods or services from multiple suppliers. In this paper, we focus on a single good market, i.e., the energy market. Nevertheless, for markets that offer multiple goods, the presented ideas can be applied multiple times in parallel. We assume that all communication is secured, i.e., communication channels are available all the time and guarantee confidentiality as well as integrity. Hence, a trade is not visible to any third party. The practical realization of such a market place requires supplier discovery and price formation services, which is beyond the scope of this work.

We deduce a formal model and its assumptions: the model consists of two participating parties, namely a set of consumers C and a set of suppliers S. Moreover, a discrete notion of time, denoted as t, is used. In each time period t, a consumer $c_i \in C$ is attributed with a demand $d_{i,t}$. Consumers can cover their demand by buying from one or multiple suppliers $s_j \in S$. As we are only interested in modelling consumption privacy instead of anonymity, it is sufficient to consider only one single consumer $c \in C$ in all following discussions.

The act of a consumer to buy a certain amount of energy in a given time period from a supplier is called trade. All trades of one consumer are denoted by a two dimensional matrix. Each entry $b_{j,t} \geq 0$ of this matrix describes the amount of the good bought by a consumer from supplier s_j at time t. Consequently, the demand at time t of the consumer is the sum of all trades with all suppliers $d_t = \sum_{s_j \in S} b_{j,t}$. In the following privacy analysis, we refer to the time series

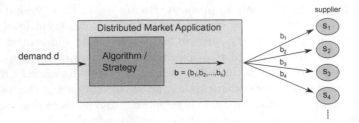

Fig. 1. Distributed market model. The consumer's demand d is split between multiple suppliers $s_1, s_2, \ldots, s_n$.

of a consumer $\mathbf{d} =< d_1, d_2, \ldots, d_n >$ as *original* load profile and for the time series that a supplier observes $\mathbf{b}_j =< b_{j,1}, b_{j,2}, \ldots, b_{j,n} >$ as *reported* load profile. Figure 1 illustrates the distribution model for a given demand d.

A consumer that cannot produce or store energy needs to cover all its demand via the market. Hence, its entire demand profile is at risk to be leaked. Contrary to consumers, so-called *prosumers* exist, who are capable of producing and storing energy to a certain extent, e.g., via a solar panel and an additional battery. Thus, by partially covering their demands through (unpredictable) third sources, they have more possibilities to protect their load profiles. We note, that given the possibility to report arbitrary and negative trades, two non-colluding suppliers are sufficient to trivially guarantee information theoretic security, by reporting $b_{1,t} = r_t$ to the first supplier with r_t being a random number and $b_{2,t} = d_t - r_t$ to the second supplier. Such a protocol guarantees correctness and privacy but is incompatible with time-of-use tariffs and practical live monitoring.

For the remainder of this paper we will focus on consumers only, as they are the more challenging case for privacy-protection. Therefore, to restrict our analysis adequately to the capabilities of consumers, we define all trades to be non-negative $b_{j,t} \geq 0$.

3.2   Attacker Model

Assuming a secure communication network, the only possible point to attack is at the end-users, namely compromising a supplier. Furthermore, we assume that the attacker is interested in reconstructing the original load profiles of consumers from reported consumption information. As this kind of attacker is completely passive, consumers are unable to differentiate between honest and compromised suppliers. Moreover, as a first step we assume that only one supplier is compromised, which is sufficient to show the impact of the considered attacker on distributed energy markets.

3.3   Privacy Metric - λ Indistinguishability

We define a Load Signature Hiding Game (LSHG) based on Bohli et al. [4] to measure the privacy of a Smart Metering Application (SMA). An adversary A

selects two possible load profiles, namely the vectors $\mathbf{d}^0 = < d_1^0, d_2^0, ..., d_n^0 >$ and $\mathbf{d}^1 = < d_1^1, d_2^1, ..., d_n^1 >$, and sends them to a challenger. After receiving the two scenarios the challenger randomly draws a bit $\beta \in \{0, 1\}$ and simulates $\mathbf{d}^\beta$. The simulation result is a transcript, which is then sent back to the adversary A. Following the described market scenario, the transcript consists of all trades with one randomly chosen supplier: $\mathbf{b} = < b_1, b_2, ..., b_n >$. The adversary outputs a bit δ and wins the game by correctly guessing which scenario was used to create the transcript, hence, iff $\delta = \beta$. The privacy of the SMA is measured by the difference between random guessing and correctly answering which of the two scenarios belongs to the transcript. As in [4] the two demand load profiles are required to have the same aggregate, since this information has to be known by the supplier for billing purposes. Otherwise, distinguishing load profiles is trivial.

To measure the privacy protection provided by the buying strategies introduced later in this paper, we present the idea of λ-IND. Even though deviating from common privacy metrics is bearing risks, we propose a new privacy metric and advocate the notions of indistinguishably, due to the following reasons:

- As discussed in Sect. 2, other common privacy metrics are either inapplicable, e.g., anonymity metrics, or provide insufficient protection in this scenario. For example, differential privacy under continual observation [9] only provides event-level protection that does not span over multiple events.
- Cryptographic games provide a strong formal tool and have successfully been applied as privacy metrics in different scenarios, e.g., for privacy preserving RFID tags [25].
- The strict indistinguishability notion for the smart grid by Bohli et al. [4] assumes a very strong adversary, who is allowed to choose arbitrary load signatures. This definition is too strong to show that only a part of the load profile is protected.

The goal of λ-IND is to show that high resolution attacks are infeasible. We are convinced that this is an important stepping stone between none and full protection, i.e., perfect indistinguishability in the LSHG. Our idea is as follows, instead of challenging the privacy mechanism with two totally different load profiles, the load samples from the same time period are restricted to be in relative distance to each other.

Formalizing this concept, we introduce the privacy parameter λ that expresses the maximal relative difference between two load samples taken from two load profiles in the privacy game, respectively. The new privacy metric λ-IND is based on the definition of the LSHG with the exception that two load samples in both scenarios are allowed to differ by at most a factor λ. Hence, given a load sample d_t^0 in the first scenario, the demand in the second scenario is restricted to $d_t^1 \in [d_t^0, \lambda \cdot d_t^0]$. Without loosing generality, $\lambda > 1$ is assumed for all further discussion. We refer to this restriction as the λ *requirement* and introduce the following definition:

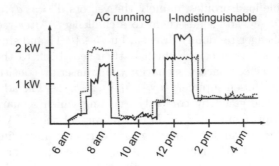

Fig. 2. Applicability of λ-IND for exemplary load profiles from two different households. At approximately 11 am both households switch on their AC, which leads to a similar power consumption. After a period of high energy usage in both households with different duration, no further activity in the household represented by the solid line is visible, whereas in the second household a TV is turned on. Thus, after 1 pm only a small λ is sufficient to show the running TV is hidden with λ-IND.

Definition 1. *Considering the LSHG(β) game fulfilling the λ requirement and the adversary A for a given distribution algorithm **Alg**, the (λ-Indistinguishability) advantage of A is defined as*

$$\mathbf{Adv}_{Alg}^{\lambda\text{-IND}} = |\Pr[\mathrm{LSHG}(0)_{\mathrm{Alg},\lambda}^{A} = 0] - \Pr[\mathrm{LSHG}(1)_{\mathrm{Alg},\lambda}^{A} = 0]|.$$

We illustrate λ-IND with an example. Given $\lambda = 1.2$ and load samples of 1000 Wh in the first profile, the maximum load sample an attacker can choose in the second profile is 1200 Wh. Thus, the chosen loads for the second profile have to be in between the corridor from 1000 Wh to 1200 Wh. Consequently, given a base load of 1000 Wh, an additional appliance with a load signature of maximal 200 Wh is undetectable. This concept is also illustrated in Fig. 2. Summarizing, a privacy mechanism guaranteeing λ-IND makes all load samples indistinguishable that are in relative distance to each other.

4   Buying Strategies

In this section, we introduce and evaluate multiple buying strategies in our formalized distributed market scenario. First, we introduce the notion of *fair* buying strategies, i.e., strategies where no supplier is favored. Second, we introduce the Temporal Diversification (TD) and Sample Diversification (SD) buying strategies and evaluate both strategies in the (unrestricted) LSHG model as well as under λ-IND.

A buying strategy is an algorithm that distributes an input demand d_t among multiple suppliers $s \in S$ in every time period. Thus, each supplier s_j observes a reported load profile of load samples $\mathbf{b}_j = <b_{1,j}, b_{2,j}, \ldots, b_{n,j}>$. By observing these load samples over a larger time period and assuming a steady input demand d, each approached supplier s_j observes an distribution $P_j(b)$ of load samples. We focus on *fair* buying strategies, i.e., buying strategies that do not favor any supplier over time. Thus, we propose the following formal definition for fair distribution algorithms:

Definition 2. *A distribution algorithm* **Alg** *with input load sample d_t and output vector consisting of $|S|$ load samples $b'_t = < b_{t,1}, b_{t,2}, ..., b_{t,|S|} >$ is called fair, iff for all $x \in [0, d_t]$ the following condition holds:*

$$\Pr[b_{t,1} = x] = \Pr[b_{t,2} - x] = ... = \Pr[b_{t,|S|} = x].$$

Note, even though unfair strategies might be interesting for the consumer, e.g., because of economic or ecological preferences, distribution algorithms that favor certain suppliers have the drawback that an attacker may obtain information on these preferences. This background information might undermine the consumers privacy. Hence, in the light of privacy protection, we recommend *fair* distribution algorithms. Among such fair algorithms are the TD and SD strategies that are introduced in the following two subsections.

4.1   Buying Strategy - Temporal Diversification (TD)

Consumers that cover their demand according to the TD strategy, have to meet their demand d_t per time period t through only one, yet changing supplier. Several variants of this strategy are possible w.r.t. the order (deterministic or stochastic) suppliers are approached.

An example for a deterministic variant is to use a round-robin scheme, i.e., suppliers are approached subsequently in an ordered sequence. Once the last supplier in the sequence is reached, the process starts with the first supplier again. In the second variant, suppliers are randomly chosen from the set of available suppliers. Several variations of such a random strategy are possible, e.g., the same supplier can be approached for k subsequent time periods. Hence, depending on the consumer's goals the granularity of the observed time frame can be controlled by parameter k.

Round-robin and random TD strategies can only offer limited privacy, as long as the number of suppliers is limited. This is because, consumers will inevitably return to the same supplier at some point. However, these strategies reduce the temporal resolution of a compromised attacker. For the indistinguishability analysis we apply LSHG and λ-IND on a randomized TD strategy and leave out the round-robin variant due to its static and predictable results. These are that each supplier is approached after at most $|S|$ time periods. An analysis of the TD strategy prepares the evaluation of the more complex SD strategy in the LSHG and λ-IND.

To analyze strategies with the help of cryptographic games, the attacker needs to construct two scenarios for the challenger. With respect to the TD strategy, it turns out that any two non-equal demand profiles are distinguishable, by setting one half of the first demand profile to an arbitrary $d^0 > 0$ and the other half to $d^1 \neq d^0$, $d^1 > 0$. The requirement for non-zero loads $d^0, d^1 > 0$ is necessary for the adversary to distinguish between zero consumption and not being approached at all. The second demand profile is constructed by swapping d^0's and d^1's. As a result of this construction, the sum of all load values is the same in both scenarios, as required. The adversaries advantage is then equivalent to the probability to observe a non-zero load sample:

$$\mathbf{Adv}_{\mathrm{TD}}^{\mathrm{LSHG}} = 1 - \left(\frac{|S| - 1}{|S|} \right)^n .$$

We further observe that the attacker advantage in the LSHG is equal to the advantage in λ-IND, $\mathbf{Adv}_{\mathrm{TD}}^{\lambda\text{-IND}} = \mathbf{Adv}_{\mathrm{TD}}^{\mathrm{LSHG}}$. This is because, the λ-requirement does not prevent the adversary from choosing load samples that uniquely identify a load profile.

4.2   Buying Strategy - Sample Diversification (SD)

Consumers that deploy the Sample Diversification (SD) strategy cover their demand by using multiple suppliers simultaneously. A randomized algorithm splits the input demand into multiple smaller samples that are sent out to different suppliers. Hence, each supplier only observes a share of the total demand.

For example, given $|S| = 3$ suppliers and a demand of $d_t = 1000$ Wh. A consumer deploying a SD strategy could meet its demand by buying $b_{1,t} = 511$ Wh from the first supplier, $b_{2,t} = 89$ Wh and $b_{3,t} = 400$ Wh from the second and third supplier. Several variations of this strategy are possible and can be differentiated by their distribution of load samples, e.g., exponential or uniform. Below we present an approach to derive the upper bound of the adversaries advantage for any SD variant.

Upper Bound for the Adversaries Advantage in the LSHG Game. We analyze the SD strategy in LSHG. For this the adversary needs to choose two load profiles that show the largest difference to maximize its advantage. However, a binary difference, namely zero and non-zero load is already sufficient, as we show. Thus, in the first load profile one half of the load samples is set to zero and the other half to a value greater than zero, e.g., one. The second scenario is constructed by swapping zeros and ones ensuring equal demands in both scenarios. Since any randomized reported consumption $b_{j,t}$ to supplier s_j is bounded by zero and the actual demand, i.e., $0 \leq b_{j,t} \leq d_t$, a smart meter has to report zero consumption in times of zero demand and non zero consumption to one or more suppliers in times of demand. In the following calculation, we denote the number n_s, as the number of suppliers being approached in every time period. Receiving a load sample greater than zero allows the challenger to deduce the simulated scenario, namely the one where the sample in the load sequence $\mathbf{b}_j$ is greater than zero. For simplicity reasons we assume an even number of load samples per profile. Since $\frac{n}{2}$ loads per scenario are greater than zero, the adversaries advantage is bound by the probability to observe such a non-zero load:

$$\mathbf{Adv}_{SD}^{LSHG} = 1 - \left(\frac{|S| - n_s}{|S|}\right)^{n/2}.$$

Upper Bound for the Adversaries Advantage under λ-IND. To derive an upper bound on the adversaries advantage under λ-IND, we first have to describe an optimal adversary. According to the Neyman-Pearson Lemma [21], the best possible advantage when distinguishing distributions is achieved when using a *maximum likelihood-ratio distinguisher*. Given such an optimal distinguisher, its advantage is equal to the statistical distance, also known as total variation distance D_{TV}. The statistical distance between two discrete[1] probability functions P_0, P_1 for a given sample x is defined as

$$D_{TV}(P_0, P_1) = \frac{1}{2}\|P_0(x) - P_1(x)\|_1 = \frac{1}{2}\sum_{x\in\Omega}|P_0(x) - P_1(x)|\,dx.$$

The singular case can be extended to multiple samples by computing the 1-norm over all possible combinations [3]. As this can be computationally expensive, Pinsker's inequality [6,22] can be used to compute an upper bound on the distinguishing advantage more efficiently. Pinsker's inequality connects the statistical distance D_{TV} with the Kullback-Leibler divergence D_{KL} and is defined for multi-samples n as

$$D_{TV}(P_0^n, P_1^n) = \frac{1}{2}\|P_0^n(x) - P_1^n(x)\|_1 \le \sqrt{2n \cdot D_{KL}(P_0\|P_1)}.$$

To minimize the adversaries advantage in λ-IND, an optimal strategy has to distribute demands d_0 and d_1, which differ by at most λ, in such a way that the distributions of observed load samples show minimal statistical distance. First, we consider the case where a load profile consists of only one demand ($n = 1$). The least statistical distance is achieved when the transport between the two distributions observed by the adversary in the LSHG is minimized. As the two distribution P_0 and P_1 have to differ, because the originate different input demands, the best possible way to construct distribution P_1 from a given P_0 is realized by transporting probability from the two extremes 0 and $\max(d_0, d_1)$. This minimizes the amount of transported probability and thus, the statistical distance. Given a number of available suppliers $|S|$ and the privacy parameter λ, the statistical distance is then bound to (cf. Appendix A):

$$\mathbf{Adv}_{SD,1}^{\lambda\text{-IND}} = \frac{\lambda - 1}{|S| \cdot \lambda}.$$

Following the same strategy for load profiles consisting of multiple samples ($n > 1$), a maximum likelihood-ratio distinguisher can only decide according the transported probabilities and has thus an advantage of at most

$$\mathbf{Adv}_{SD,n}^{\lambda\text{-IND}} = 1 - \left(1 - \frac{\lambda - 1}{|S| \cdot \lambda}\right)^n.$$

---

[1] For simplification purposes, in this work we make use of discrete instead of continuous probability distributions. This is reasonable when considering a finite metering resolution (e.g., $10^{(-7)}$ kWh).

4.3   Heuristics for the SD Strategy

A distribution strategy as presented above cannot directly be deployed in practical settings. This is because, in a real world deployments of a smart meter all values from zero to a households maximum consumption will be observed at some point. Thus, the static assignment with minimal transport from and to a single value has to be replaced by a continuous approach. Furthermore, the values for upcoming d_t are unknown to the distribution algorithm, and therefore a *proportional* distribution scheme is desirable. Thus, the fraction of the demand observed by an individual supplier is independent of the input demand. Moreover, a heuristic should function with little computational cost to avoid expensive smart meter hardware. Finally, a practical heuristic should reduce the communication costs and should only report noticeable consumption. Thus, tiny load samples could be grouped and sent out to only one supplier. However, this variation impacts the privacy and is evaluated further in Sect. 5.

We present an efficient heuristic that considers the afore-mentioned thoughts. It is uses the idea that the probability transport is kept minimal and that the distribution should become uneven towards the extremes. Moreover, as a variant, all samples below a threshold τ can aggregated and grouped together to avoid the communication of arbitrarily small samples. The core idea of the heuristic, as presented in Algorithm 1, is to iteratively draw the reported samples according a uniform distribution over the remaining demand:

Algorithm 1. Communication Optimized Distribution Algorithm

1: **input** $d, |S|, \tau$
2: $b_2 \leftarrow \cdots \leftarrow b_{|S|} \leftarrow 0$
3: $b_1 \leftarrow \text{rand}()$ ▷ First load is drawn uniformly from $[0, d]$
4: $l \leftarrow 1 - b_1$ ▷ Remaining load
5: **for** $i = 2, \ldots, |S| - 1 \wedge l > 0$ **do**
6:        $b_i \leftarrow \text{rand}() \cdot l$
7:        $l \leftarrow l - b_i$
8:        **if** $l < \tau$ **then**   ▷ Threshold variant: Compare with threshold
9:               $b_i \leftarrow b_i + l$ ▷ Aggregate the rest
10:               $l \leftarrow 0$
11:        **end if**
12: **end for**
13: $b_{|S|} \leftarrow l$
14: $\mathbf{b} \leftarrow \text{shuffle}(< b_1, b_2, \ldots, b_{|S|} >)$ ▷ Shuffle for fair distribution
15: $\mathbf{b} \leftarrow d \cdot \mathbf{b}$
16: **output** $\mathbf{b}$

The algorithm takes a demand d, a number of suppliers $|S|$ and (optional) a threshold τ as input and outputs a vector of load samples, whose sum is the given input demand. In a first step the interval $[0, 1]$ is split into two parts according to a value b_1 drawn uniformly from the same interval. The left part of the interval becomes the first reported load. The remaining load $l_1 = d - b_1$ is further split by a random value b_2 drawn from the uniform distribution on the interval $[0, l_1]$. In the further steps the remaining load is updated, $l_2 = l_1 - b_2$. This iterative procedure continues for all suppliers or until the remaining load reaches the threshold (if given). In both cases, the last reported load $b_{|S|}$ is set to $l_{|S|-1}$ to distribute the remaining load. As a result, earlier drawn b_j are more likely to be larger than those which have been drawn at the end of the recursive procedure. To achieve a *fair* distribution for all suppliers, in its final steps the algorithm performs a random permutation (shuffle) on $b_1, \ldots, b_{|S|}$ and multiplies each fraction b_j with the total demand.

5   Evaluation

We discuss the applicability of our results in an evaluation on real world data sets in this section. First, we identify a reasonable value for the privacy parameter λ. Then, we study the influence of different parameter choices, e.g., the number of suppliers, on the adversaries advantage against the SD strategy.

5.1   Privacy Sensitive Appliances

To show that λ-IND has practical relevance, we identify appliances that in our opinion show the highest privacy risk. In a second step, we evaluate their energy consumption in comparison with the total consumption. The latter give us an insight on a reasonable choice for λ.

One group of privacy sensitive appliances are digital screens. Recently Greveler et al. [12] showed that the TV program can be identified in the aggregate power consumption. Moreover, Clark et al. [5] showed an attack, where rendered websites could be identified through power analysis. Since LC-Displays also display private information, we are convinced that digital devices need special protection. Similar concerns have been raised by Backes et al. [2]. Another example of noteworthy appliances are alarm systems. A remote detection of their functionality can compromises the households inhabitants safety [13].

We evaluate the energy consumption of the mentioned appliances on two larger public data sets that are used in NILM research:

The *Reference Energy Disaggregation Data Set (REDD)* was published by J. Zico Kolter and Matthew J. Johnson [16]. It contains fine granulated energy data collected from six houses around Boston, Massachusetts. Kolter et al. measured not only the total consumption but also monitored multiple labeled sub-circuits within the households. The dataset consists of low (1 Hz) and high frequency (15 kHz) measurements.

The *Almanac of Minutely Power data set (AMPds)* was released by Stephen Makonin et al. [19]. The AMPds provides one year of data from a single household from the Vancouver region in British Columbia. Similar to the *REDD* data set, the *AMPds* provides readings of 21 sub-metered circuits with a frequency of one reading per minute.

For our evaluation we used the statistics programming language R. First, all incomplete and implausible entries are removed from the data sets, e.g., entries where sub-metered circuits are not measured or the power consumption of appliances exceeds the total consumption. Second, all load samples are aggregated in 15 min intervals. Third, all time periods with zero consumption of sensitive devices are removed. Finally, a histogram is created over the fraction of energy used by the sensitive devices.

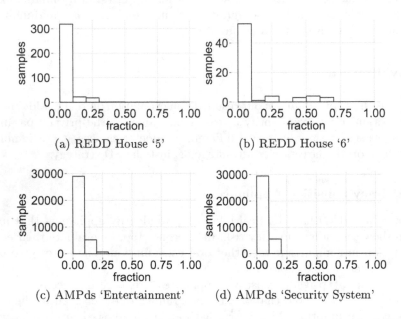

Fig. 3. Fraction of energy spent on electronic devices for two houses in the REDD and the energy spent on entertainment and security system in the AMPds.

Figure 3a and b show the results for the *REDD* for two distinct households, which have a sub-metered circuits labeled electronics. The histograms illustrate the number of time periods in which the fraction energy consumption of entertainment appliances is within the range printed on the x-axis. Figure 3c illustrates the fraction of energy used entertainment appliances in the *AMPds* and Fig. 3d illustrates the same for the alarm system. Taking these numbers into account, in more than 80 % of all time periods the measured fraction is below or equal 10 %. Furthermore, with the exception of 'house 6', in more than 95 % of all time periods, the sensitive appliances consume less than 20 % of the total energy. The alarm systems always require less than 20 % of the total energy consumption. Unfortunately, no breakdown of the sub-metered circuits is given. Thus, the actual consumption of a individual sensitive appliances could be even less. The results support the idea that λ-IND with small λ, e.g., $\lambda = 1.2$, is of practical use to measure the protection of privacy sensitive appliances.

5.2   λ-IND Evaluation of the SD Strategy

In Sect. 4, we have introduced the SD strategy and have proposed a theoretical distribution strategy as well as heuristics. In this section, we evaluate both with different parameters under λ-IND. Thus, the relationship between the λ, the number of suppliers, and the adversaries advantage is studied.

In Sect. 4 a formula for computing an upper bound on the adversaries advantage for given distribution is presented. The described heuristics, however, require a further investigation, as the resulting distribution are not described in closed-form. Therefore, to evaluate these we follow a numerical Monte Carlo approach. First, we distribute a constant demand onto $|S|$ suppliers by applying the heuristics. Repeating this experiment $k = 10^7$ times, a probability distribution of load samples is observed. Given this distribution, an optimal likelihood-ratio distinguisher is used to calculate the adversaries advantage under λ-IND. The heuristic and the evaluation itself are written and executed in R.

The upper bound on the advantage of the adversary as computed in Sect. 4 depending on the number of samples for a different number of suppliers is illustrated in Fig. 4a. The parameter λ is fixed to 1.2 and we observe that, as expected, an increasing number of suppliers decreases the adversaries advantage. Figure 4b shows the distinguishing advantage in dependence on the number of samples for different choices of λ using a fixed number of suppliers $|S| = 16$. When increasing λ, the maximal advantage of the attacker also increases. Thus, the consumer faces the trade-off between the protected time span and the level of protection, i.e., the maximal fraction of energy that can be protected. However, we observe that the advantage is never negligible. Moreover, as others have already discussed [8], the question which advantage is acceptable is of social concern and not of technical interest.

The results of the numerical evaluation of the heuristic described in Algorithm 1 are presented in Fig. 4. The advantage of the heuristics with/out threshold are compared with the earlier computed boundary. A value of $\lambda = 1.2$ is chosen and the number of suppliers is set to $|S| = 16$. We note that both heuristics perform close to the computed bound, with the threshold variant providing slightly less privacy. However, we observed that the threshold algorithm communicates on average with suppliers 3.29 per time period, which is far less than the available 16 suppliers. Thus, aggregating small samples reduces the required communication effort with minimal privacy trade-off.

5.3   Computation and Communication Complexity

The computation costs for distribution algorithms that implement the TD and SD strategy are very low in comparison to the proposed cryptographic aggregation protocols. The costs depend on a few, at most linear in the number of suppliers, symmetric cipher operations per time period. This is because the TD strategy only requires the generation of one secure random number per time period. The non-optimized heuristic for the SD strategy requires at most two random numbers per approached supplier.

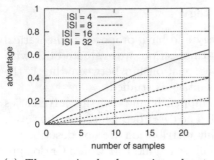
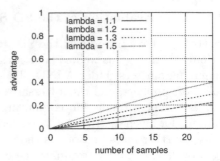

(a) The maximal adversaries advantage when distinguishing load profiles with n samples distributed onto $|S|$ suppliers. The samples are allowed to differ by a factor of $\lambda = 1.2$.

(b) The maximal adversaries advantage when distinguishing load profiles distributed between $|S| = 16$ suppliers for a different number of load samples and various values for λ.

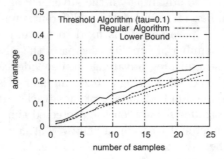

Fig. 4. Distinguishing advantage against both variants of the distribution algorithm.

Studying the communication patterns of both strategies, we observe that unidirectional communication is sufficient. Yet, the communication complexity varies for the TD and SD strategy. The TD strategy requires the same number of messages as an unprotected SMA, namely one message per load sample. In contrast, the SD strategy requires messages linear in the number of used suppliers $O(|S|)$. When using the presented threshold algorithm, on average the number of required messages reduces significantly.

In summary, being dependant on only symmetric ciphers and unidirectional communication, the computational and communication costs are very low when compared with other proposed solutions.

6   Conclusion

In this paper, we have introduced privacy-preserving, randomized buying strategies for an application in smart grids. Contrary to most approaches in the state of the art, these strategies do not presume the cooperation of suppliers nor expensive hardware at consumer side.

Our approach employs a distributed market to buy energy from multiple sources in order to protect the privacy of consumers. Our results indicate that it is not possible to conceal the complete energy consumption of a consumer, but at least it is feasible to conceal sensitive appliances, e.g., an alarm system. Based upon a formal model, we propose the indistinguishability notion of λ-IND that is capable of measuring the protection of such privacy sensitive appliances, which is supported by an evaluation on real-world data sets. Moreover, we have been able to show boundaries in the LSHG and under λ-IND in dependence on the number of readings to be protected and the number of available suppliers. Furthermore, we have developed an heuristic that approximates the SD strategy with low computational and communication overhead.

However, the provided level of privacy protection is fairly low compared to other approaches suggested so far. Even under the comparable weak definition of λ-IND, an adversary achieves non-negligible advantage when observing a larger number of samples. Privacy solutions in which consumers and utilities cooperate, e.g., aggregation protocols, provide stronger privacy protection.

Further work will be a detailed analysis of attackers with access to the information of multiple suppliers, e.g., colluding suppliers. Furthermore, hybrid strategies as well as algorithms that utilize unfair distribution strategies might be interesting candidates for a privacy analysis. Additionally, attacks against diversification strategies through pricing strategies could be evaluated.

Acknowledgments. This work has been co-funded by the German Federal Ministry of Education and Research (BMBF) within CRISP, by the DFG as part of project A.1 within the RTG 2050 "Privacy and Trust for Mobile Users" and by the Hessian LOEWE excellence initiative within CASED. At the time this research was conducted, Stefan Schiffner and Mathias Fischer were part of CASED at TU Darmstadt. Stefan Schiffner is currently employed at the European Union Agency for Network and Information Security (ENISA). The content of this article does not reflect the official opinion of ENISA. Responsibility for the information and views expressed in therein lies entirely with the authors.

A   Constructing Minimal Distinguishable Distributions

To derive an optimal distribution strategy under λ-IND, multiple steps are necessary. First, we discuss the idea of probability transports. Then, given an input distribution and a new desired mean, we construct a new distribution with the specified mean, which has the least statistical distance to the input distribution. Finally, we compute the distinguishing advantage against this construction.

Probability Transport. A probability transport is the change of occurrence probabilities of two values in a (discrete) distribution. Transporting probability $y > 0$ from x_s to x_d implies that the likelihood to observe x_s decreases, while the likelihood to observe x_d increases by y. Given two distributions P_0 and P_1 that are separated by one transport, the change of mean $\Delta\mu = \mu^1 - \mu^0$ can be computed by $\Delta\mu = (x_d - x_s) \cdot y$, where y describes the transported probability, x_s the source, and x_d the destination value.

Optimal Construction. Given the definition of a transport and an input distribution P_0 with mean μ_0, we show how to construct the least distinguishable distribution P_1 that has a mean of $\mu_1 = \lambda \cdot \mu_0$. The best construction of P_1 is by transporting probability from the smallest possible x_s, where $P_0(x_s) > 0$ holds, to the largest possible $x_d = d^1 = \lambda \cdot d^0$. By this construction the mean increases with the least increase in the statistical distance, which only depends on the transported probability y. The accurate value y that is necessary for the transport to achieve a mean μ^1 is

$$y = \frac{\Delta\mu}{x_d - x_s} = \frac{\mu^1 - \mu^0}{d^1 - x_s}.$$

Note that multiple transports might be required if $P_0(x_s)$ does not provide sufficient probability.

Distinguishing Advantage. Given this construction, we show how the first distribution P_0 should be chosen, such that construction produces a pair of distributions that is the least distinguishable pair of distributions for the means μ_0 and μ_1. A transport from $x_s = 0$ to $x_d = d^1$ provides the best and thus least increase in the adversaries advantage while increasing the mean. Thus, we deduce that distribution P_0 needs sufficient probabilities $P_0(0) \geq y$ for a transport from 0. If this is the case then only one transport from 0 to d^1 is necessary to construct P_1 from P_0. A transport from some $x_s > 0$ implies that a larger amount has to be transported and therefore would result in a larger statistical distance.

Given two distributions constructed according the derived properties, we are able to link the advantage with the privacy parameter λ and the number of available suppliers $|S|$. The latter determines the required mean, when assuming a fair distribution algorithm. With only one transport, we can deduce the following distinguishing advantage:

$$
\begin{aligned}
\mathbf{Adv}_{SD,1}^{\lambda\text{-IND}} &= y = \frac{\Delta\mu}{x_d - x_s} = \frac{\mu^1 - \mu^0}{d^1 - 0} = \frac{d^1/|S| - d^0/|S|}{d^1} \\
&= \frac{\lambda \cdot d^0 - d^0}{|S| \cdot \lambda \cdot d^0} = \frac{(\lambda - 1) \cdot d^0}{|S| \cdot \lambda \cdot d^0} \\
&= \frac{\lambda - 1}{|S| \cdot \lambda}.
\end{aligned}
$$

References

1. Ács, G., Castelluccia, C.: I have a DREAM! (DiffeRentially privatE smArt Metering). In: Filler, T., Pevný, T., Craver, S., Ker, A. (eds.) IH 2011. LNCS, vol. 6958, pp. 118–132. Springer, Heidelberg (2011)
2. Backes, M., Meiser, S.: Differentially private smart metering with battery recharging. In: Garcia-Alfaro, J., Lioudakis, G., Cuppens-Boulahia, N., Foley, S., Fitzgerald, W.M. (eds.) DPM 2013 and SETOP 2013. LNCS, vol. 8247, pp. 194–212. Springer, Heidelberg (2014)

3. Baignères, T., Sepehrdad, P., Vaudenay, S.: Distinguishing distributions using chernoff information. In: Heng, S.-H., Kurosawa, K. (eds.) ProvSec 2010. LNCS, vol. 6402, pp. 144–165. Springer, Heidelberg (2010)

4. Bohli, J.-M., Sorge, C., Ugus, O.: A privacy model for smart metering. In: 2010 IEEE International Conference on Communications Workshops, pp. 1–5. IEEE, May 2010

5. Clark, S.S., Mustafa, H., Ransford, B., Sorber, J., Fu, K., Xu, W.: Current events: identifying webpages by tapping the electrical outlet. In: Jajodia, S., Mayes, K., Crampton, J. (eds.) ESORICS 2013. LNCS, vol. 8134, pp. 700–717. Springer, Heidelberg (2013)

6. Csisz, I., et al.: Information-type measures of difference of probability distributions and indirect observations. Studia Sci. Math. Hungar. **2**, 299–318 (1967)

7. Danezis, G., Kohlweiss, M., Rial, A.: Differentially private billing with rebates. In: Filler, T., Pevný, T., Craver, S., Ker, A. (eds.) IH 2011. LNCS, vol. 6958, pp. 148–162. Springer, Heidelberg (2011)

8. Dwork, C.: Differential privacy. In: Bugliesi, M., Preneel, B., Sassone, V., Wegener, I. (eds.) ICALP 2006. LNCS, vol. 4052, pp. 1–12. Springer, Heidelberg (2006)

9. Dwork, C., Naor, M., Pitassi, T., Rothblum, G.N.: Differential privacy under continual observation. In: Proceedings of the 42nd ACM Symposium on Theory of Computing (STOC), pp. 715–724 (2010)

10. Efthymiou, C., Kalogridis, G.: Smart grid privacy via anonymization of smart metering data. In: International Conference on Smart Grid Communications (SmartGridComm), pp. 238–243. IEEE (2010)

11. Garcia, F.D., Jacobs, B.: Privacy-friendly energy-metering via homomorphic encryption. In: Cuellar, J., Lopez, J., Barthe, G., Pretschner, A. (eds.) STM 2010. LNCS, vol. 6710, pp. 226–238. Springer, Heidelberg (2011)

12. Greveler, U., Justus, B., Loehr, D.: Multimedia content identification through smart meter power usage profiles. Computers, Privacy and Data Protection CPDP, Brussels, Belgium (2012)

13. Hart, G.W.: Residential energy monitoring and computerized surveillance via utility power flows. IEEE Technol. Soc. Mag. **8**(2), 12–16 (1989)

14. Jawurek, M., Kerschbaum, F., Danezis, G.: Privacy technologies for smart grids - a survey of options. Technical report, Microsoft Research - Tech Report - 2012 - 119 (2012)

15. Kalogridis, G., Efthymiou, C., Denic, S.Z., Lewis, T.A., Cepeda, R.: Privacy for smart meters: towards undetectable appliance load signatures. In: IEEE International Conference on Smart Grid Communications (SmartGridComm), pp. 232–237 (2010)

16. Kolter, J.Z., Johnson, M.J.: REDD: a public data set for energy disaggregation research. In: SustKDD Workshop on Data Mining Applications in Sustainability, San Diego, CA, pp. 1–6 (2011)

17. Kursawe, K., Danezis, G., Kohlweiss, M.: Privacy-friendly aggregation for the smart-grid. In: Fischer-Hübner, S., Hopper, N. (eds.) PETS 2011. LNCS, vol. 6794, pp. 175–191. Springer, Heidelberg (2011)

18. Lin, H.-Y., Tzeng, W.-G., Shen, S.-T., Lin, B.-S.P.: A practical smart metering system supporting privacy preserving billing and load monitoring. In: Bao, F., Samarati, P., Zhou, J. (eds.) ACNS 2012. LNCS, vol. 7341, pp. 544–560. Springer, Heidelberg (2012)

19. Makonin, S., Popowich, F., Bartram, L., Gill, B., Bajic, I.V.: AMPds: a public dataset for load disaggregation and eco-feedback research. In: IEEE Electrical Power and Energy Conference, pp. 1–6 (2013)

20. Molina-Markham, A., Shenoy, P., Fu, K., Cecchet, E., Irwin, D.: Private memoirs of a smart meter. In: Proceedings of the 2nd ACM Workshop on Embedded Sensing Systems for Energy-Efficiency in Building, pp. 61–66. ACM (2010)
21. Neyman, J., Pearson, E.S.: On the problem of the most efficient tests of statistical hypotheses. In: Kotz, S., Johnson, N. (eds.) Breakthroughs in Statistics. Springer Series in Statistics, pp. 73–108 (1992)
22. Pinsker, M.S.: Information and information stability of random variables and processes (1960)
23. Rial, A., Danezis, G.: Privacy-preserving smart metering. In: Proceedings of the 10th Annual ACM Workshop on Privacy in the Electronic Society, pp. 49–60. ACM (2011)
24. Varodayan, D., Khisti, A.: Smart meter privacy using a rechargeable battery: minimizing the rate of information leakage. In: IEEE International Conference on Acoustics, Speech and Signal Processing (ICASSP), pp. 1932–1935 (2011)
25. Vaudenay, S.: On privacy models for RFID. In: Kurosawa, K. (ed.) ASIACRYPT 2007. LNCS, vol. 4833, pp. 68–87. Springer, Heidelberg (2007)
26. Wang, S., Cui, L., Que, J., Choi, D.-H., Jiang, X., Cheng, S., Xie, L.: A randomized response model for privacy preserving smart metering. IEEE Trans. Smart Grid 3(3), 1317–1324 (2012)

Selected Cloud Security Patterns to Improve End User Security and Privacy in Public Clouds

Thomas Länger[1]($\boxtimes$), Henrich C. Pöhls[2], and Solange Ghernaouti[1]

[1] Swiss Cybersecurity Advisory and Research Group (SCARG),
Université de Lausanne, Lausanne, Switzerland
thomas.laenger@unil.ch
[2] Institute of IT-Security and Security Law (ISL),
Universität Passau, Passau, Germany

Abstract. Cloud computing has the potential to dramatically reduce the cost and complexity of provisioning information technology resources for end users. However, to make it secure and privacy-preserving for end users, additional technical safeguards must be added—the application of strong cryptography is such a safeguard. The Horizon 2020 project PRISMACLOUD surveys and advances several cryptographic protocols and primitives usable to cryptographically address common cloud security and privacy issues. The cryptographic functionality will entirely be encapsulated in five configurable tools, from which cloud services providing end-to-end security can be constructed. This approach relieves cloud service designers from dealing with the complex and error prone correct application of cryptographic functionality and shall spark the emergence of a multitude of privacy and security preserving cloud applications for the benefit of the end-users—who will no longer have to rely on contractual and legal instruments for ensuring, that privacy and security is enforced by cloud providers on their behalf. In order to support the privacy-by-design development of the tools, we developed several cloud security patterns for common critical situations in the cloud—in the three fields of data storage in the cloud, user privacy protection and data minimisation, and authentication of stored and processed data.

Keywords: Cloud computing · Privacy · Security · User centric security · Cloud security pattern · End-to-end security · Cryptography · Security-by-design

1 Introduction

1.1 Significance of Cloud Computing

Cloud computing[1] is the major growth area in information and communication technologies today, and with its huge processing capabilities and data storage

---

[1] The authors' work is supported by the European Union Horizon 2020 research activity n° 644962 PRISMACLOUD: "Privacy and security maintaining services in the cloud" [17]; duration 2/2015–7/2018; 16 partners; https://www.prismacloud.eu.

S. Schiffner et al. (Eds.): APF 2016, LNCS 9857, pp. 115–132, 2016.
DOI: 10.1007/978-3-319-44760-5_8

architectures, and with all the data which is amassed, and even created through its use, it is closely related to another major growth area in Information and Communication Technologies (ICT), that of big data aggregation, processing and analysis. With an estimated size of about 150 billion US-Dollar an enormous rush to move into cloud computing is observed [23,28]. The American business magazine Forbes has an overview of several forecasts and market estimates [13]. As a recent report by the Economist says: "Cloud technologies have gone mainstream" [27]. Today's biggest players to provide these capabilities are in fact companies which have enormous financial power at their disposal and are proficiently experienced in the field of ICT. They now aim at increasing revenue and domination in the developing information age, and invest huge efforts in the construction of new data centres and in new technologies for asserting their leading positions.

The biggest cloud provider today [24], Amazon.com Inc., started as an online book store in 1994 and has been generating enormous wealth as an e-commerce retailer. Since 2006, Amazon offers public cloud services (Platform as a service—PaaS, which it initially has developed to cater for its own retail infrastructures) on a commercial basis. The second and third biggest providers are Microsoft Corp. and Google Inc. (now the holding company Alphabet. Inc.) [24], who made their fortunes in Personal Computer operating systems and office software, and in search engines and internet advertising business, respectively. Besides the above mentioned three cloud providers, there are many other providers and players competing in this field over markets and governance of our future society.

1.2   Security Problems

In the history of ICT innovation several comparable situations are known, when companies have rushed into a newly developing market, while at the same time also shaping the market. In such a hurry, developments often do not respect the requirements and needs of the end users—but rather the needs of the companies, which want to grow quickly. The price in these situations is often paid by the end users: Systems and services are made available on a large scale before the data privacy and security concerns of the customers are fully addressed and resolved.

This situation, for valid reasons, keeps security aware customers currently away from the cloud—be it because they are forced by regulation to guarantee a certain degree of confidentiality for the data they are operating with (e.g. in the health sector, or in e-government), or that they are just companies, or individuals, who highly value the security of their data.

A comprehensive and authoritative Cloud Computing Security Risk Assessment is maintained by the European Union Agency for Network and Information Security (ENISA) [8,9]. It references data protection risks, risks connected to governance and control, as well as technical risks related to cloud computing. Many of these risks can effectively be countered in the secure cloud services, that can be built from the PRISMACLOUD toolbox.

1.3   Proposed Solutions to Improve Cloud Privacy and Security

The European Commission, in its endeavour to strengthen European competitiveness and in its struggle to maintain European sovereignty over the data which is being moved to the cloud, has developed a proprietary European Cloud Computing Strategy [11], and supports the development of secure cloud systems in their Horizon 2020 strategic programme [10] of which the project PRISMACLOUD [17] is a part. The Commission recognises the enormous cost reduction potential of a move to the cloud for companies and entities of all sizes. Foremost, it recognises the strategic importance of a European share and participation in the development and commercialisation of cloud computing products and services, and what is more, the strategic importance of maintaining sovereignty by not losing "European data" to opaque conglomerates beyond European data protection legislation and control.

Whether European research and development will be able to economically contest with its American competitors on providing the basic cloud services on a large scale is questionable: Today, almost the entire cloud business is based in the United States of America, in the area of Seattle, Washington and in California in the San Francisco Bay Area. It is also there, and in huge data centres all across the United States, where the clouds are physically hosted, and the data is stored and processed.[2] European industries compete in the shadow of the American market giants, like in many other major fields of ICT. Yet, the European Commission sees an opportunity to focus on original European strengths of data security and privacy protection for the benefit of the end-users and customers.

The PRISMACLOUD project will use a privacy-and-data-protection-by-design approach [6,16] and provide the *advanced cryptographic tools* (in form of a software library which can be parametrized in various ways) for implementing privacy and security aware services on top of a potentially untrusted cloud. Thus, end users' effective governance and control over the storage and processing of their data shall be reinstated, following the spirit of the new European General Data Protection Regulation which has been adopted in June 2016. The feasibility of the PRISMACLOUD approach shall be validated in *eight sample cloud services* which will be provided as reference implementations: Data sharing service, secure archiving service, privacy enhancing identity management service, selective authentic exchange service, verifiable statistics service, infrastructure attestation service, anonymisation service, and encryption proxy service. The applicability of the services in real-world applications shall be verified in *three pilot applications* in the fields of Smart Cities, e-Health, and e-Government.

---

[2] It is now, that cloud providers have started to host their data centers in multiple locations world-wide, including Asia, South America, and countries of the European Union (see e.g. Amazon: http://docs.aws.amazon.com/AWSEC2/latest/UserGuide/using-regions-availability-zones.html). Nevertheless, the headquarters and main installations of these businesses are certainly under U.S. American jurisdiction and it is at least possible that data, in whichever form and state of aggregation, might be consolidated with data residing in the U.S.A.

1.4 Contributions and Outline

This paper concentrates on the very tangible problem of how to practically tighten and increase for end users the security and privacy of data and computations in cloud settings, by applying suitable cryptographic tools. The PRIS-MACLOUD paradigm provides the tools encapsulating cryptographic protocols and primitives, thus enabling the required end-to-end security—much in the same way as encryption and digital signatures enable end-to-end security for communications over untrusted networks. In order to secure the aspired results, developers and application designers need to develop and use the suitable cryptographic tools right. To this goal, we developed nine cloud security design patterns, communicating and addressing the often conflicting requirements from different actors and explaining which existing cryptographic building blocks can be used to achieve the required functionalities.

In the Introduction (Sect. 1) we framed the security context for end users in untrusted clouds. In Sect. 2 we provide an introduction to the capabilities of design patterns in general by a historical approach on their evolution from architectural design patterns through software design patterns to cloud security patterns. In Sect. 3 we present an overview of the *nine patterns* developed in the framework of the PRISMACLOUD project in the fields of *(i) data storage in the cloud, (ii) user privacy protection and data minimisation*, and *(iii) authentication of stored and processed data* and go into detail for one pattern of each of the three fields.[3] In Sect. 4 we introduce the *five configurable tools* which will be developed in the project, and list the cryptographic protocols and primitives they are composed of, as well as example services which can be built from them. The services' functionality and practicability will be evaluated by three pilot applications in the fields of Smart Cities, e-Health, and e-Government by project end. In Sect. 5 we present conclusions.

2 Design Patterns

2.1 Representation of Knowledge in Design Patterns

The Viennese Christopher Alexander, who has since 1963 been living and teaching in Berkeley, California, published his book "A Pattern Language: Towns, Buildings, Construction" [1][4] in 1977, where he and his co-authors introduced the concept of reusable design solutions for architectural problems. The idea behind the architectural patterns is to provide a collection of proven solutions for problems which occur over and over again. The 253 presented patterns contain the concentrated knowledge and experience of designers and are intended to be reused. Alexander defines a pattern language as a collection of patterns

---

[3] The other patterns can be studied in the public PRISMACLOUD deliverable D2.2 "Domain independent generic security models", available on the project web site www.prismacloud.eu.

[4] The entire book, 1218 pages, can be downloaded as pdf from archive.org/details/APatternLanguage.

from a specific domain. The proposed patterns were intended to be "alive and evolving". Alexander viewed them as "hypotheses", as "current best guess", to be improved and possibly replaced with more profound patterns, as a result of "new experience and observation". The idea of design patterns was taken up again in 1994 by computer scientists and especially software engineers who tried to tackle the reusability of software with a software design pattern approach. Reusability of software was then, after about 20 years of object oriented design, a big issue. The resulting book "Design Patterns: Elements of Reusable Object-Oriented Software" [14] has become a standard and has not lost its significance and relevance in software engineering today. The problem setting in software engineering is comparable to that in the field of architecture: Not to "solve every problem from first principles", but instead use a proven solution to a design problem.

The idea of design patterns was applied to other contexts as well. Security patterns, or security design patterns "codify basic security knowledge in a structured and understandable way" [25]. They represent a practical means to communicate end user needs and requirements. Security patterns are connected to one or more specific security goals. The Internet Privace Engineering Network (IPEN) of the European Data Protection Supervisor supports "(re)-usable building blocks, design patterns and other tools for selected Internet use cases where privacy is at stake".[5] IPEN's objective is "to integrate data protection and privacy into all phases of the development process (...) It supports networking between engineer groups and existing initiatives for engineering privacy into the Internet."[6] A comprehensive collection of security patterns which were discussed at the annual "Pattern Languages of Programs" (PLoP) conferences since 1997, is available on the homepage of the security researcher Munawar Hafiz (Auburn University, Alabama, USA).[7] It currently contains a catalogue of 97 security patterns. There is also on-going work on privacy patterns, which connect problems to solutions within the context of user privacy. The ability of design patterns to communicate and address the often conflicting requirements from different actors in different domains, is ideal for their application in designing information privacy into information systems: "Privacy Patterns that span across usability, engineering, security and other considerations can provide sharable descriptions of generative solutions to common design contentions. Since patterns focus on describing the resolutions of contradictory forces in a design context, the pros and cons of a specific solution can be easily debated. Unlike guidelines, regulations or best practices, patterns are descriptive, rather than normative, facilitating discussion and debate and providing education rather than insisting on particular solutions or practices" [7]. There are several websites

---

[5] https://secure.edps.europa.eu/EDPSWEB/edps/EDPS/IPEN.

[6] ibid.

[7] www.munawarhafiz.com/securitypatterncatalog/index.php. Munawar Hafiz is also author of several papers on security patterns, e.g. [15], which presents "4 design patterns that can aid the decision making process for the designers of privacy protecting systems".

online for joint development of privacy design patterns, like privacypatterns.org
by researchers of the University of California, Berkeley, School of Law (funded
with grants from the U.S. Department of Homeland Security and from the NIST,
among others), and the privacypatterns.eu—resulting from the European FP7
project PRIPARE (Preparing industry to privacy-by-design by supporting its
application in research).[8]

2.2 Assumptions and Categories for the Pattern Descriptions

The cloud security patterns do not represent "hard requirements" on cloud applications and services, the patterns represent more a way of communicating a user
need (and specifically a security need) to the system architects and developers
of the services in an informal way. The system architects and developers themselves shall read from the pattern the information enabling them to develop the
cryptographic building blocks in such a way, that the applications and systems
using these building blocks, satisfy end users' security and privacy needs.

Different publications about security patterns (and about design patterns
in general) define the patterns along different categories. We have taken into
consideration the categories used in [1,14,25], as well the categories used on
the security pattern websites cloudcomputingpatterns.org and cloudpatterns.org
and have chosen a synthesis that seems suitable for us. We use the same main
categories as in Alexander's et al. seminal pattern book [1] (problem, solution), as
do all the other sources and complement them with other categories (intention,
building block, consequences and countered threats).

3 PRISMACLOUD Cloud Security Patterns

3.1 Overview of Cloud Security Patterns

The nine cloud security patterns have been developed in the first year of the
PRISMACLOUD project, in order to better understand the end user "situation"
currently prevailing in cloud storage and computing. In the practical project
context, the patterns will serve as additional input in the design phase of the
PRISMACLOUD tools in another project work package. But the cloud security
patterns will also provide input to an "impact analysis of cloud usage for end
users", a main deliverable of the project, providing guidance for corporate, governmental, and individual end users in their confrontation with cloud services.

The nine cloud security patterns have been designed to varying level of detail
and will, as design patterns are generally intended to be "alive and evolving"
[1], be further developed while the PRISMACLOUD research activity continues.
Because of space constraints, we will present here only one selected pattern from
each of the categories (i) data storage in the cloud, (ii) user privacy protection
and data minimisation, and (iii) authentication of stored and processed data.
For the other patterns (which are not presented in detail), we give a summary

---

[8] www.pripareproject.eu.

description after the short introductions to the single fields, in order to telegraph the basic "situation", and the idea behind the solution.[9]

3.2   Field 1: Data Storage in the Cloud

The security of data at rest represents one of the most fundamental problems regarding privacy. Too often data confidentiality is regarded as being easily fix-able by "just employing client-side encryption". While this solution is viable, it requires the effort of a fully fledged infrastructure for managing cryptographic keys in order to still enjoy one of the true cloud benefits—the ability to share data with ease. There are two patterns in this specific field:

- *Pattern 1: Secure cloud storage by default* is applicable in any context where a user wants to securely store or share data objects in a cloud infrastructure.
- *Pattern 2: Moving a legacy application's database to the cloud* is applicable when an end user wants to deploy an existing database to a public cloud.

We describe only Pattern 1 as an example in the following.

Pattern 1: Secure Cloud Storage by Default

Summary. Describes the qualities of a cloud storage service, as most users would expect it when moving their digital assets to the cloud: The data in the cloud storage remains readily available when needed, and dependably and securely confidential against the cloud provider and other tenants in the vicinity of the cloud, as well as against other third parties which are not entitled by the user to access the data. The data may easily be shared with others, and easily be transferred to another cloud provider when the user wants to do so.

Intention. Provide a cloud storage service with strong confidentiality, integrity, and availability, from which the cloud user can anytime effectively pull away the stored data.

Problem. Currently, most cloud storage providers store the data either unen-crypted, or apply encryption which remains completely under their control; some cloud users locally encrypt their data before they store it in the cloud in order to maintain the confidentiality of the data.

   Whether the cloud provider encrypts or does not encrypt the data it stores, the cloud provider has in practice full access to the data—if it is not encrypted by the user in the first place. In many cases, especially in free-of-charge public cloud services from the big cloud providers, the end users have to consent to terms-of-reference granting the provider full rights to the data (including rights to store, combine, or otherwise use the data in ways non-anticipated and not explicitly consented to by the user, in order to be able to sell or commercialise the data in any other imaginable way). Nevertheless, also in commercial cloud services, the

---

[9] For a more detailed description of all cloud security patterns we want to direct the attention to PRISMACLOUD deliverable D2.2 "Domain independent generic security models", available on the project web site www.prismacloud.eu.

cloud provider has to be trusted to maintain the confidentiality of the data—by not looking at the stored data itself, and by effectively protecting it against access by unauthorised third parties. This includes all copies and replications of the data which are created for availability purposes in all layers of a storage architecture.

Also with respect to availability of data and of cloud services, the user is dependent on the provider. There are cases known, where bankruptcy of a cloud provider led to sudden loss of access to customer data. Deletion of data in clouds is also a big issue and it is not sufficiently solved how an effective deletion of data in all replications and backups can be achieved and substantiated.

When cloud users use end-to-end encryption to mitigate some of the mentioned problems and threats they are required to implement and maintain a cryptographic key management system and an access control mechanism, with all its known complexities and implications.

Solution. Cloud users do not want to give up their property rights and privacy rights on the data. Cloud users want to maintain full control over their cloud storage by default. They want strong confidentiality guarantees by default, while being able to share data with other cloud users or with the cloud provider at their own discretion. The data needs to be protected against loss by some kind of redundancy in a way that the confidentiality remains upheld. The cloud user wants to be able to withdraw the data from one cloud provider and give it to another provider for hosting at any time without having to rely on any form of cooperation with the cloud provider. The cloud user wants to be sure that the data can be completely withdrawn, with no copies of the plain information remaining at the provider.

Building Block. PRISMACLOUD proposes the *cryptographic storage solution tool* with increased practical usability for the secure, distributed storage of data. This tool uses information dispersal, based on a *secret sharing primitive* [2,4,26].

Consequences and Countered Threats. The pattern *secure cloud storage by default* counters almost all identified risks related to confidentiality, integrity, and availability of stored data in the cloud and therefore constitutes a disruptive technology of highest potential. A cryptographically secure storage solution can potentially entirely transform cloud provisioning world-wide. One new assumption which is introduced by this tool is the non-collusion assumption, i.e. that sufficiently many of the cloud providers do not maliciously cooperate to discover the secret. This means, that the number of shares necessary to reconstruct the secret in the threshold scheme of the information dispersal algorithm is a crucial design parameter. The non-collusion assumption can only be substantiated by other assumptions on the trustworthiness of the single involved cloud providers. However, that risk can be deliberately reduced by continuous renewal and replacement of the shares. This reduces the attack window for procuring a sufficient number of shares for reconstructing the information. On the other hand, the data owner does not have to rely on computational assumptions for the confidentiality of the data. The pattern covers the following threats:

- *Loss of governance* with respect to losing the authority to effectively decide about access to the data, about moving the data and deleting the data.
- *Lock-in* is effectively countered by the ability to exclude shares from the data set and to generate new shares to be stored at a different providers.
- Many other technical risks are covered by the implicit encryption, e.g. *isolation failure, management interface compromise, data protection failure, insecure or incomplete data deletion, malicious insider.*
- *Availability* improves as even in the case of one storage provider being off-line, the secret still may be reconstructed with the shares from other providers. On the other hand, if many providers would be off-line simultaneously, the reconstruction may (temporarily) not be possible.

The leakage of metadata, which occurs during storage and retrieval of the single shares, and by synchronisation activity between the single storage providers during share renewal, may still present a privacy problem.

3.3   Field 2: User Privacy Protection and Data Minimisation

Privacy protection requires to minimise the access to information following a need-to-know principle, which means, that the cloud provider shall only have access to what is needed to fulfil the delegated task. This is a known principle with respect to data, but it also applies for the meta-data created through the interaction of the user with the cloud. The most common interaction of a user with a cloud is to prove that he or she is authorised to use a service, but doing so shall not reveal more information than necessary, and shall not allow user tracking by the cloud.

- *Pattern 3: Non-identifiable and untrackable use of a cloud service* has anonymity as its goal, and linkable data is to be completely excluded, while in pattern 4 some information is revealed.
- *Pattern 4: Minimise exposure of private data during authentication in the cloud* assumes that some information is revealed in order to get authorised, but which information exactly is revealed, remains under the control of the user.
- *Pattern 5: Big data anonymisation* is applicable when user privacy is at stake in big data analysis.

The patterns 3 and 4 are closely related to each other—both are concerned with effectively reducing the amount of data which is exposed during interaction with cloud services and applications, and both can be realised with the cryptographic building block of anonymous credentials. We describe pattern 4 as an example next.

Pattern 4: Minimise Exposure of Private Data During Authentication

Summary. Only expose the minimum amount of data necessary when authenticating for a cloud service. During the process of authentication, a user wants to present some attributes, without revealing other attributes he or she may additionally have. The user may also only want to prove the possession of an attribute, or some quality of an attribute (e.g. a statement on a range it is in) without revealing the exact value of the attribute. Moreover, the user may want to show or prove attributes to different sites in a manner, that the single showings cannot be linked to the same user.

Intention. The pattern wants to reduce the data which is unnecessarily exposed during authentication situations.

Problem. Disclosing more data than necessary for performing or delegating a specific task represents a severe privacy threat for the user. Such data is prone to being accumulated and data-mined by the cloud provider and by other parties eventually getting in possession of the data. For example, authentication for a service in the cloud is often performed by the use of an identity certificate. The user shows the certificate to the verifier who verifies the digital signature on the certificate with the public key of a certifier. The verifier thus learns all the data contained in the identity certificate, although for a proper authentication it might be sufficient to access only a small subset of the data. Identity certificates also make interactions attributable to the bearer of the identity certificate, i.e. interactions can be tracked across services. All these side effects are problematic from a privacy point of view and the principle of data minimisation actually calls for avoiding such unnecessary disclosure of data in information infrastructure transactions.

Solution. Authentication allows a claimant in a protocol to convince the verifier that the required set of attributes is correctly held by the claimant. A solution must enable this functionality without revealing any additional attributes and potentially also without being able to link several interactions of the same user.

Building Block. PRISMACLOUD proposes the *flexible authentication with selective disclosure tool* to achieve the desired solution. This tool could implement the technology of "anonymous credentials" following [5].

Consequences and Countered Threats. The pattern allows an effective reduction of the amount of data which is revealed during authentication and other transactions requiring the presentation of user data. The pattern enables, that statements about the encoded attributes can be proven to a verifier without revealing the values of the attributes. The pattern enables, that different credential shows are unlinkable or can be implemented to be unlinkable. If events need to be linkable, it is possible to anonymously prove the possession of a pseudonym. The most important technical risks can be excluded because of the cryptographic security of the primitives which are used for its implementation. The current pattern is also effective for countering data protection risks. It allows a fine grained control of which data is exposed to whom. It thus reduces risks connected to the processing of personal data collected by the service provider without effective necessity. It reduces the lack of transparency, and all the risks involved by chain processing involving multiple processors and by moving data between jurisdictions, especially also out of the control of a local data protection regulation.

3.4   Field 3: Authentication of Stored and Processed Data

The patterns in this field are concerned with integrity of data and with a verifiable authentication of origin of data. This is particularly of interest when data is entrusted to cloud systems outside the immediate control of the data owner. But the rigidity of previously used data authentication schemes, e.g. digital signature schemes, did not allow to authorise certain subsequent modifications. Thus, using them did increase the security of a cloud service, but still represented a severe privacy threat as the authenticity proof required to show the entire authenticity protected data to the third party. Moreover, verifiable authenticity is also required for the results of processing and for properties of the involved infrastructures, which cannot be achieved with previously used schemes.

- *Pattern 6: Protect the authenticity of a data set and possible subsets* is applicable whenever data originates at a credible source and its trustworthiness depends on (a) the source staying verifiably authentic and (b) the data being subjected only to authorised subsequent modifications. It is applicable as a substitute for integrity protection by standard signatures.
- *Pattern 7: Authorise controlled subsequent modifications of signed data* is closely related to a pattern known as "delegation". It applies whenever a third party shall be authorised to do subsequent changes, for which the verifier is able to cryptographically verify the authorisation by the original signer. It maintains the confidentiality of processing steps and the original data, as the verifier does not know the changes done nor the original data.
- *Pattern 8: Controlling the correctness of delegated computations* is relevant whenever cloud providers are performing computations on data but cannot be considered fully trustworthy or immune to attacks on data integrity.
- *Pattern 9: Controlling your virtual infrastructures* applies to situations where a customer or end user rents a virtual infrastructure from a cloud service provider. Using recently developed methods for representing the topology of virtualised infrastructure as a graph and issuing a signature on that graph, one can extend current audit procedures with a means for proving the correct configuration of virtualised infrastructures.

In the following we will display Pattern 6 as a selected example.

Pattern 6: Protect the Authenticity of a Data Set and Possible Subsets

Summary. It shall be possible to subsequently cloak and/or remove information from an authentic data set, e.g. a signed data structure, while attaining two additional properties: (1) to protect the confidentiality of the information that was removed, (2) to retain (or have only minimal impact on) the authenticity guarantee of the remaining data.

Intention. The pattern allows for future subsequent removal of data from a data set for which integrity and authenticity protection mechanisms such as digital signatures are usually applied to protect the data set (1) against unauthorised subsequent changes and (2) to authenticate the source of the data.

Problem. Currently well accepted and widely used standard digital signatures do not support any subsequent editing of the data. Whether authorised or not, it will be detected and as a result the integrity and authenticity can no longer be established for the remaining unchanged data. Obvious and naïve solutions to the integrity problem exist, but offer no privacy with sufficient cryptographic strength.[10] Assume, a number of tests is carried out an a blood sample and a report is being created, containing e.g., (1) blood sugar, (2) total cholesterol, (3) haemoglobin, (4) vitamin D, (5) tuberculosis (TB). If only blood sugar, cholesterol and vitamin D (tests 1, 2, and 4) are given to the patient's ecotrophologist, the problem, generally also known as the document sanitization problem [19], is how the remaining data is protected against malicious tampering and the credible source remains verifiable. Moreover, the removal must eliminate all traces such that the ecotrophologist as a potential attacker is prohibited from reconstructing removed data. This must go as far as to even remove any trace that there ever has been done a tuberculosis test (test 5), as it is only conducted for patients in high risk groups or already treated for TB, which reveals private information.

Solution. Employ a different set of cryptographic functionalities, or conventional digital signature schemes in a different way, such that malleability is enabled while authenticity for the remaining data and confidentiality of the removed data is preserved. The allowed modifications must be formally described and the special digital signature for the data set is created. Subsequently the authenticity of the modified data set can be verified, thus giving the cryptographic assurance about the origin of the modified data and that only allowed modifications were made.

Building Block. PRISMACLOUD proposes the *flexible authentication with selective disclosure tool* which enables transparent redactable signature functionality [22], as e.g. to authorise a subsequent removal while keeping the authenticity of the remaining data protected and to hide the fact that something was removed. The tool can be tailored, e.g. [3], to offer a similar legal assurance [21,29].

Consequences and Countered Threats. The pattern combines the strength of cryptographic end-to-end integrity protection with the ability to remove data for data minimisation purposes. The pattern counters at least the following threats:

- *Loss of data integrity*: The remaining data is still integrity protected, any unauthorised change will be detected.
- *Loss of accountability*: The origin of the remaining data can still be authenticated using the public key that is used for digital signature verification. Further accountability depends on the tool and can be tailored.
- *Data leakage*: Unneeded data, if marked as removable, can be removed without reducing the remaining data's verification of origin and integrity.

---

[10] Whenever the signature mathematically still depends on some removed data, like in hash trees, they cryptographically do not offer a sophisticated level of privacy [3].

– *Insecure or incomplete data deletion*: Data requested to be removed is marked as removable in an integrity protected data structure and can be removed with no negative effects on the integrity of the other data. This removes a potential hinderance to delete data at all occurrences.

4 PRISMACLOUD Tools

4.1 Introduction

The PRISMACLOUD project proposes a set of five configurable tools, encapsulating several cryptographic protocols and primitives. Without exception, the cryptographic protocols and primitives are either extensions or adaptations of existing cryptographic protocols or primitives of Technology Readiness Level [12] (TRL) 3 or higher. The novelty and added value of the project is, that the single primitives are advanced to TRL 7 ("system prototype demonstration in operational environment").

The encapsulation of complex cryptographic functionality shall leave the complex and error-prone correct implementation and application to cryptographers and specialised software engineers and prevent likely mistakes by service developers. The tools will be provided as a software library. The single tools can be parametrised in various different ways and thus be customised for use in a specific service. The services provide interfaces in form of (restful) application programming interfaces (APIs) and are suitable to be deployed in the cloud [18].

Table 1 presents which tools can be applied as solution to which patterns.

4.2 Prismacloud Tools and Employed Cryptographic Primitives

In the following, we provide a summary of the functionalities of the single tools used in the single patterns, as well as the cryptographic protocols and primitives they are based on. A detailed descriptions of the tools and primitives, including references can again be found in [18].

Tool 1: Secure Object Storage Tool. PRISMACLOUD proposes to split the data to be stored into a number of shares which are distributed to several cloud storage providers in a way, that no single provider can access the plain data, which can only be reconstructed from a fixed number of shares. Under the assumption that a certain number of providers do not maliciously cooperate, the secret sharing algorithm itself is considerably stronger than commonly used cryptographic systems and is capable of long-term security [20]. Therefore, it can be applied also in scenarios with highest confidentiality requirements, like in e-Health or e-Government. It requires an explicit access control system to the split shares, but then provides a kind of key-less encryption with provable security. The tool allows checking the integrity of remotely stored shares without having to retrieve the shares first. It also solves the availability problem at the user level, without the need of explicit backups. Single shares can also be taken out of the system and be replaced by newly generated ones. This prevents vendor lock-in

Table 1. Cloud security patterns and related cryptographic building blocks

Field 1: Data storage in the cloud
Pattern 1: Secure cloud storage by default
Tool 1: Secure object storage tool
Pattern 2: Moving a legacy application's database to the cloud
Tool 5: Data privacy tool
Field 2: User privacy protection and data minimisation
Pattern 3: Non-identifiable and untrackable use of a cloud service
Tool 2: Flexible authentication with selective disclosure tool
Pattern 4: Minimise exposure of private data during authentication
Tool 2: Flexible authentication with selective disclosure tool
Pattern 5: Big data anonymisation
Tool 5: Data privacy tool
Field 3: Authentication of stored and processed data
Pattern 6: Protect the authenticity of a data set and possible subsets
Tool 2: Flexible authentication with selective disclosure tool
Pattern 7: Authorise controlled modifications of signed data
Tool 2: Flexible authentication with selective disclosure tool
Pattern 8: Controlling the correctness of delegated computations
Tool 3: Verifiable data processing tool
Pattern 9: Controlling your virtual infrastructures
Tool 4: Topology certification tool

and, when shares are continuously renewed, enables long-term data security as it minimises the chance of an attacker to get a sufficient number of shares for reconstructing the information by attacking one cloud provider after the other. The used cryptographic protocols and primitives are:

- *Secret sharing schemes*: A secret sharing protocol is used to split the information into several parts, of which any subset of a given number of shares is necessary to access the information.
- *Remote data checking*: Allows for efficient checking of the availability and correctness of remote shares
- *Private information retrieval*: Allows clients to retrieve data items from a storage provider without revealing to the provider which items were retrieved

Tool 2: Flexible Authentication with Selective Disclosure Tool. PRIS-MACLOUD supports the authentication of arbitrary messages (or documents). This tools encapsulates cryptographic primitives to offer three abstract functionalities: *authentication*, *selective disclosure*, and *verification*. The data originator authenticates by signing a message, together with a disclosure policy describing which parts of the message can be selectively disclosed. Selective disclosure allows to disclose parts of the information from such a signed message to other receiving parties. The verification functionality checks if only authorised modifications, i.e. modifications conforming to the disclosure policy, were done. The selective disclosure is achieved by the concept of malleable signature schemes—although the direct application of a selective disclosure primitive would also be possible. The desired granularity of verification can be controlled by the signature primitive used. The cryptographic protocols and primitives are:

- *Malleable signatures schemes*: Allows to authorise subsequent modifications of certain parts of the signed data without the signature losing its validity; integrity against unauthorised modifications and authentication of origin are as protected as by classical digital signatures.
- *Attribute-based credentials*: Provides anonymous authentication; a multi-show credential system allows an arbitrary number of unlinkable showings.
- *Functional signatures schemes*: Allow to certify computations and processes; allow to delegate signature generation to other parties for a class of messages meeting certain conditions.
- *Zero-knowledge proofs*: Allow one party to convince another party of the validity of a statement without revealing any more information than the validity of the statement.
- *Group signature schemes*: Allow the signer to stay anonymously towards the verifier as the verifier only sees a signature that is valid for a group of signers.

Tool 3: Verifiable Data Processing Tool. This tool allows the verification of results of computations on signed data, delegated to a computing cloud. When a client gets back the result of the computation, he or she can efficiently decide whether the requested function was correctly applied to the data. The used cryptographic protocols and primitives are:

- *Secret sharing schemes*: see tool 1.
- *Malleable signatures schemes*: see tool 2.
- *Functional signature schemes*: see tool 2.
- *Zero knowledge proofs*: see tool 2.

Tool 4: Topology Certification Tool. Current cloud audit procedures can be extended with a means for proving security properties of virtualised infrastructures. An auditor (a human or a software agent) verifies an actual infrastructure, represents it as a graph, and issues a digital certificate on the graph. A prover component issues a zero-knowledge proof on the certificate, capable of convincing a cloud customer of the requested security properties, without revealing to the customer actual details of the topology. The tool encompasses the following:

- *Graph signature schemes*: Allows digitally signing a set of vertices and edges.
- *Zero-knowledge proofs*: see tool 2.

Tool 5: Data Privacy Tool. This tool provides the functionalities of the following two cryptographic primitives:

- *Format- and order-preserving encryption*: Adds a layer of cryptography directly into the data fields of a database applications: Format preserving encryption applies encryption in a manner such that the ciphertext has the same format as the plaintext (e.g. a social security number is mapped to a cryptogram with the format of a social security number).
- *k-anonymity*: K-anonymisation of data anonymises data in a way, that for each entry, there are at least $(k-1)$ other entries, from which it cannot be distinguished. While k-anonymity is a NP hard problem, new, more efficient approaches to anonymising big sets of data have improved in efficiency and are now capable of anonymising very large data sets.

5   Conclusions

In the current article we pointed out how cloud security patterns can be used to support the privacy-by-design process of a large scale development effort for reusable software tools, enabling the construction of privacy and security aware cloud services. In this context, the patterns act as medium between two groups: towards developers of cryptographic protocols and primitives, and to software engineers they communicate the problems which need to be cryptographically solved—and towards cloud service developers they convey which functionalities of existing software libraries ("the tools") can be re-used for the creation of cloud services. In addition to a commonly employed requirements approach, the cloud security patterns are used in the on-going H2020 PRISMACLOUD project to communicate the security requirements of involved stakeholders in a descriptive and informal way, thus enabling an on-going discussion, resulting in a generative approach towards resolving design contentions.

References

1. Alexander, C., Ishikawa, S., Silverstein, M.: A Pattern Language: Towns, Buildings, Construction. Oxford University Press, Oxford (1977)
2. Backes, M., Datta, A., Kate, A.: Asynchronous computational VSS with reduced communication complexity. In: Dawson, E. (ed.) CT-RSA 2013. LNCS, vol. 7779, pp. 259–276. Springer, Heidelberg (2013). http://dx.doi.org/10.1007/978-3-642-36095-4_17
3. Brzuska, C., Pöhls, H.C., Samelin, K.: Non-interactive public accountability for sanitizable signatures. In: De Capitani di Vimercati, S., Mitchell, C. (eds.) EuroPKI 2012. LNCS, vol. 7868, pp. 178–193. Springer, Heidelberg (2013). http://dx.doi.org/10.1007/978-3-642-40012-4_12
4. Buchmann, J., Demirel, D., Happe, A., Krenn, S., Lorünser, T., Traverso, G.: PRISMACLOUD D4.1: secret sharing protocols for various adversary models (2015). www.prismacloud.eu. H2020 project PRISMACLOUD deliverable
5. Camenisch, J., Herreweghen, E.V.: Design and implementation of the *idemix* anonymous credential system. In: ACM CCS, pp. 21–30. ACM (2002). http://doi.acm.org/10.1145/586110.586114

6. Danezis, G., Domingo-Ferrer, J., Hansen, M., Hoepman, J.H., Le Mtayer, D., Tirtea, R., Schiffner, S.: Privacy and data protection by design. Technical report, European Union Agency for Network and Information Security (ENISA) (2015)
7. Doty, N., Gupta, M.: Privacy design patterns and anti-patterns. In: Workshop "A Turn for the Worse: Trustbusters for User Interfaces Workshop" at SOUPS 2013 Newcastle, UK (2013)
8. ENISA European Union Agency for Network and Information Security: Cloud computing repository. http://www.enisa.europa.eu/activities/Resilience-and-CIIP/cloud-computing. 31 Mar 2015
9. ENISA European Union Agency for Network and Information Security: Cloud computing; Benefits, risks and recommendations for information security; Rev. B., December 2012. https://www.enisa.europa.eu/act/rm/files/deliverables/cloud-computing-risk-assessment/at_download/fullReport. 1 Mar 2016
10. European Commission: Establishing Horizon 2020 - The Framework Programme for Research and Innovation (2012). http://eur-lex.europa.eu/LexUriServ/LexUriServ.do?uri=CELEX:52011PC0809:EN:NOT. 1 June 2016
11. European Commission: European Cloud Computing Strategy "Unleashing the Potential of Cloud Computing in Europe" (2012). http://ec.europa.eu/digital-agenda/en/european-cloud-computing-strategy. 31 Mar 2015
12. European Commission: Technology readiness levels (TRL) (2014). http://ec.europa.eu/research/participants/data/ref/h2020/wp/2014_2015/annexes/h2020-wp.1415-annex-g-trl_en.pdf. 1 June 2016
13. Forbes magazine: Roundup of cloud computing forecasts and market estimates Q3 update (2015). http://www.forbes.com/sites/louiscolumbus/2015/09/27/roundup-of-cloud-computing-forecasts-and-market-estimates-q3-update-2015/#35e2a3576c7a. 1 Mar 2016
14. Gamma, E., Helm, R., Johnson, R., Vlissides, J.: Design Patterns: Elements of Reusable Object-Oriented Software. Addison-Wesley, Boston (1994). ISBN: 0-201-63361-2
15. Hafiz, M.: A collection of privacy design patterns. In: Proceedings of the 2006 Conference on Pattern Languages of Programs, PLoP 2006, pp. 7:1–7:13. ACM, New York (2006). http://doi.acm.org/10.1145/1415472.1415481
16. Lorünser, T., Länger, T., Slamanig, D.: Cloud security and privacy by design. In: Katsikas, K.S., Sideridis, B.A. (eds.) E-Democracy 2015. CCIS, vol. 570, pp. 202–206. Springer, Heidelberg (2015). http://dx.doi.org/10.1007/978-3-319-27164-4_16
17. Lorünser, T., et al.: Towards a new paradigm for privacy and security in cloud services. In: Cleary, F., Felici, M. (eds.) CSP Forum 2015. CCIS, vol. 530, pp. 14–25. Springer, Heidelberg (2015). doi:10.1007/978-3-319-25360-2_2
18. Lorünser, T., Slamanig, D., Länger, T., Pöhls, H.C.: PRISMACLOUD tools: a cryptographic toolbox for increasing security in cloud services. In: Proceedings of the International Conference on Availability, Reliability and Security (ARES 2016). IEEE (2016) (to be published Sept 2016)
19. Miyazaki, K., Hanaoka, G., Imai, H.: Digitally signed document sanitizing scheme based on bilinear maps. In: Proceedings of the 2006 ACM Symposium on Information, Computer and Communications Security, ASIACCS 2006, pp. 343–354. ACM, New York (2006). http://doi.acm.org/10.1145/1128817.1128868
20. Müller-Quade, J., Unruh, D.: Long-term security and universal composability. In: Vadhan, S.P. (ed.) TCC 2007. LNCS, vol. 4392, pp. 41–60. Springer, Heidelberg (2007). http://dx.doi.org/10.1007/978-3-540-70936-7_3

21. Pöhls, H.C., Höhne, F.: The role of data integrity in EU digital signature legislation—achieving statutory trust for sanitizable signature schemes. In: Meadows, C., Fernandez-Gago, C. (eds.) STM 2011. LNCS, vol. 7170, pp. 175–192. Springer, Heidelberg (2012)
22. Pöhls, H.C., Samelin, K.: On updatable redactable signatures. In: Boureanu, I., Owesarski, P., Vaudenay, S. (eds.) ACNS 2014. LNCS, vol. 8479, pp. 457–475. Springer, Heidelberg (2014)
23. PRWeb: A Cloud Computing Forecast Summary for 2013–2017 from IDC, Gartner and KPMG, citing a study by Accenture (2013). http://www.prweb.com/releases/2013/11/prweb11341594.htm. 31 Mar 2015
24. RightScale Inc.: State of the Cloud Report (2015). http://assets.rightscale.com/uploads/pdfs/RightScale-2015-State-of-the-Cloud-Report.pdf. 31 Mar 2015
25. Schumacher, M., Fernandez-Buglioni, E., Hybertson, D., Buschmann, F., Sommerlad, P.: Security Patterns - Integrating Security and Systems Engineering. Wiley, West Sussex (2006)
26. Shamir, A.: How to share a secret. Commun. ACM 22(11), 612–613 (1979). http://doi.acm.org/10.1145/359168.359176
27. The Economist Intelligence Unit: Mapping the cloud maturity curve, May 2015. http://www.economistinsights.com/analysis/mapping-cloud-maturity-curve. 31 Mar 2015
28. Transparency Market Research: Cloud Computing Services Market - Global Industry Size, Share, Trends, Analysis and Forecasts 2012–2018 (2012). http://www.transparencymarketresearch.com/cloud-computing-services-market.html. 31 Mar 2015
29. Van Geelkerken, F., Pöhls, H.C., Fischer-Hübner, S.: The legal status of malleable- and functional signatures in light of Regulation (EU) No. 910/2014. In: Proceedings of 3rd International Academic Conference of Young Scientists on Law & Psychology 2015 (LPS 2015), pp. 404–410. L'viv Polytechnic Publishing House, November 2015. https://drive.google.com/file/d/0B-Yu3Ni9z3PXM2lBajhCXzhoWk0/view

Privacy (Privacy Policies and Privacy Risk Representation)

PrivacyInsight: The Next Generation Privacy Dashboard

Christoph Bier(✉), Kay Kühne, and Jürgen Beyerer

Fraunhofer Institute of Optronics, System Technologies
and Image Exploitation IOSB, Karlsruhe, Germany
{christoph.bier,kay.kuehne,juergen.beyerer}@iosb.fraunhofer.de

Abstract. Transparency is an integral part of European data protection. In particular, the right of access allows the data subject to verify if his personal data is processed in a lawful manner. The data controller has the full obligation to provide all information on personal data processing in an easily accessible way. Privacy dashboards are promising tools for this purpose. However, there is not yet any privacy dashboard available which allows full access to all personal data. Particularly, information flows remain unclear. We present the next generation privacy dashboard *PrivacyInsight*. It provides full access to all personal data along information flows. Additionally, it allows exercising the data subject's further rights. We evaluate PrivacyInsight in comparison with existing approaches by means of a user study. Our results show that PrivacyInsight is the most usable and most feature complete existing privacy dashboard.

Keywords: Privacy · Data protection · Right of access · Privacy dashboard · Usability · Data subject · Transparency · User interface

1 Introduction

The exceptional role of data protection in shaping our modern information society cannot be overestimated. European data protection is not only the "right to be let alone" [26] as some still understand the concept of privacy. It is much more. Due to the social dimension of information sharing and data processing, it regulates the terms and conditions of modern data processing.

An integral condition of data protection is transparency. It is a prerequisite for exercising all further rights of the data subject, such as the rights to rectify, to erase, and to restrict the processing.[1] The comprehensive transparency framework of data protection law consists of transparency measures before access (ex ante transparency) and after access (ex post transparency) to personal data by a data controller. Ex ante, the data controller has to provide information to the data subject in cases of collection from the data subject (Article 13 of the General Data Protection Regulation (GDPR) 2016/679) as well as whenever personal data has been obtained from a third party (Article 14 GDPR).[2]

---

[1] CJEU, 07.05.2009 - C-553/07.

[2] http://eur-lex.europa.eu/legal-content/EN/TXT/?uri=CELEX:32016R0679.

© Springer International Publishing Switzerland 2016
S. Schiffner et al. (Eds.): APF 2016, LNCS 9857, pp. 135–152, 2016.
DOI: 10.1007/978-3-319-44760-5_9

Ex post, the data controller has to make all provisions necessary to inform the data subject according to his right of access. The right of access is called the "magna carta of data protection" [23,24,29]. Without the right of access, the data subject would not be able to verify if his personal data is processed in a lawful manner and according to the given purpose.

Privacy dashboards are means to provide access to personal data in a structured and interactive manner. We introduce a next generation privacy dashboard called *PrivacyInsight*. It is designed along legal and usability requirements. PrivacyInsight's new features include (1) automated collection and processing of the required information, (2) visualization of personal data along information flows, (3) customizable depth of information, (4) selective views on data of interest, and (5) immediate exercise of the further rights of the data subject. Additionally, we set up a user study and compared our tool to existing approaches.

The rest of the paper is structured as follows. First, we discuss existing research on transparency enhancing tools (TETs) in Sect. 2. Afterwards, we derive the legal requirements of the right of access (Sect. 3.1) and the usability requirements on privacy dashboards (Sect. 3.2). In Sect. 4, we present the architecture, model, and design of PrivacyInsight based on these requirements. We outline our implementation in Sect. 5. Our user evaluation is presented and discussed in Sect. 6. Finally, we provide some conclusions and discuss ideas for future work (Sect. 7).

2   Related Work

We refer to the surveys of Hedbom [11] and Janic et al. [13] for a broad overview of earlier approaches on TETs. Tools which simplify the expression of user preferences towards privacy are one area of research. The P3P[3] (Platform for Privacy Preferences) user agent privacy bird [7] is a representative of this field. As P3P never got broad support, proprietary, server-side tools for privacy settings dominate the market. Early adopters of this approach are Google,[4] a technology company, and acxiom,[5] a marketing and information management service. In addition, browser plug-ins, e.g., Mozilla Lightbeam,[6] uncovering the interdependence of cookie tracking by different parties from the client-side have been developed.

One of the most impressing stories in TET research is the European FP6 project PRIME[7] and its FP7 successors PrimeLife[8] and A4Cloud.[9] They brought up the Data Track privacy dashboard [27], one of the first tools providing transparency on data disclosures. Initially, Data Track was a client-side transaction

---

[3] https://www.w3.org/P3P/.
[4] https://www.google.com/dashboard/.
[5] https://aboutthedata.com/portal/.
[6] https://www.mozilla.org/de/lightbeam/.
[7] https://www.prime-project.eu/.
[8] http://primelife.ercim.eu/.
[9] http://www.a4cloud.eu/.

log for personal data. It was renewed as a server-side privacy dashboard for the cloud called GenomSynlig[10] within A4Cloud [2,8]. GenomSynlig provides two perspectives on past data sharing: the trace view and the timeline view. [3] Unfortunately, it provides only information if the data subject is the source of personal data. It does not provide any information on controller-internal data flows. Recipients of personal data are not visible in the given views.

Another privacy dashboard has been developed by Kolter et al. [15]. It is a controller independent Java application which lays the burden of transparency on the data subject. The information on the disclosed data originates in a web browser transaction log. A crowd-sourced data base provides information on data controllers' further data processing. Kani-Zabihi and Helmhout [14] introduce an online interactive tool called translucene map. It visualizes the flow of personal data for a particular purpose in a general manner. The user is able to highlight the flow in the presented graph per data category.

Visualization is one thing. But as far as a privacy dashboard should not be limited to static information, the collection and storage of the actual lineage of personal data is required. Such information is called personal data provenance. Provenance tracking originates from scientific computing [9,25]. Aldeco-Perez and Moreau [1] proposed to use provenance also for auditing the usage of personal data. Pulls et al. [22] introduced a scheme to collect personal data provenance without revealing the linkage between different logs.

Data provenance does not provide any means to enforce the further rights of the data subject. Hence, a combination with usage control has been proposed [5]. Usage control allows to specify and enforce the usage of personal data after access to it has been granted. Park and Sandhu introduced the first usage control model in [18,19]. An alternative unified model was described by Pretschner et al. [20]. The unified model has the advantage to integrate an information flow model [10,21] which can directly feed into a data provenance model.

3   Requirements

The design of a privacy dashboard has to fulfill the requirements given by current and future data protection law. These requirements will be discussed in the next section. Afterwards, we introduce a set of usability requirements.

3.1   Legal Requirements for a Privacy Dashboard

The right of access is a fundamental right codified in Article 8 (2) of the Charter of Fundamental Rights of the European Union (the Charter). It is in conjunction with Article 6 (1) of the Treaty on European Union part of the Union law. The data subject is entitled to the right of access according to Article 12 of the European Data Protection Directive (EDPD) 95/46/EC.[11] The directive is

---

[10] http://hci.cse.kau.se:8000/.

[11] http://eur-lex.europa.eu/legal-content/EN/TXT/?uri=CELEX:31995L0046.

implemented in national law, e.g., in Germany by the Federal Data Protection Act (FDPA). Article 12 is reflected in Paragraph 34 FDPA.

In a nutshell, the data subject has the right to obtain from the controller information on (1) the personal data stored as well as their categories, (2) the source and the recipients of personal data to whom the data is disclosed, (3) knowledge of the logic involved in automatic processing of data concerning him, and (4) the purpose of processing personal data. The right of access is uphold and even strengthened in Article 15 GDPR.

The right can be exercised by every data subject without constraint or pre-condition. It is the obligation of the controller to assure that he is able to provide all information listed above. The data subject shall not be bound to use a particular kind of technology in advance or during the request such as a set of cryptographic credentials or a certain software. The data subject is not even obliged to request the information in an electronic way. So, if the provenance of personal data is automatically collected and stored, it mus be retrievable by the data subject as well as by a substitute such as the data protection officer.

Requirement 1. *The controller must not establish any formal or technical, especially client-side, constraints for the data subject w.r.t. the right of access.*

On the other hand, Recital 63 of the GDPR states that, wherever possible, the controller shall provide the data subject with remote access to his personal data. Particularly, controllers which provide online services based on personal are beholden to provide an online tool, i.e., a privacy dashboard

Requirement 2. *The controller shall provide a privacy dashboard accessible by every data subject.*

As stated in Article 12 (a) EDPD first and second indent, the controller shall communicate the personal data undergoing processing together with their categories to the data subject. This is rephrased in Article 15 (1) GDPR as the right to access the personal data.

Requirement 3. *The controller shall provide access to all personal data and their categories to the data subject.*

There is also the rule that the form of response must follow the form of the request. According to Article 15 (3) GDPR, the controller shall provide an electronic copy of the personal data in a commonly used format as far as the request was made electronically. This right is strengthened by the right to data portability in Article 20 GDPR. According to that, a common format which is machine readable must be offered as well.

Requirement 4. *All information must be downloadable in a common, machine readable form.*

Article 12 (a) EDPD first indent includes the recipients in the information which has to be provided. According to Article 2 (g) EDPD, recipient means any person or body to whom data are disclosed. Artice 4 (9) GDPR clarifies that the term "body" is not limited to third parties. The perimeters of a body are defined by the organizational structure of the controller and by the purpose for which departments and IT systems process personal data. Therefore, relevant parts of the internal data flow of a controller must be disclosed to the data subject.

Requirement 5. *The controller shall provide all recipients of personal data, including the internal data flow, to the data subject.*

In contrary to the recipients, sources of personal data must only be disclosed if they are stored by the controller anyway. Article 12 (a) EDPD second indent requires to provide any available information. However, sources must be disclosed because recipients must be disclosed in all cases but collection.

Requirement 6. *The controller shall provide all sources of personal data, whenever available, to the data subject.*

In line with Article 12 (a) EDPD first indent, the purpose of processing must be communicated to the data subject. This includes the purpose specified at collection time as well as any subsequently changed purposes (cf. Recital 61 GDPR).

Requirement 7. *The controller shall provide the purpose of every step of processing to the data subject.*

The right of access is not intended to be an end in itself. Awareness of data processing makes not much sense if one cannot intervene in unlawful or unwanted processing. Therefore, the further rights of the data subject, the rights to rectify, to erase, and to restrict the processing of personal data, must be well integrated into a privacy dashboard.

Requirement 8. *The controller shall provide means to exercise the rights to rectify, to erase, and to restrict the processing of personal data in context with access to the personal data.*

We omit further requirements on the logic involved as well as on new mandatory information according to the GDPR due to page limitations.

Article 12 (a) EDPD second indent requires the controller to communicate to the data subject in an intelligible form. This means that the information provided shall be understandable by all ordinary citizens. The GDPR upholds this and requires in Article 12 (1) to provide information in concise, transparent, intelligible and easily accessible form, using clear and plain language. Therefore, it is necessary to define usability requirements for a privacy dashboard.

3.2   Usability Requirements for a Privacy Dashboard

The ISO standard 9241-11 [12] defines three guiding criteria for the usability of software: the effectiveness of task completion, the efficiency of usage, and the satisfaction of the users.

We will discuss five selected requirements out of 16 due to page limitation. First, it is important to provide the user with meaningful information on each object at all time to better perspicuity and minimize unnecessary clicks. So called tooltips offer a lean way to provide additional information on an object. They also help to reduce unwanted actions by the user by clarifying possible actions and therefore optimizing efficiency.

Requirement 9. *All control elements shall provide meaningful tooltips upon hovering with the (mouse) pointer.*

The potentially most frequently asked question on side of the data subject is what personal data is disclosed and to whom. Therefore, the data subject shall be able to get an immediate overview on all transferred and processed personal data and on all sources, processors and recipients. As good starting point for further investigations this improves efficiency.

Requirement 10. *The data subject shall be able to get an immediate overview of all transferred and processed personal data.*

Requirement 11. *The data subject shall be able to get an immediate overview of all sources, processors and recipients of his personal data.*

The larger the amount of data, the harder is a clear, intelligible overview in text form. Symbols offer a way to represent personal data categories in a lean and recognizable way. This requires meaningful and self-explanatory graphical representations of the data.

Requirement 12. *All used symbols shall be self-explanatory and meaningful.*

Learnability is an important factor of user satisfaction. If the user can not get his head around a problem, he will be unsatisfied and stop using the software.

Requirement 13. *The data subject shall be able to solve all realistic tasks successfully after a brief introduction to the privacy dashboard.*

These five usability requirements basically require a presentation of information in a transparent, intelligible form and a baseline for learnability and efficiency and therefore should enable everybody to use a privacy dashboard.

4   Design

The PrivacyInsight framework consists of three parts: The system architecture, the information flow and provenance model, and the actual design of the privacy dashboard. The architecture describes how personal provenance is collected, stored, and retrieved for presentation. Additionally, it integrates measures for enforcing the further rights of the data subject. The information flow and provenance model is the background model behind the privacy dashboard. Provenance storage and presentation are based on it.

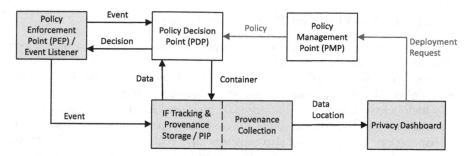

Fig. 1. Overview of the architecture

4.1 System Architecture

The provenance of personal data is collected by *event listeners* (cf. Fig. 1). They are integrated in all system layers processing or storing personal data. This includes applications, operating systems, and databases. Event listeners intercept system events and forward them to the information flow tracking component.

The *information flow tracking* component hosts an information flow model of the system and a provenance store (cf. Sect. 4.2). The provenance store contains the full lineage of personal data per system while the information flow model tracks only the current state of the system. This allows us to separate the granularity of information flow tracking from the granularity of provenance storage. Fine grained information flow tracking is necessary to avoid label creep.

Personal data provenance is collected from multiple systems. It is aggregated only when there is a request by the data subject. Only the provenance for the requesting subject is retrieved. This is possible as the relationship between personal data and data subjects is maintained in a pseudonymous database. The personal data provenance is provided to the *privacy dashboard* (cf. Req. 5) where it is presented to the data subject (cf. Sect. 4.3).

According to requirement 8, the further rights of the data subject must be exercisable via the privacy dashboard as well. Consequently, a data usage control infrastructure is connected to the presented provenance infrastructure. The main difference between provenance event listeners and *policy enforcement points (PEPs)* is that the former do not modify or inhibit the events detected. Because of that, we used the PEPs of the existing unified usage control infrastructure (cf. Sect. 2). Therefore, the integration is straight forward. We just need to deploy an additional *policy decision point (PDP)* and a *policy management point (PMP)*. The PDP evaluates policies and triggers the execution of compensating actions at the PEPs. The PDP queries the information flow tracking component, the *policy information point (PIP)*, for the location of personal data [5, 21]. The PMP is responsible to translate requests made by the data subjects into policies and to deploy them on the PDPs of the systems where the data is processed or stored.

4.2   Information Flow and Provenance Model

Our formal information flow model is a tuple (D, C, F, Σ, E, R) as introduced by Harvan and Pretschner [10,21].

The set of states $\Sigma = (C \to 2^D) \times (C \to 2^C) \times (F \to C)$ of the information flow model consists of three mappings. The *storage function* $s : C \to 2^D$ represents which personal *data* $d \in D$ is stored or processed in which *container* $c \in C$. A container is, e.g., the address space of a system process, a file, an e-mail, a network connection, etc. The state also captures *alias relations* $l : C \to 2^C$ between containers, which are used to express that a container is implicitly updated whenever some other container is being updated. This can for instance happen when processes share memory. Finally, the state comprises all *names* under which a container is currently accessible ($f : F \to C$). A file container may for instance not only be accessible by means of its file name, but also by a corresponding file handle.

Transitions of the state $R \subseteq \Sigma \times E \times \Sigma$ are triggered by characteristic events $e \in E$ in the system that are observed by event listeners. The information flow tracking component interprets these events according to a given information flow semantic.

The provenance model is based on this information flow model. A *provenance graph* is a directed acyclic forest $\mathscr{G} = (\mathscr{R}, \mathscr{L})$ consisting of the nodes $\mathscr{R} \subseteq \mathscr{D} \times \mathscr{C} \times \mathbb{N}$ and the edges $\mathscr{L} \subseteq \mathscr{R} \times \mathscr{R}$ between these nodes. The provenance graph contains a provenance tree for each personal data. The root is the source of the data. Each node $\mathscr{R}$ represents a datum in a container together with a time stamp of its creation time. *Representations* (nodes) are created and (partially) eliminated based on the updates of the storage function in the information flow model.

Additionally, the functions $termTime : \mathscr{R} \to \mathbb{N}$, $purpose : \mathscr{R} \to PURPOSE$ (cf. Req. 7), and $repType : \mathscr{R} \to REPTYPE$ are defined on a representation. The representation type (*repType*) marks which role a representation has in personal data processing. This is an important fact for a structured visualization on the privacy dashboard.

4.3   User Interface and Visual Design

The PrivacyInsight main view consists of three parts: The navigation bar, the data flow visualization and the status bar.

The navigation bar provides functionality that is not linked to elements in the data flow visualization and has a more global effect. These are the possibilities to undo the last step in the graph, to reset the whole graph to the initial state, and to download all data (cf. Req. 4).

The main feature is to visualize the flow of personal data into, through and out of an organization. The approach for this is a provenance graph. Organizational units like relevant IT systems and departments are represented as nodes while the data flows between the units are directed edges (cf. Sect. 4.2).

Organizational units are automatically aggregated to not overwhelm the user with too many nodes. The user has to be able to incrementally expand a unit into contained child units. For example, the starting node "company" would be expanded into "department 1", "department 2", and "department 3", which again would be expandable.

Sinks and sources are clearly separated nodes at the opposing ends of the visualization with a symbol list of all data categories that passed through (cf. Fig. 2). Thereby, the requirements 3, 6 and 5 are fulfilled. Every data is listed in the main view (cf. Req. 10) and, with good symbol selection, every data category is distinguishable (cf. Req. 12).

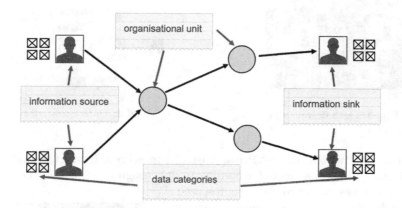

Fig. 2. Mockup of the data flow visualization

In the initial state, only sinks and sources plus a central node representing the organization offering the dashboard are displayed together with tooltips (cf. Req. 9). That way, the user can get an instant overview over of all sources, processors and recipients of his personal data without any interaction (cf. Req. 11).

Regarding interactions with the graph and the data itself, only four actions plus the activities for the further rights of the data subject are necessary. First, there is the possibility to isolate the data flow of a singe data in the graph for easier tracking by blanking out the rest of the graph. This action is available at all lists of data categories in the view. The next interaction is the opening of a detail view on nodes. Every unit has a list of all contained data categories together with their purpose (cf. Req. 7) and the time of the first appearance in the unit. In addition, every non-elementary unit offers the possibility to expand itself and show subsidiary units. The last interaction is linked to every data in the data category list. It opens a detail view on data which displays the personal data in full and offers the possibility to exercise the further rights of the data subject (cf. Req. 8).

5   Implementation

The user interface is an interactive web application built with current state of the art technologies. HTML5 and less are the groundwork upon which d3.js builds the graph. The parts of the graph are scalable vector graphics. The whole interface is easily configurable via parameters in a JSON file. The infrastructure has a HTTP interface which offers API endpoints for getting the data flow, getting a specific data, and requesting for policy deployment. The data flow comes in form of a JSON object consisting of representations (cf. Sect. 4.2).

Fig. 3. Data details view

Fig. 4. Data categories

All interactive features of PrivacyInsight are accessible via the main view (cf. Fig. 6a). It is implemented according to our design concept (cf. Fig. 2).

Data sources and sinks are represented with nodes which show a company logo or a user symbol. The data are represented by small symbols of their category floating next to the node (cf. Fig. 4). By clicking the symbol, it is possible to view only the flow of this personal data in the graph. Hovering the symbol reveals an eye icon which provides access to the detail view on personal data.

The detail view on personal data reveals the full personal data and offers interaction opportunities. From left to right these are: download of the datum, request a change, request deletion and contact the controller (cf. Fig. 3).

The organizational units, represented by nodes, offer an expansion button and a button to view a list of all data that passed

Fig. 5. Data per unit view

through (cf. Fig. 5). Each list item states the data category and the associated symbol, the time of the first appearance in the unit, and the purpose of processing. Symbols indicate if the personal data was processed or only stored. By clicking the category of a data, it is possible to view only this data in the graph. A click on the eye icon opens the data detail view (cf. Fig. 3)).

6   Evaluation

6.1   Setting and Scenario

PrivacyInsight (cf. Fig. 6a) was evaluated against two different systems: *Genom-Synlig* (cf. Fig. 6b) as the current state of the art and a *JSON document* (cf. Fig. 6c), which represents the common response from companies. Genom-Synlig provides with the trace view a visualization comparable with PrivacyInsight.[12] We used it with filters set for only one company. The JSON document consists of 45 pages in PDF format. At the beginning of the document, an intro states the company name and a postal contact address. PrivacyInsight itself was used in a slightly changed version. All logos and external links were removed to reduce possible bias.

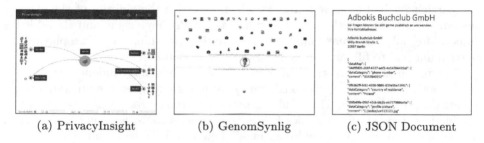

(a) PrivacyInsight   (b) GenomSynlig   (c) JSON Document

Fig. 6. Systems evaluated in comparison

31 persons took part in the evaluation over five days. 38 % of the participants were female and three-quarter came from an urban environment. All participants were between 20 and 60 years old with 45 % in the age band between 20 and 29 years. With 70 %, the majority graduated university. All participants with the exception of one person had a high-school diploma. 61 % stated they were currently employed, 32 % currently in education and two persons in retirement. Regarding the technical background, three-quarter stated they solve technical problems most of the time on their own and only 13 % that they barely do. 30 % of the participants had already developed web applications by themselves and further 50 % use them regularly. Concluding, our participants were educated above average.

The whole evaluation took place in a laboratory at Fraunhofer IOSB. The participant had a separate workplace for the tasks and for filling out the paper questionnaires. This way, the examiner was able to prepare the tasks without the participant noticing. Additionally, our computer system was equipped with an eye tracking device.

The scenario was presented as follows: "The user shops at an online bookshop called AdBokis at which the participant signs-up for an account. Two days later, a newsletter from the company Extreme Advertisement leaves the participant

---

[12] http://hci.cse.kau.se:8000/Datatrack_views/datatrack-traceview.html.

questioning where they got his personal data from. After a failed attempt to get information from Extreme Advertisement directly, the participant now turns to Adbokis."

The evaluation consisted of two parts: The first part compared the three systems. The second part evaluated PrivacyInsight in more detail. The *first part* let the user solve five tasks with every system. The tasks were identical for every system but the correct solution varied. The order of the systems was randomly but equally distributed permutated beforehand to get an as independent as possible result. The used time to solve the task and whether the solution was correct or not was logged. The maximum time for a solution was set to two minutes with no answer in this time frame counting as not correctly solved. After the participant finished all tasks for a system he had one minute of free play with the system before filling out the usability questionnaire. The *second part* started with the examiner giving an introduction into how to use PrivacyInsight. Afterwards, the participant had to solve ten tasks which exceeded the abilities of the other systems. They showed the user the full scale of PrivacyInsight and its added value. After all tasks were completed and another two minutes of free play, the participant had to fill out two more usability questionnaires.

The first usability questionnaire was the quick, technology independent *System Usability Scale (SUS)* [6] consisting of 10 items with possible answers on a Likert scale from 1 to 5. The resulting score on a range from 0 to 100 is translatable to extended school grades from *worst imaginable* to *best imaginable* [4]. While originally designed unidimensional, Lewis and Sauro found out that it contains learnability (requirement 13) as a second factor [17]. In the first part, we used the SUS to compare the subjective usability rating between the three systems. The SUS in the second part provided in combination with the results in the first part a measure of the change in perception through better knowledge on the abilities of PrivacyInsight. The PET-Uses questionnaire [28], designed for privacy-enhancing technologies, was not used here because some of the questions did not match privacy dashboards. The first bit of PET-Uses has actually a high overlapping with the SUS.

The second usability questionnaire was the more complex *User Experience Questionnaire (UEQ)* [16]. It consists of 26 items which each are seven-stage scales between semantic differentials. The items group up to the 6 scales *attractiveness, perspicuity, efficiency, dependability, stimulation*, and *novelty*, which again can be grouped in pragmatic quality and hedonic quality plus attractiveness as a pure valence dimension.

6.2   Results

First Part. The first task asked the participants to find out if Adbokis got a picture of them. With GenomSynlig only 40 % of the participants gave the right answer while PrivacyInsight enabled 70 % and the JSON document full 90 % to give the right answer. The mean solving time was 60 s for GenomSynlig, 51 for PrivacyInsight and 39 for JSON. With GenomSynlig, 7 participants were unable to give an answer in the two minute time frame while with the other two systems it was only three each.

The second task asked the participants to find out which mail address Adbokis got from them. Again, GenomSynlig scored worse than the other systems: While PrivacyInsight and the JSON enabled 90 % to give a correct answer, GenomSynlig only enabled half of them. With averaging 24 s, the JSON document was the fastest solution followed by 39 s with PrivacyInsight and 43 s with GenomSynlig. It is noticeable that all participants answered correctly with PrivacyInsight if they were able to answer in time. GenomSynlig misled often to fast but wrong answers. Probably because even with filters set, the information on the data still shows all services.

Task three asked which ip addresses Adbokis associated with the participants. JSON reached only 39 % correct answers at 52 s mean and GenomSynlig had 52 % correct answers at an average of 58 s for an answer. PrivacyInsight enabled 68 % of the participants to give a correct answer at a medium time of 55 s.

The fourth task asked the participants to request a deletion of their phone number. With just one incorrect answer, PrivacyInsight was by far the most successful system at this question. The mean process time of just 25 s was clearly under the 50 s with JSON and the 75 s with GenomSynlig. JSON enabled 65 % to answer correctly and GenomSynlig 45 %. The incorrect answers with the JSON document were mostly participants who did not read the textual introduction on the first page. The problem with GenomSynlig was that the interaction with the data is not by data item but rather at the data list of the service.

The last task in the first part was to display the data flow of the first name to Adbokis. This was for all systems by far the most difficult question. JSON reached only 16 % correct answers, GenomSynlig 35 % and PrivacyInsight 58 %. On average, the participants needed 85 s for a solution with JSON where 32 % had a time out. GenomSynlig had a mean of 71 s and nearly a fifth time outs and PrivacyInsight 66 s and also 32 % time outs. For most of the participants it was simply not clear when they reached the goal without an introduction to the system.

In the SUS, the JSON document scored a median of 27,5 points which translates to awful till poor (cf. Fig. 7). GenomSynlig got a median of 45 points which translates to poor till okay in school grades. PrivacyInsight scored with a median of 67,5 point clearly better than the other systems but still only reached an okay till good. The learnability dimension had a mean of 45 points with the JSON, 48 points with GenomSynlig and 68 points with PrivacyInsight. The JSON has compared to the overall score a good learnability but still way worse then the other systems which scored roughly like their overall score. Concluding, the JSON document scored expectedly bad while PrivacyInsight and GenomSynlig hit upon strongly divided opinions. For most of the participants the usability of PrivacyInsight was better than GenomSynlig.

Thanks to our eye tracking device, we were able to record the direction and course of gaze and the duration of eye fixation. We did not interpret all data yet. But the heat map of the first 12 s of user interaction with PrivacyInsight shows

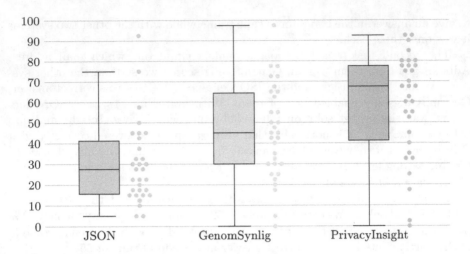

Fig. 7. SUS scores of the evaluated systems

that the visualization guides the user to the right spots. The data controller and the personal data collected from the data subject are in main focus (cf. Fig. 8). The fixation for GenomSynlig was less durable and more scattered. Hence, it is more difficult to analyze. We omitted this as well as visualizations of direction and course of gaze due to page limitation.

Second Part. The second part had 10 tasks which had the purpose to test the full abilities of PrivacyInsight and to show the participants the provided added value. All tasks were specifically designed for PrivacyInsight and were not solvable with the other systems. Therefore, no comparison was doable. In the following, we will only present selected observations.

We found out that the participants understood the principle of expanding nodes after a while. They could find specific units without problems. Binding of the purpose to processes instead of data led to some confusion but was ultimately no problem for the participants. Most of the tasks were solved quickly and correctly by nearly every participant.

The SUS in the second part had a median of 65 points with quartiles at 50 and 71 points while the whiskers were at 32,5 and 87,5 points. In comparison with the SUS in the first part, the individual scores in the second part were far less scattered. The introduction and the further knowledge about the system consolidated the opinions of the participants. The permutation in the first part did not seem to have any influence on the rating and/or the solutions in the second part. A control question asked for an adjective score of the system in extended school grades. With a correlation coefficient of 0,8, we observed a clear positive correlation.

The User Experience Questionnaire calculates values on a range from -3 to $+3$ for all scales and groups. Values from -3 to $-0,8$ are considered to be negative, values from $-0,8$ to $+0,8$ as neutral and $+0,8$ to $+3$ as positive.

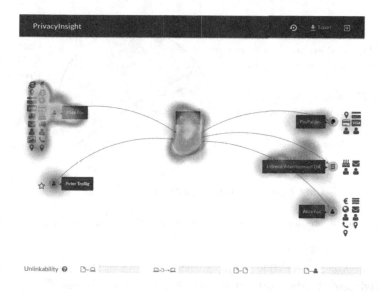

Fig. 8. Heat map displaying the user focus in the first 12 s

In reality, participants usually avoid extreme answers so the values mostly vary between −2 and +2. A comparison data set is provided with the UEQ but consists mostly of established systems. So, the comparison has to be treat with caution. Attractiveness scored a mean of 1,25 which is in comparison above average. The pragmatic quality scored only slightly positive with an average of 0,88. Efficiency reached average value of 1,27. Dependability scored an average of 0,87. This is in comparison below average. Perspicuity was the worst scale with an average of 0,49 which is neutral but in comparison in the 25 % of the worst results. The result is so bad because the system is percepted confusing (0,2) and complicated (0,1). However, it is rather easy to learn (0,9). The hedonic quality scores with a mean of 1,39 as the best group. Stimulation has a mean of 1,26 which is in comparison above average. This is mostly because PrivacyInsight was considered interesting. Novelty is the best scale with a mean of 1,5. This is in comparison in the best 10 % of the results. In the scales, it is seen mostly inventive (2,0) and leading edge (2,0). In conclusion, PrivacyInsight was seen as new and inventive but with clear deficits in perspicuity where it was rather complicated and confusing. On the other hand, the participants thought it would be easy to learn.

An additional question asked if the further information offered by PrivacyInsight in comparison with GenomSynlig is worth the increased complexity. The participants rated this question with a median of 6, a step before total agreement. Another question asked if the integration of the right of access with further rights of the data subject in one platform is considered useful. Three-quarter of the participants fully agreed. Except for one outlier, all participants gave the

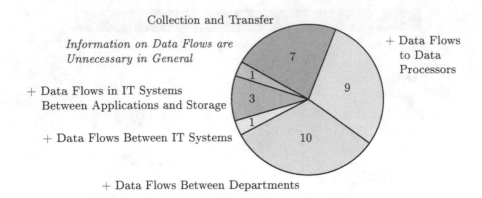

Fig. 9. Expected Information on Data Flows in a Privacy Dashboard (Clockwise)

second strongest answer. Therefore, an combination of the right of access with further rights of the data subject is regarded as absolutely useful.

The last question assessed the expected amount of information in personal data provenance. We found out that 87 % of the participants would be satisfied with collection, transfer, the flow between departments and the flow to data processors (cf. Fig. 9). This finding strongly supports the need of a system like PrivacyInsight.

7   Conclusion

We designed and implemented the next generation privacy dashboard PrivacyInsight based on well-funded legal requirements. The presented back-end system architecture and model allow the automated collection and processing of comprehensive personal data provenance. PrivacyInsight's visualization of personal data along information flows is attuned to user needs. Data subjects are able to understand the purpose of every step of processing. The transfer of personal data to processors and third parties is immediately apparent. PrivacyInsight's customizable depth of information and its selective views on data of interest lead to a higher usability than existing systems. The combination with usage control technology allows us the immediate exercise of the further rights of the data subject.

Further optimizations will include a user tutorial and faster access to information, e.g., via a search tool. Moreover, extending PrivacyInsight as an internal risk analysis tool for data protection officers is future work.

References

1. Aldeco-Pérez, R., Moreau, L.: Provenance-based auditing of private data use. In: Proceedings of the 2008 International Conference on Visions of Computer Science: BCS International Academic Conference, VoCS 2008, pp. 141–152. British Computer Society, Swinton (2008)
2. Angulo, J., Bernsmed, K., Fischer-Hübner, S., Froystad, C., Gjaere, E.A., Wästlund, E.: D: D-5.1 user interface prototypes v1. Deliverable, KAU, SINTEF (2014)
3. Angulo, J., Fischer-Hübner, S., Pulls, T., Wästlund, E.: Usable transparency with the data track: a tool for visualizing data disclosures. In: Proceedings of the 33rd Annual ACM Conference Extended Abstracts on Human Factors in Computing Systems, pp. 1803–1808. ACM (2015)
4. Bangor, A., Kortum, P., Miller, J.: Determining what individual sus scores mean: adding an adjective rating scale. J. Usability Stud. 4(3), 114–123 (2009)
5. Bier, C.: How usage control and provenance tracking get together - a data protection perspective. In: IEEE Security and Privacy Workshops (SPW), pp. 13–17 (2013)
6. Brooke, J., et al.: Sus-a quick and dirty usability scale. Usability Eval. Ind. 189(194), 4–7 (1996)
7. Cranor, L.F., Guduru, P., Arjula, M.: User interfaces for privacy agents. ACM Trans. Comput.-Hum. Interact. 13(2), 135–178 (2006)
8. Fischer-Hübner, S., Angulo, J., Pulls, T.: How can cloud users be supported in deciding on, tracking and controlling how their data are used? In: Hansen, M., Hoepman, J.-H., Leenes, R., Whitehouse, D. (eds.) Privacy and Identity 2013. IFIP AICT, vol. 421, pp. 77–92. Springer, Heidelberg (2014)
9. Freire, J., Koop, D., Santos, E., Silva, C.T.: Provenance for computational tasks: a survey. Comput. Sci. Eng. 10(3), 11–21 (2008)
10. Harvan, M., Pretschner, A.: State-based usage control enforcement with data flow tracking using system call interposition. In: Proceedings of the 3rd International Conference on Network and System Security (NSS 2009), pp. 373–380. IEEE, Saint Malo (2009)
11. Hedbom, H.: A survey on transparency tools for enhancing privacy. In: Matyáš, V., Fischer-Hübner, S., Cvrček, D., Švenda, P. (eds.) The Future of Identity. IFIP AICT, vol. 298, pp. 67–82. Springer, Heidelberg (2009)
12. ISO: ISO 9241–11: Ergonomic requirements for office work with visual display terminals (VDTs). Technical report, International Organization for Standardization, Geneva, Switzerland (2000)
13. Janic, M., Wijbenga, J.P., Veugen, T.: Transparency enhancing tools (TETs): an overview. In: Third Workshop on Socio-Technical Aspects in Security and Trust (STAST), pp. 18–25 (2013)
14. Kani-Zabihi, E., Helmhout, M.: Increasing service users' privacy awareness by introducing on-line interactive privacy features. In: Laud, P. (ed.) NordSec 2011. LNCS, vol. 7161, pp. 131–148. Springer, Heidelberg (2012)
15. Kolter, J., Netter, M., Pernul, G.: Visualizing past personal data disclosures. In: International Conference on Availability, Reliability, and Security (ARES 2010), pp. 131–139 (2010)
16. Laugwitz, B., Held, T., Schrepp, M.: Construction and evaluation of a user experience questionnaire. In: Holzinger, A. (ed.) USAB 2008. LNCS, vol. 5298, pp. 63–76. Springer, Heidelberg (2008)

17. Lewis, J.R., Sauro, J.: The factor structure of the system usability scale. In: Kurosu, M. (ed.) HCD 2009. LNCS, vol. 5619, pp. 94–103. Springer, Heidelberg (2009)
18. Park, J., R.: Towards usage control models: beyond traditional access control. In: Proceedings of the Seventh ACM Symposium on Access control models and technologies (SACMAT 2002), pp. 57–64. ACM, Monterey (2002)
19. Park, J., Sandhu, R.: The UCON ABC usage control model. ACM Trans. Inf. Syst. Secur. 7(1), 128–174 (2004)
20. Pretschner, A., Büchler, M., Harvan, M., Schaefer, C., Walter, T.: Usage control enforcement with data flow tracking for X11. In: Proceedings of the 5th International Workshop on Security and Trust Management (STM), pp. 124–137, Saint Malo (2009)
21. Pretschner, A., Lovat, E., Büchler, M.: Representation-independent data usage control. In: Garcia-Alfaro, J., Navarro-Arribas, G., Cuppens-Boulahia, N., de Capitani di Vimercati, S. (eds.) DPM 2011 and SETOP 2011. LNCS, vol. 7122, pp. 122–140. Springer, Heidelberg (2012)
22. Pulls, T., Peeters, R., Wouters, K.: Distributed privacy-preserving transparency logging. In: Proceedings of the 12th ACM Workshop on Workshop on Privacy in the Electronic Society, WPES 2013, pp. 83–94. ACM, New York (2013)
23. Roßnagel, A.: Handbuch Datenschutzrecht. C.H. Beck, München (2003)
24. Simitis, S. (ed.): Bundesdatenschutzgesetz. Nomos, Baden-Baden, 7 auflage (2011)
25. Simmhan, Y.L., Plale, B., Gannon, D.: A survey of data provenance in e-science. ACM Sigmod Record 34(3), 31–36 (2005)
26. Warren, S.D., Brandeis, L.D.: The right to privacy. Harvard Law Rev. 4(5), 193–220 (1890)
27. Wästlund, E., Hübner, S.F.: End user transparency tools: UI prototypes. Technical report, KAU (2010)
28. Wästlund, E., Wolkerstorfer, P., Köffel, C.: PET-USES: privacy-enhancing technology – users' self-estimation scale. In: Bezzi, M., Duquenoy, P., Fischer-Hübner, S., Hansen, M., Zhang, G. (eds.) IFIP AICT 320. IFIP AICT, vol. 320, pp. 266–274. Springer, Heidelberg (2010)
29. Weichert, T.: Auskunftsanspruch in Verteilten Systemen. Datenschutz und Datensicherheit (DuD) 30(11), 694–699 (2006)

A Framework for Major Stakeholders in Android Application Industry to Manage Privacy Policies of Android Applications

Shi-Cho Cha[1(✉)], Chuang-Ming Shiung[2], Tzu-Ching Liu[1], Sih-Cing Syu[1], Li-Da Chien[1], and Tsung-Ying Tsai[1]

[1] Department of Information Management,
National Taiwan University of Science and Technology, Taipei, Taiwan
csc@cs.ntust.edu.tw
[2] Criminal Investigation Bureau, Taipei, Taiwan
saxbear@gmail.com

Abstract. As Android's permission-based system cannot fulfill the requirements of personal data protection, several countries around the world are requesting application developers to provide privacy policies for their applications. To address the issue, this study proposes a framework to Manage Privacy Policies of Android Applications (MaPPA). MaPPA provides standard format for application providers to present privacy policies in machine processable format and to embed the policies into applications. Application verifiers or marketplace providers can then verify whether an application complies with embedded privacy policies and envelop verification reports in the application. Therefore, users can extract privacy policies and verification reports from applications directly. Compared to providing URL links to privacy policies in marketplaces, the proposed framework can reduce the cost for application developers to maintain additional servers to provide privacy policies. Moreover, application users can obtain verification reports in an application to comfirm the consistency between privacy policies and application behavior. In light of this, the study can hopefully solve current problems of privacy policy notification for Android applications.

1 Introduction

Smartphones are very popular recently. According to the statics of International Data Corporation (IDC), vendors sold more smartphones than feature phones for the first time in the first quarter of 2013 [31]. Currently, there are several different smartphone platforms, such as iOS, Android, Window Phone, and so forth. Current smartphone platforms usually provide Application Programming Interfaces (APIs) for application developers to develop applications. In addition, there are several application marketplaces for developers to submit their applications to the marketplaces. Therefore, users can download applications from marketplaces and install the downloaded applications on their smartphones to

S. Schiffner et al. (Eds.): APF 2016, LNCS 9857, pp. 153–170, 2016.
DOI: 10.1007/978-3-319-44760-5_10

enhance functionality. In this case, invasions of privacy occur if a user installs an application that collects user behaviors and transfers the behavioral data to others secretly.

Current smartphones are usually equipped with different kinds of sensors. When a user uses an mobile application, the application may obtain context information through the sensors. Compared to using applications on traditional laptops or personal computers, using mobile applications may pose new risks to user privacy [9,15].

Among major smartphone platforms, this study focuses on the Android platform because the Android platform is currently the most popular smartphone platform [16]. Android smartphones have permission-based systems for users to control whether applications can access their personal data. Simply speaking, the Android platform has defined several types of permissions. Applications need to obtain permission to access personal data and sensors on user smartphones [7].

There are two different ways for an application to request permission from a user: If an application was developed with Android API prior to API level 23, the smartphone of a user asks the user to give permission to the application while the user installs the application. Beginning in Android API level 23, the Android platform requires applications to obtain permission to perform sensitive actions before executing them [20].

Several researchers have pointed out that the requested permission of an application is not enough for users to determine whether or not to use the application: First, users may not understand the meaning of the permission items [11,18] and the security risks of giving applications permission to access their personal data [13]. Moreover, when applications request permission to access user data, users can only know that the applications are going to collect their data. Users usually cannot know how the applications use their data [2]. To overcome the deficiencies, Liccardi et al. [21] and Gates et al. [12,13] have proposed approaches to calculate privacy risks of giving a permission to an application based on what permission the application requests. Therefore, in addition to requested permission, users can decide whether or not to install an application based on its privacy risk values. Moreover, Lin et al. proposed to collect feedbacks from crowds and provide information about how many percentage of users are surprised that an application requests such permission [23].

To protect user privacy, government agencies in different countries are starting to request application developers to provide privacy policies about their applications. For example, the US California Attorney requests application developers to provide privacy policies along with their applications [38]. Although current marketplaces usually enable application developers to submit applications along with the URL of associated privacy policies, application developers may not provide the URLs or forget to maintain sites hosting the application privacy policies so that users cannot obtain the policies. Also, users may forget to check privacy policies of an application while they download and install applications from marketplaces. Even if a user obtains privacy policies of an application, the user may not be able to ensure that the application behaves as the stated in the policies.

In light of this, this study proposes a framework to Manage Privacy Policies of Android Applications (MaPPA). MaPPA fulfills the requirements of major stakeholders in the Android application market – application developers, trusted third party application verifiers, marketplace providers, and application users – to manage privacy policies. Generally, MaPPA links the stakeholders based on the proposed scheme to embed privacy policies and additional information into existing Android applications (or Android application package (APK) files). Application developers can generate machine processable privacy policies for their applications based on the specifications of privacy policies provided by MaPPA and embed generated privacy policies into their applications. Moreover, to help users to decide whether or not to install an application, MaPPA enables third party verifiers and marketplace providers to present verification reports or notes (such as user feedback and other security indicators) about an application in a standard format and embed the data into the application. Application users can install supporting applications provided by MaPPA to browse privacy policies, verification reports, and additional notes of an application.

Compared to furnishing URL links to privacy policies in marketplaces, the proposed MaPPA framework provides easy means for application developers, application verifiers, and marketplace providers to present privacy policy related information about an application to application users via the application itself. Therefore, application developers, application verifiers, and marketplace providers of the application do not need to maintain additional servers to provide such information. Moreover, application users can read the verification reports in the application to ensure that the application complies with the associated privacy policies. This study can hopefully solve current problems of privacy policy notification for Android applications.

The rest of the paper is organized as follows. Section 2 provides preliminary information on privacy regulations about smartphone applications and briefly introduces related application privacy analysis and protection techniques. Section 3 overviews the proposed framework. Section 4 describes machine processable format of privacy policies and the means of embedding privacy policies and additional information in applications. Section 5 summarizes suggested verification items to check that an application behaves as its privacy policies describes. This study also introduces how to generate and to validate verification reports in this section. Conclusions are finally drawn in Sect. 6 along with recommendations for future research.

2   Background Knowledge and Related Work

2.1   Privacy Policy Requirement and Representation

Many countries around the world have recognized the privacy risks of smartphone applications and request application developers to provide privacy policies for their applications. For example, the US California Attorney General Harris started to request application developers to provide privacy policies based on the California Online Privacy Protection Act (CalOPPA) in 2012 [38]. Harris

also achieved agreement with major smartphone application platforms to provide optional data field for application developers to provide privacy policies
when they submit applications to the application marketplaces. In addition to
requesting application developers to provide privacy policies, Canada Office of
the Privacy Commissioner (OPC) recommended application developers provide
easy access to privacy policies before users download and install applications [26].
The Article 29 Data Protection Working Party (WP29) of European Commission
analyzed the scenario of applications accessing personal data in smartphones.
The working party then clarified that application developers play the role of
data collectors defined in the EU Data Protection Directive (95/46/EC), and
therefore application developers should comply with the Directive [9]. Therefore,
the working party stated that application developers must provide readable and
understandable privacy policies based on the EU Data Protection Directive.

Current regulations and guidelines about smartphone application privacy
usually provide suggested components of privacy policies for smartphone applications. Because smartphones usually have smaller screen size than laptops or
personal computers, US NTIA (National Telecommunications and Information
Administration) recommends that application developers provide short form
notices about collecting and sharing user data with others to users before users
download and install their applications [37]. Simply speaking, short form notices
can be viewed as the subset of privacy policies. Application developers should
still publish full privacy policies.

To help application developers to establish privacy policies for their applications, organizations such as Mobile Marketing Association [25] and Terms-
Feed [34] provide template of smartphone application privacy policies and guidelines on how to use the template to generate privacy policies. Moreover, several organizations, such as iubenda[1], TermsFeed[2], MEF (Mobile Ecosystem
Forum)[3] and so forth, provide wizard-based privacy policy generators for application developers to generate privacy policies step by step. In addition, Tomuro
et al. proposes a system to generate privacy policies of an application using
privacy policies of similar applications [36].

Even if application developers provide qualified privacy policies, users may
just ignore the policies because they do not wish to take efforts to read the
policies. If there is a machine processable format for privacy policies, users can
set their privacy preferences to their agents or something on their smartphones,
the agents can then decide whether or not to accept privacy policies based on
user preferences. In this case, W3C have defined the Platform for Privacy Preferences (P3P) [24]. P3P provides a vocabulary and specification for a Web site
to express its privacy policies in XML-based machine readable format. Users can
set their privacy preferences in browsers (or P3P agents). Therefore, when users
use browsers to surf Web sites that do not have P3P-based privacy policies or

---

[1] http://www.iubenda.com/en/mobile.

[2] https://termsfeed.com/privacy-policy/generator/.

[3] http://www.appprivacy.net/.

have policies that do not satisfy user preferences, the browsers will warn the users or block functions, such as cookies, requested by the sites.

Although P3P has become less popular recently, to the best of our knowledge, P3P is still the most well-known specification to express privacy policies. Therefore, researchers use and adapt the specifications in the areas of database accessing [1], e-Commerce [32], RFID applications [6], cloud computing [27], and so on. This study also borrows the concept of P3P specification and modify the specification for smartphone applications. This study provides the details in Sect. 4.

2.2 Application Privacy Invasion Behavior Identification

Marketplace providers and other application analyzers can use static or dynamic analysis tools to identify whether applications access personal data and transfer personal data to other places. Static analysis tools analyze application source code or analyzable binary codes without executing applications. If analyzers cannot obtain source codes from application developers, the analyzers may also use reverse engineering technologies to transfer applications into analyzable format.

To understand practices about how an application collects and uses user data, static analysis tools, such as AppIntent [43], FlowDroid [3] and BlueSeal [33], usually identify codes (or sources) where user data is collected. Then, static analysis tools track the flow of collected data to discover dangerous functions (or sinks) used to process the data. Static analysis tools can also use backward dataflow analysis techniques to find out whether data processed by dangerous functions are originated from personal data.

One of the biggest challenges faced by static analysis tools is that more and more application developers use code obfuscating in their applications to prevent software piracy. Therefore, more and more researchers are proposing dynamic analysis tools. Dynamic analysis tools usually execute applications in emulated environments (or emulators) to detect application personal data behavior. Researchers and dynamic tool developers usually build their emulated environments by compiling modified Android source codes. Generally, the emulators should detect the events where applications access personal data and then track how the application use the data. There are several different ways for emulators to detect that an application is trying to collect personal data:

To begin with, dynamic analysis tools such as VetDroid [44], intercept application system calls to request permission. In addition to knowing that an application requests permission to collect associated data, analyzers can use DroidScope [42] or RiskMon [17] to obtain information about personal data collected by applications through API calls and callbacks. Moreover, analyzers can add hooks on Android application framework or system kernel to monitor events of data accessing. For example, SemaDroid embeds hooks on several sensor modules to monitor sensor usage of applications [41].

After identifying whether applications collect personal data, dynamic analysis tools track the flow of the data. Current dynamic analysis systems, such as TaintDroid [8], DroidScope [42], and VetDroid [44], usually add "taint tags" on the data to be tracked. The systems can then recognize data objects "tainted" by tagged data by intercepting Dalvik VM instructions, native codes, and IPC calls about the data. Therefore, dynamic analysis tools can identify the situations where applications leak personal data or data tainted by personal data.

Because traditional dynamic analysis tools usually execute applications in emulated environment, malicious applications may detect emulated execution environments and act as normal applications in emulators [29,39]. Therefore, analyzers can prepare analysis environment in physical smartphones and use emulator detection mitigation technologies to prevent applications from detecting the presence of emulators [40].

Moreover, to trigger malicious behavior of applications automatically, dynamic analysis tools may adopt UI automation techniques to imitate users interaction with applications [14]. Since dynamic analysis tools may need to test a large number of possibilities based on user input, dynamic analysis systems can utilize static analysis techniques to reduce test cases. For example, AppsPlaygrounds examine GUI components on application screens to decide the sequence of user input to explore applications efficiently [30]. A5 uses static analysis techniques to identify Intents received by applications and send generated Intents to applications for dynamic analysis [40].

To prevent reinventing the wheel, this study does not propose new static and dynamic analysis tools. This study proposes to use the tools to verify the consistency between application behavior and associated privacy policies.

2.3   Privacy Policy Notification

Providing privacy notices or policies about applications explicitly may help users to perceive privacy risk more accurately [4]. Generally, there are different timing for users to obtain privacy policies of applications: If application developers provide URLs to privacy policies of their applications in marketplaces, users can browse the policies and decide whether to download applications. Applications can popup their privacy policies when users first use their applications or when the users are executing the applications. Researchers have surveyed the effectiveness of privacy notification in different timing [5,10]. Based on the survey of Balebako et al., the effectiveness of providing privacy notices when users are using applications is better than displaying notices when users first use the applications [5]. Also, the effectiveness of showing notices before application usage is better than providing links of privacy notices in marketplaces.

To help users to understand privacy policies, additional information can be included in privacy notices. For example, marketplace providers or anti-virus applications on user smartphones can provide the risk level of using an application based on permissions requested by the application and application behavior to enhance privacy notice of the application [12,21]. Moreover, marketplace providers can summarize user reviews of an application to enable users to understand potential privacy and security issues of the application [19,35]. At this point, this study proposes a means to enable marketplace providers and other parties to append information to application privacy policies.

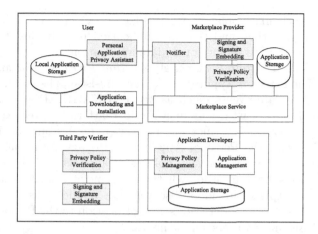

Fig. 1. Framework overview

3   Overview of the Proposed Framework

Figure 1 illustrates the framework proposed in this article. As depicted in this figure, this study uses colored rectangles to specify major components of the framework. This study overviews the components of the proposed framework by major stakeholders as follows:

First, application developers can store their developed applications (or APK files) in the *Privacy Policy Management* mechanism. After parsing the application files, the Privacy Policy Management mechanism decomposes the applications into components, such as activities, broadcast receivers, services, and request the application developers to provide associated privacy policies. The Privacy Policy Management mechanism will provide GUI interfaces for applications to generate privacy policies for their applications. Then, the application developers can embed generated policies in associated applications using the Privacy Policy Management mechanism.

Second, before application developers upload their application with privacy policies to marketplaces, application developers can send their applications to trusted third parties verifiers. Third party verifiers evaluate whether the behavior of an application is consistent with the privacy policies embedded in the application. Then, the verifiers generate verification reports with signatures for further validation.

After receiving applications submitted from application developers, marketplace providers check whether the applications have embedded privacy policies and reject applications without privacy policies. Marketplace providers may request applications to be verified by trusted third parties. Otherwise, marketplace providers may need to verify the applications themselves. Then, marketplaces providers add applications to their marketplaces. Because it would cost a lot of time for a marketplace provider to verify applications, this study does not request marketplace providers to finish application verification before adding applications to their marketplaces. Marketplace providers can analyze applications continuously. If they find that an application is malicious, they can use *Notifier* to notify users to remove or update applications.

Finally, users can install *Personal Application Privacy Assistants* on their smartphones. The Personal Application Privacy Assistants listen for application installation and update events (such as the PACKAGE_ADDED and PACKAGE_CHANGED broadcast events in Android Platform). After extracting privacy policies (if any) and verification results (if any) from the installed or updated applications, the Personal Application Privacy Assistants will notify users. Users can then browse privacy policies of applications as well as associated verification results and decide whether to remove suspicious applications. Moreover, if marketplace providers discover that applications downloaded by users are malicious, the providers will send notification to the Personal Application Privacy Assistants in users smartphones.

4   Embedding Privacy Policies and Additional Information in Applications

Android platform uses application package (APK) files to store contents of applications. Users download APK files from marketplaces to install applications on their smartphones. This study extends traditional Android APK file format by embedding privacy policies and verification reports of third party verifiers into the APK files. Generally, APK files are zip format archive files per se [7]: An APK file of an application archives files and directories about compiled programs, resources (such as images, screen layouts, and other resources), application settings, and libraries used by the application. To enable users to check the integrity of an application, when an application developer generates an APK file of the application, the APK generation tool will list the names of every file to be archived and generate digests of the files based on contents of the files(using SHA-1, SHA-256, SHA-512 and other secure hash algorithm). Then, the APK generation tool produces a file named *MANIFEST.MF* containing each filename and associated digest value.

To discover the modification of the MANIFEST.MF file, for every file to be archived, the APK generation tool concatenates its filename and digest of file contents to generate a new digest. Therefore, the APK generation tool can generate a signature file called *CERT.SF*, which contains every filename and digest value of concatenated filename and associated digest of file contents. Furthermore, the APK generation tool uses the private key of the developer to sign the CERT.SF file and store the generated signature along with the certificate of the developer into a *CERT.RSA* file. The APK file generation tool creates a special directory called *META-INF* to store the file of MANIFEST.MF, CERT.SF, and CERT.RSA. Finally, the APK file generation tool archives the original program files and files in META-INF directory to generate the final APK file.

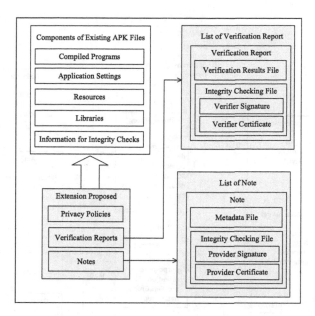

Fig. 2. Extension to the existing APK file format

Therefore, when a user downloads an APK file, the user can unzip the APK file to obtain CERT.SF and CERT.RSA. Then, the user can use the certificate in CERT.RSA to verify that the owner of the certificate has signed the CERT.SF file with associated private key. The user can further use CERT.SF to verify integrity of MANIFEST.MF and use MANIFEST.MF to verify integrity of other files zipped in the APK file.

Figure 2 illustrates how to embed privacy policies, verification reports and notes about the applications in APK files. First, application developers can generate privacy policies of applications and store the policies in the file with the name *PRIVACYPOLICY*. As the attributes in the class PRIVACYPOLICIES in Fig. 3, a PRIVACYPOLICY file includes four major components:

– At least one privacy policy. Current applications usually include components (such as advertising components) developed by other application developers. As the opinion issued by the European Commission WP 29 [9], if the component developers collect and use personal data for their own purposes, the component developers should be treated as joint data collectors with the application developers. Therefore, application developers should obtain the practices of personal data from component developers and include the practices in privacy policies of the application developers. To reduce the communication cost among application developers and component developers, this study enables component developers to provide privacy policies of their components to application developers. Therefore, the application developers can embed component privacy policies to their applications directly.

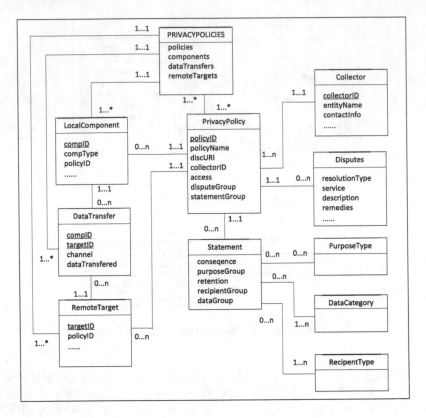

Fig. 3. Data schema for privacy policies about an application

This study adopts the format of privacy policies in P3P and adapt the specifications for smartphone applications. For example, P3P specify categories of personal data collected and used for Web browsing. In this case, this study adopts the categories recommended by Harris [15]. Furthermore, this study use JSON to present privacy policies and other components because JSON is lighter than XML [22]. This study skips the detailed specification of a privacy policy. Interested people can see the P3P specification [24].

- Internal components in an application. The components element in the PRIVACYPOLICY file is an array of JSON Objects. Each object represents a component in an application. A component object has compID attribute to identify each component, compType attribute to show what type (such as an Activity, a BroadcastReceiver, a Service, or a ContentProvider) the component is, and the privacy policy applied to the component.
- Targets that an application may transfer personal data to. If an application is going to transfer personal data to places outside the application, a RemoteTarget object should be generated to store the identity of the target and the privacy policy applied to the target.

- Means for personal data to be transferred from internal components of an application to remote targets.

MaPPA stores the PRIVACYPOLICY file in the META-INF directory of the corresponding application's APK file. Embedding privacy policies and verification reports in the META-INF directory of APK files has the following benefits:

- Third party verifiers can add verification reports to APK files of applications without requesting application developers to sign the applications again[4].
- When a user updates an application with updated privacy policies, the user may not know the update of the policies unless the user checks the Web site hosting the policies. Embedding privacy policies in application APK files enables users to obtain the updated privacy policies when they update applications.
- Application developers can notify users about the update of privacy policies using the same way of updating applications.

Third-party verifiers or marketplace providers may verify applications and provide verification results to application users. In general, a verifier can store verification results of an application in a verification results file, which includes the following components:

- Information about the verifier.
- Date of Verification result establishment.
- List of verification items and corresponding results. This study provides the details about common verification items suggested to be performed by verifiers in Sect. 5.

MaPPA presents the above verification results file in a JSON object and serialize the JSON object into the verification result file. In addition, the verifier generates an integrity checking file for users to validate the integrity of a verification results file. This study illustrates how to generate the integrity checking file and how to use the file to validate the verification results in Sect. 5. Moreover, to enable users to identify the relationship between a verification results file and its associated integrity checking file, MaPPA requests the files for the same verification report to use the same name but with different extension. For example, if a verification results file of an application is A.josn, the corresponding integrity checking file should be A.RSA.

A verifier can embed the verification results file and the integrity checking file into the META-INF directory of the application's APK file. The reason is similar to the reason mentioned when embedding an application's PRIVACYPOLICY file into the META-INF directory. This study will skip duplicate statements.

---

[4] Note that if applications need to support over-the-air (OTA) updates, the whole APK files need to be signed by OTA servers assigned by smartphone vendors [7]. This study does not address the OTA updates scenario because normal applications do not need to support OTA updates.

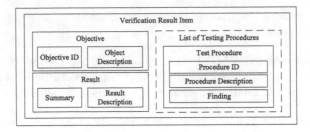

Fig. 4. Contents of a verification result item

Note that different parties may verify an application and embed their verification reports in the application. A verifier can embed a new verification report into an application if there is no verification report that has the same name with the report to be embedded. In this case, people may challenge that application developers may remove verifier reports with bad results. Current design of MaPPA just accepts the situation because users can decide not to install an application if there is no verification report signed by trusted third verifier. Otherwise, a notary service should keep the verification history of each application to enable users to check the consistency between verification reports embedded in an application and verification history of the application.

In addition to verification reports, MaPPA allows marketplace providers or third party verifiers to embed notes of an application. A note includes a metadata file and an integrity checking file. A metadata file contains information about the entity providing the note (or the note provider) and one or more name/value pairs to describe the attributes. Also, a note provider should prepare an integrity checking file for users to validate the note. Embedding a note into an application follows the same rule of embedding a verification report. This study skips the details.

5   Privacy Policy Verification and Verification Reports Generation

A verification results file includes verifier profiles, the date of when the file was created, and a list of verification results. As its name implies, the list of verification results is the major component of a verification results file. At this point, MaPPA adopts the report format of the Payment Card Industry (PCI) Data Security Standard report on compliance [28]. Generally, an verification result item shows whether an application complies with an object.

Figure 4 illustrates components of an item for verification result. First, a verification result is for an objective, which has identity and description. Second, a verifier may follow a process to test whether an application complies with an object step by step. A verifier can provide procedure identity or sequence number, description of the procedure, and key findings for each step. Note that this study uses dotted rectangle to represent a list of testing procedures because a

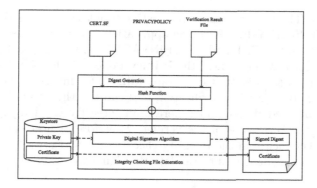

Fig. 5. The process to generate an integrity checking file

verifier can choose not to disclose detailed test results to prevent leaking sensitive information of tested applications. Finally, a verifier provides summarized results of an verification item, such as pass, not pass, not appliable, and so on, along with detailed description of the item.

MaPPA recommends verifiers to perform the following verification:

- To verify whether privacy policies cover every component of an application: Verifiers can first use static or analysis tools to obtain a list of components used in an application. Then, verifiers can discover components that are not covered by the PRIVACYPOLICY file in the application.
- To check whether an application only collects data mentioned in privacy policies: For each component of an application, verifiers can recognize personal data collected by the application. Recall the format of privacy policies in Fig. 3. Verifiers can extract a list of data categories from the dataGroup element in statements of associated privacy policies. Then, if verifiers find that a data item collected by an application component is not covered in the list of data categories, the verifiers can declare that the application does not comply with the embedded privacy policies.
- To identify malicious personal data leakage: With current static and dynamic analysis technologies, analyzers can know that a component of an application leaks personal data to other applications or remote sites. To help verifiers to understand targets for data leakage, application developers may provide mappings between computer-based target names and owners of the names. For example, if a verifier finds that an application transfers smartphone IMEI to a specific IP address, the verifier may need to know the owner of the IP address to determine that whether the application has leaked the IMEI data to other parties.

This study depicts the process for a verifier to generate an integrity checking file in Fig. 5. First, a verifier has his/her private key and associated certificate stored in the KeyStore. After the verifier has established a verification result file, the verifier can input the verified application into the Privacy Policy Verification tool of MaPPA. The Privacy Policy Verification tool then extracts the CERT.SF and PRIVACYPOLICY files from the application and uses a hash function to generate digests of the CERT.SF, the PRIVACYPOLICY file, and the verification result file respectively. Then, the Privacy Policy Verification tool performs XOR operation on the digests to generate a digest for integrity checking. Consequently, the Privacy Policy Verification tool can use the verifier's private key to sign the generated digest and generate an integrity checking file with the signature and the certificate of the verifier. Therefore, a user can extract the signature and certificate in the integrity checking file and use the public key in the certificate and related files to validate the signature.

6   Conclusion and Future Work

This study has proposed a framework to Manage Privacy Policies of Android Applications (MaPPA). The key concept of MaPPA is to enable application developers, third party application verifiers, and marketplace providers to embed machine processable privacy policies as well as associated verification reports and notes into Android applications without modifying the original Android APK file format. Current marketplace providers usually request application providers to provide URL links to application privacy policies when submitting applications to marketplaces. Comparatively, MaPPA reduces the cost of application developers and verifiers to maintain additional servers. Also, users can obtain verification reports and notes about application privacy policies to determine whether or not to trust the privacy policies. As a result, this study can hopefully provide an efficient and effective communication scheme for application privacy policies.

This study has certain limitations that point the way for future research. First, this study only suggests verification items for application privacy policies. We can further define specifications and ontologies for verification reports to enable user agents to process verification reports automatically. Moreover, as MaPPA allows different verifiers to provide their verification reports, this study is going to develop conflict resolution schemes. Users may adopt results with majority of the conflict results or request a conflict resolution service. Furthermore, although users can obtain verification reports about whether applications comply with associated privacy policies, we can further adopt runtime privacy protection technologies to enforce the policies. Last but not least, if an application transfers personal data to a back-end service, a verifier usually cannot ensure that the server follows associated privacy policies to process personal data by analyzing the application. It would be an interesting challenge to define guidelines for a verifier to audit back-end services.

Acknowledgement. This work was supported in part by the Taiwan Ministry of Science and Technology under grants 103-2221-E-011-092-MY2.

References

1. Agrawal, R., Bird, P., Grandison, T., Kiernan, J., Logan, S., Rjaibi, W.: Extending relational database systems to automatically enforce privacy policies. In: 21st International Conference on Data Engineering 2005 (ICDE 2005), Proceedings, pp. 1013–1022, April 2005
2. Alhamed, M., Amiri, K., Omari, M., Le, W.: Comparing privacy control methods for smartphone platforms. In: 2013 1st International Workshop on the Engineering of Mobile-Enabled Systems (MOBS), pp. 36–41, May 2013
3. Arzt, S., Rasthofer, S., Fritz, C., Bodden, E., Bartel, A., Klein, J., Le Traon, Y., Octeau, D., McDaniel, P.: Flowdroid: precise context, flow, field, object-sensitive and lifecycle-aware taint analysis for android apps. SIGPLAN Not. **49**(6), 259–269 (2014)
4. Bal, G.: Explicitness of consequence information in privacy warnings: experimentally investigating the effects on perceived risk, trust, and privacy information quality. In: Myers, M.D., Straub, D.W., (eds.) ICIS. Association for Information Systems (2014)
5. Balebako, R., Schaub, F., Adjerid, I., Acquisti, A., Cranor, L: The impact of timing on the salience of smartphone app privacy notices. In: Proceedings of the 5th Annual ACM CCS Workshop on Security and Privacy in Smartphones and Mobile Devices (SPSM 2015), New York, NY, USA, pp. 63–74. ACM (2015)
6. Cha, S.-C., Huang, K.J., Chang, H.M.: An efficient and flexible way to protect privacy in RFID environment with licenses. In: 2008 IEEE International Conference on RFID, pp. 35–42, April 2008
7. Elenkov, N., Internals, A.S.: An In-Depth Guide to Android's Security Architecture. No Starch Press, San Francisco (2014)
8. Enck, W., Gilbert, P., Chun, B.-G., Cox, L.P., Jung, J., McDaniel, P., Sheth, A.N.: Taintdroid: an information-flow tracking system for real time privacy monitoring on smartphones. In: Proceedings of the 9th USENIX Conference on Operating Systems Design and Implementation (OSDI 2010), Berkeley, pp. 393–407. USENIX Association (2010)
9. European Commission Article 29 Data Protection Working Party. Opinion 02/2013 on apps on smart devices. 00461/13/EN, Wp. 202 (2013)
10. Felt, A.P., Greenwood, K, Wagner, D.: The effectiveness of application permissions. In: Proceedings of the 2nd USENIX Conference on Web Application Development (WebApps 2011), Berkeley, CA, USA, p. 7. USENIX Association (2011)
11. Felt, A.P., Ha, E., Egelman, S., Haney, A., Chin, E., Wagner, D.: Android permissions: user attention, comprehension, and behavior. In: Proceedings of the Eighth Symposium on Usable Privacy and Security (SOUPS 2012), New York, NY, USA, pp. 3:1–3:14. ACM (2012)
12. Gates, C.S., Chen, J., Li, N., Proctor, R.W.: Effective risk communication for android apps. IEEE Trans. Dependable Secure Comput. **11**(3), 252–265 (2014)
13. Gates, C.S., Li, N., Peng, H., Sarma, B., Qi, Y., Potharaju, R., Nita-Rotaru, C., Molloy, I.: Generating summary risk scores for mobile applications. IEEE Trans. Dependable Secure Comput. **11**(3), 238–251 (2014)
14. Hao, S., Liu, B., Nath, S., Halfond, W.G.J., Govindan, R.: PUMA: programmable UI-automation for large-scale dynamic analysis of mobile apps. In: Proceedings of the 12th Annual International Conference on Mobile Systems, Applications, and Services (MobiSys 2014), New York, NY, USA, pp. 204–217. ACM (2014)

15. Harris, K.D.: Privacy on the go, recommendations for the mobile ecosystem. California Dept. of Justice Recommendations (2013)
16. IDC Research, Inc. Smartphone os market share, 2015 q2. IDC Research Report (2013). http://www.idc.com/prodserv/smartphone-os-market-share.jsp. Accessed 24 June 2016
17. Jing, Y., Ahn, G.-J., Zhao, Z., Hu, H.: RiskMon: continuous and automated risk assessment of mobile applications. In: Proceedings of the 4th ACM Conference on Data and Application Security and Privacy (CODASPY 2014), New York, NY, USA, pp. 99–110. ACM (2014)
18. Kelley, P.G., Consolvo, S., Cranor, L.F., Jung, J., Sadeh, N., Wetherall, D.: A conundrum of permissions: installing applications on an android smartphone. In: Blyth, J., Dietrich, S., Camp, L.J. (eds.) FC 2012. LNCS, vol. 7398, pp. 68–79. Springer, Heidelberg (2012)
19. Kong, D., Cen, L., Jin, H.: AUTOREB: automatically understanding the review-to-behavior fidelity in android applications. In: Proceedings of the 22nd ACM SIGSAC Conference on Computer and Communications Security (CCS 2015), New York, NY, USA, pp. 530–541. ACM (2015)
20. Lake, I.: Building better apps with runtime permissions. Android Developers Blog (2015). http://android-developers.blogspot.tw/2015/08/building-better-apps-with-runtime.html. Accessed 24 June 2016
21. Liccardi, I., Pato, J., Weitzner, D.J.: Improving mobile app selection through transparency and better permission analysis. J. Priv. Confidentiality **5**(2), 1–55 (2013)
22. Lin, B., Chen, Y., Chen, X., Yu, Y.: Comparison between JSON and XML in applications based on AJAX. In: Proceedings of the 2012 International Conference on Computer Science and Service System (CSSS 2012), Washington, DC, USA, pp. 1174–1177. IEEE Computer Society (2012)
23. Lin, J., Amini, S., Hong, J.I., Sadeh, N., Lindqvist, J., Zhang, J.: Expectation and purpose: understanding users' mental models of mobile app privacy through crowdsourcing. In: Proceedings of the 2012 ACM Conference on Ubiquitous Computing (UbiComp 2012), New York, NY, USA, pp. 501–510. ACM (2012)
24. Egelman, S., Cranor, L., Dobbs, B., Hogben, G., Humphrey, J., Langheinrich, M., Marchiori, M., Presler-Marshall, M., Reagle, J., Schunter, M., Stampley, D.A., Wenning, R.: The platform for privacy preferences 1.1 (P3P1.1) specification. In: W3C Specification (2006). https://www.w3.org/TR/P3P11/. Accessed 24 June 2016
25. Mobile Marketing Association Privacy and Advicacy Committee. Mobile application privacy policy framework. MMA White Paper (2011). http://www.mmaglobal.com/news/mobile-marketing-association-releases-final-privacy-policy-guidelines-mobile-apps. Accessed 24 June 2016
26. Office of the Privacy Commissioner of Canada, IPC of Alberta external, and IPC for British Columbia. Seizing opportunity: good privacy practices for developing mobile apps. OPC Guidance Documents (2012). https://www.priv.gc.ca/information/pub/gd_app_201210_e.asp
27. Olurin, M., Adams, C., Logrippo, L.: Platform for privacy preferences (P3P): current status and future directions. In: 2012 Tenth Annual International Conference on Privacy, Security and Trust (PST), pp. 217–220, July 2012
28. Payment Card Industry (PCI) Security Standards Council, LLC. Template for report on compliance for use with PCI DSS v3.1, PCI reporting templates (2015). https://www.pcisecuritystandards.org/documents/PCI_DSS_v3_1_ROC_Reporting_Template.pdf

29. Petsas, T., Voyatzis, G., Athanasopoulos, E., Polychronakis, M., Ioannidis, S.: Rage against the virtual machine: hindering dynamic analysis of android malware. In: Proceedings of the Seventh European Workshop on System Security (EuroSec 2014), New York, NY, USA, pp. 5:1–5:6. ACM (2014)

30. Rastogi, V., Chen, Y., Enck, W.: Apps playground: automatic security analysis of smart phone applications. In: Proceedings of the Third ACM Conference on Data and Application Security and Privacy (CODASPY 2013), New York, NY,USA, pp. 209–220. ACM (2013)

31. Reed, B.: IDC: smartphone shipments to top feature phone shipments for first time ever in 2013. Yahoo! News (2013). http://news.yahoo.com/ idc-smartphone-shipments-top-feature-phone-shipments-first-020026360.html. Accessed 24 June 2016

32. Said, A.A., Hussin, A.R.C., Dahlan, H.M., Pour, M.M.H.: Privacy policy preference (P3P) in e-commerce: key for improvement. In: 2012 International Conference on Information Retrieval Knowledge Management (CAMP), pp. 177–181, March 2012

33. Shen, F., Vishnubhotla, N., Todarka, C., Arora, M., Dhandapani, B., Lehner, E.J., Ko, S.Y., Ziarek, L.: Information flows as a permission mechanism. In: Proceedings of the 29th ACM/IEEE International Conference on Automated Software Engineering (ASE 2014), New York, NY, USA, pp. 515–526. ACM (2014)

34. Terms feed. Sample privacy policy template. Online document (2014). https:// termsfeed.com/blog/sample-privacy-policy-template/. Accessed 24 June 2016

35. Tian, Y., Liu, B., Dai, W., Ur, B., Tague, P., Cranor, L.F.: Supporting privacy-conscious app update decisions with user reviews. In: Proceedings of the 5th Annual ACM CCS Workshop on Security and Privacy in Smartphones and Mobile Devices (SPSM 2015), New York, NY, USA, pp. 51–61. ACM (2015)

36. Tomuro, N., Lytinen, S., Hornsburg, K.: Automatic summarization of privacy policies using ensemble learning. In: Proceedings of the Sixth ACM Conference on Data and Application Security and Privacy (CODASPY 2016), New York, NY, USA, pp. 133–135. ACM (2016)

37. US NTIA. Short form notice code of conduct to promote transparency in mobile app practices (2013). https://www.ntia.doc.gov/files/ntia/publications/july_25_ code_draft.pdf. Accessed 29 Mar 2016

38. US State of California Department of Justice. Attorney general Kamala D. Harris notifies mobile app developers of non-compliance with california privacy law. US California Dept of Justice Press News (2012). https://oag.ca.gov/news/pre ss-releases/attorney-general-kamala-d-harris-notifies-mobile-app-developers-non-compliance. Accessed 24 June 2016

39. Vidas, T., Christin, N.: Evading android runtime analysis via sandbox detection. In: Proceedings of the 9th ACM Symposium on Information, Computer and Communications Security (ASIA CCS 2014), New York, NY, USA, pp. 447–458. ACM (2014)

40. Vidas, T., Tan, J., Nahata, J., Tan, C.L., Christin, N., Tague, P.: A5: automated analysis of adversarial android applications. In: Proceedings of the 4th ACM Workshop on Security and Privacy in Smartphones and Mobile Devices (SPSM 2014), New York, NY, USA, pp. 39–50. ACM (2014)

41. Xu, Z., Zhu, S.: Semadroid: a privacy-aware sensor management framework for smartphones. In: Proceedings of the 5th ACM Conference on Data and Application Security and Privacy (CODASPY 2015), New York, NY, USA, pp. 61–72. ACM (2015)

42. Yan, L.K., Yin, H.: Droidscope: seamlessly reconstructing the OS and Dalvik semantic views for dynamic android malware analysis. In: Proceedings of the 21st USENIX Conference on Security Symposium (Security 2012), Berkeley, CA, USA, p. 29. USENIX Association (2012)
43. Yang, Z., Yang, M., Zhang, Y., Gu, G., Ning, P., Wang, X.S.: AppIntent: analyzing sensitive data transmission in android for privacy leakage detection. In: Proceedings of the 2013 ACM SIGSAC Conference on Computer and Communications Security (CCS 2013), New York, NY, USA, pp. 1043–1054. ACM (2013)
44. Zhang, Y., Yang, M., Xu, B., Yang, Z., Gu, G., Ning, P., Wang, X.S., Zang, B.: Vetting undesirable behaviors in android apps with permission use analysis. In: Proceedings of the 2013 ACM SIGSAC Conference on Computer and Communications Security (CCS 2013), pp. 611–622. ACM (2013)

Qualitative Privacy Description Language

Integrating Privacy Concepts, Languages, and Technologies

Jasper van de Ven[✉] and Frank Dylla

Bremen Spatial Cognition Center, University of Bremen, Bremen, Germany
{vandeven,dylla}@cs.uni-bremen.de

Abstract. Privacy is a major concern regarding acceptance of technology. Although, general concepts, privacy languages, and technology to implement privacy exist, these aspects are considered rather independently yet. We propose a logic based qualitative privacy description language (QPDL), which allows for an integrated view of these three perspectives and system analysis based on policy formalizations, e.g., system conformance or policy conflicts.

1 Introduction

In our everyday life vast amount of data is collected and processed with the help of technology, not only about individuals, but also private and public organizations. *Privacy* has been identified as a key factor for acceptance of these technologies. Data handling organizations and companies promise to follow certain privacy policies. However, predominantly systems are not transparent, such that everyone has to trust that promises are kept. This is somehow unsatisfactory. A solution to show that privacy issues are really dealt with would be much more beneficial for both sides: service providers as well as their clients.

In computer science literature privacy remains a vague concept which is either assumed to be known to the audience or being controversially discussed. In order to grasp privacy treatment in software we review computer science literature from three perspectives, which are dealt with rather independently: (a) concepts (Sect. 2), i.e., general definitions and data of interest, (b) existing privacy languages (Sect. 3), i.e., frameworks to describe and define privacy preferences and requirements, and (c) privacy enhancing approaches and technology (Sect. 4), i.e., methods and algorithms to implement privacy.

Based on this review we propose a qualitative privacy description language (QPDL) which allows for an integrated view of concepts, policy, and applied privacy-enhancing technology (Sect. 6). Furthermore, in contrast to existing policy and security languages we are not only aiming at machine processability, but also human comprehensibility. QPDL is based on a qualitative extension of the Linear Temporal Logic (QLTL) (Sect. 5). LTL was introduced as a method for formal software verification based on sequences of state descriptions. Nowadays a significant amount of tools are available in order to deal with LTL efficiently.

© Springer International Publishing Switzerland 2016
S. Schiffner et al. (Eds.): APF 2016, LNCS 9857, pp. 171–189, 2016.
DOI: 10.1007/978-3-319-44760-5_11

The qualitative extension is based on methods from the research area of qualitative spatial and temporal reasoning (QSTR), which deals with formal specifications of commonsense understanding of space and time.

We detail our approach by sketching how the three perspectives interrelate and how QPDL can be applied as an integrated framework. We give a definition of policies in QPDL and illustrate this with several examples (Sect. 6.1). Furthermore, we show how QPDL allows for system analysis, for example, to what extent policies are considered by a system or how violations are handled (Sect. 6.2).

2   Concepts of Privacy in Computer Science

In many publications the concept of privacy is assumed to be public knowledge. That is, no explicit definition is provided, at least in many papers from the field of computer science. Furthermore, if privacy definitions are considered, they are controversially discussed. One reason for this is that "privacy issues are fundamentally not technical"(Görlach et al. [1]). They are highly dependent on the individuals or groups concerned, situational context, and cultural background [2], i.e., user expectations and preferences, also called privacy assumptions [3]. In literature we identified four dominating concepts of how to understand and model privacy:

Information Privacy. (e.g., [4,5]) addresses the accessibility and availability of information, including but not limited to personally identifiable information (PII) or sensitive personal information (SPI), to other individuals or groups. That is, understanding and modeling privacy as an abstract data-protection and access-control problem, i.e., stating theoretic access rights that groups, individuals, and systems should conform to.

Personal Privacy. (e.g., [6]) follows the concept of information privacy with a focus on personally identifiable information (PII) and sensitive personal information (SPI). However, it also includes aspects of information security, i.e., encryption, as being a vital part of the concept of privacy.

Territorial Privacy. (e.g., [7–9]) models privacy as a spatial and temporal problem. That is, information is only available to entities present at a certain location at a certain time, e.g., only a person present in the same room is assumed to be able to hear another person talking.

Location Privacy. (e.g., [1,10]) originated due to the increasing number of available location-based services. It explicitly addresses location information, i.e., information about the (current) location of an individual or entity. Thus, this concept of privacy is restricted to a very specific set of information and can not provide a general understanding of privacy.

These concepts provide an abstract understanding and neglect to include additional and general properties of technical systems, e.g., ownership of hardware, implicit vs. explicit information, or meta-information. However, these additional properties play a vital role as users often do not share the trust a developer or service provider presumes.

In addition, if vast amounts of data are collected, it is often possible to apply inference methods to gain further information unnoticed by a user. This directly effects the informational self-determination users assume. These assumptions or the promises are generally stated as privacy policies.

3   Privacy Policy Languages

As privacy has long since been identified as being central to the general acceptance of technology a number of languages have been proposed to specify privacy policies (e.g., [11,12]), i.e., assumptions and promises regarding the availability and usage of information. We provide a brief overview of existing privacy policy languages and some of their properties. Furthermore, we include a number of security policy languages[1] that have been used or are easily adaptable to a privacy context. We focus on languages available in the general field of computer science[2] and investigate the following groups of properties: *focus*, *aspects*, and *syntax*.

The first group of properties addresses the *focus* of a language, i.e., what is the language intended to achieve. That is, we state if a language is designed to be understood by a *machine* or *human*. Furthermore, we state whether the original aim was to describe policies in the context of *privacy* or *security*.

The properties of the group *aspects* address what a language intends to constrain and from which perspective. That is, we state if the language allows to describe access–and/or *authorization* restrictions, restrictions or relations based on contextual constraints (*context*), e.g., allowing access only for certain tasks, information disclosure by the provided policy itself (*meta*), or *spatial* and *temporal* constraints, e.g., policies are only applicable at specific times or locations, or access is not allowed at a specific time or location. Furthermore, we differentiate between policy perspectives of the respective languages that explicitly address *user* assumptions, *enterprise* promises, combinations of assumptions and promises (*multi-party*), or explicitly addressing formalization of laws (*law*).

The group *syntax* addresses the syntax the language utilizes or is based on. *XML/RDF*[3] indicates that the language is based on an XML syntax and a

---

[1] These are languages whose authors stated that the aim was to address security issues. However, we acknowledge that these languages are very similar to privacy policy languages.

[2] We restrict ourselves to this literature and languages as they provide representations interpretable by computers. However, we acknowledge that their also exists a vast amount of privacy policy languages in other fields, e.g., humanities and social sciences.

[3] We acknowledge that XML and RDF are two separate formalisms with different properties. However, these differences are not essential for the presented work and thus are neglected.

respective schema or DTD is available. Languages that are either based on programming languages or are expressed as macros within source code are classified as *high-level*. If the language uses an existing logical formalism as basis, it is classified as *logical* and languages that use their own syntax are classified as *specific*.

Table 1 presents our review of existing policy languages. The languages are sorted regarding to the property of aiming at *security*, *privacy*, or neither. Then by their date of publication.

One unexpected result of this review is that only two (GeoXACML [13, 14] and LPU/CI [15,16]) out of all investigated languages state what kind of privacy concept (as presented in Sect. 2) is addressed. However, regarding the language GeoXACML, the concept itself is also neither explicitly introduced nor explained. It is also interesting that almost all languages are designed to express access-control and authorization constraints and thus implicitly seem to relate to the concept of informational privacy.

The fact that almost all investigated languages are designed to be machine-readable is due to their roots in the field of computer science. That is, the languages were created in conjunction with respective devices and technology. However, it is interesting that none of the languages was explicitly designed to be easily understandable by humans. Only five languages (SecPAL [17–19], P-RBAC [20,21], SecPAL4P [22], AAL/A-PPL [23,24], and APPEL [25]) try to provide some kind of human-readability, e.g., by providing policy wizards or through the use of natural language key-words.

Regarding aspects most languages include some form of access-control and authentication. An interesting observation related to the perspective is, that on the one hand only three languages (APPEL (P3P) [26], XPref [27], and P2U [28]) are specifically designed to express the preferences and assumptions of users. On the other hand, ten (see Table 1) are specifically designed to express the requirements and promises of enterprises.

Regarding the syntax, the preference of using XML/RDF as a foundation is based on the fact that many of the languages originated in the context of the Internet. In this context, XML/RDF are standard description languages to formalize machine parseable descriptions of rules, policies, or general data. Utilizing these standards also allows to apply existing software to implement further functionality, e.g., most XML/RDF based languages provide syntax validation.

There also exist work on describing privacy policies and laws with mathematical logics or temporal modal logics, e.g., [29,30]. We did not include this kind of work in our overview, as the used languages are not explicitly designed to represent policies. These languages exploit existing logical frameworks to analyze privacy policies and allow to utilize logical methods in order to investigate them. For example, this allows to check if a given policy contains contradictions regarding the handling of information.

4 Privacy-Enhancing Approaches and Technology

Next to languages to describe and define privacy policies, there is also a long history of research related to general methods, approaches, and techniques aiming to provide or create privacy in a technological environment or application. These technological approaches are investigated in the field of *Privacy-Enhancing Technology* (PET, e.g., [55–57]). As privacy is at its core not a purely technical problem, social aspects are also considered in this context and social means to provide privacy are employed (e.g., [55,58,59]), e.g., governmental laws, codes of conduct, and general education related to consequences. Based on the reviewed literature, we identified and collected groups of methods, abstracted from the explicit means of implementation or applied technology to create and protect

Table 1. Overview of privacy policy languages (legend see Table 2)

LANGUAGE	FOCUS				ASPECTS									SYNTAX			
	machine	human	privacy	security	authorization	context	meta	spatial	temporal	user	enterprise	multi-party	law	XML/RDF	high-level	logical	specific
XACL [31] (2000)			✓	✓					○[a]					✓			
Ponder [32,33] (2000)			✓	✓	✓				○[a]	✓	✓						✓
PSLang [34] (2000)	✓		✓	✓					○[a]			✓[i]			✓		
SAML [35,36] (2001)	✓		✓	✓							✓			✓			
Rei [37] (2002)			✓	✓			✓							○[f]	○[k]	✓	
Polymer [38] (2004)	✓		✓	✓								✓[i]			✓		
XACML [39] (2005)	✓		✓	✓							✓			✓			
GeoXACML [13,14] (2007)	✓		✓	✓	✓		✓	✓						✓			
SecPAL [17–19] (2007)	✓	○	✓	✓	✓	✓				✓		✓		✓		✓	✓
ConSpec [40] (2008)		○	✓	✓							✓					✓[d]	✓
ASLan++ [41] (2010)			✓	✓							✓				○	○	✓
P3P [42,43] (1999)	✓	✓	✓	✓					○[a]			✓[b]		✓			
CPEExchange [44] (2000)			✓	✓						✓	✓			✓			
APPEL (P3P) [26] (2001)	✓		✓	✓	✓		✓				✓			✓			
E-P3P [45,46] (2002)	✓	✓	✓	✓							✓			✓			
EPAL [47] (2003)	✓	✓	✓	✓							✓			✓			
XPref [27] (2005)	✓	✓	✓	✓						✓				✓			
LPU/CI [15,16] (2006)	○		✓	✓	✓			✓			✓	✓				✓	
Privacy APIs [48] (2006)	✓		✓	✓							✓			○	○		✓
P-RBAC [20,21] (2007)	✓	○	✓	✓	✓				✓	✓				✓			
PPL [49,50] (2009)	✓		✓	✓	✓			✓			✓			✓			
SecPAL4P [22] (2009)	✓	○	✓	✓	✓	✓[a]		✓			✓			✓		✓	✓
PrivacyLFP [51] (2010)	○		✓	✓	✓			✓			✓		✓				✓
AIR [52] (2010)	✓		✓			○[h]								✓[f]		○[g]	
S4P [53] (2010)			✓					✓			✓			✓			
Jeeves [54] (2012)	○		✓	✓						✓					✓	✓	
P2U [28] (2014)	✓		✓	✓			✓[e]	✓						✓			
AAL/A-PPL [23,24] (2014)	✓	✓	✓	○	✓	✓		✓	✓		✓			○[l]			✓
APPEL [25] (2003)	✓	○[j]							○[a]					✓			

Table 2. Legend for Table 1

o	Either not completely supported or not stated in paper
a	It allows to differentiate between *namespaces*, *domains*, *scopes*, or other (virtual) concepts
b	Policies are proposed and the user can only acknowledge or reject
d	Can be transformed into a logical automata
e	Planned, see future work of original paper
f	Focusing on RDF
g	A translation method to LP (Logic Programming) is provided
h	It is acknowledged that knowledge about rules might pose a conflict
i	The programmers are implementing the enterprise policy as part of a program
j	Supported through user friendly wizards to create policies
k	A Prolog interface is provided
l	A (semi-)automatic translation is provided

privacy: *authorization, accountability, encryption, obfuscation, fragmentation, data-hiding,* and *social means.*

Authorization addresses methods to validate and enforce a users authentication and authorization to access certain information. That is, provide functionality to an application or system to implement some form of access control.

Accountability includes methods like digital signatures or log-files. These allow to relate actions or information to specific entities, e.g., for identification of whom created or accessed certain information.

Encryption addresses methods to encrypt and decrypt information. This includes methods like synchronous or asynchronous encryption algorithms.

Obfuscation provides possibilities to prevent the complete disclosure of detailed information, but allows to present or access abstracted versions. For example, a person does not provide her exact geographic location, but states the name of the city she is in.

Fragmentation includes methods to distribute information in order to dissolve sensitive relational information. That is, information is stored in fragments at different locations and each individual fragment does not provide any sensitive information.

Data-hiding addresses methods to prevent the availability or visibility of information. This includes methods like client-side computation (hiding data or algorithms from a server), steganography (hiding data in other data), or pseudonymity (replacing information with other information).

Social means are methods applied by a society to restrict and enforce actions conducted by other individuals or groups. This includes the creation and implementation of contracts and laws controlling the usage of information.

Applying these technologies is intended to enable applications and systems to provide privacy, i.e., conform to certain privacy policies, while also providing support, i.e., desired functionality. One important difference regarding the methods introduced is if privacy is enforced, i.e., the addressed privacy functionality is guaranteed, or not, i.e., an entity is able to simply ignore addressed functionality. Contrary to the other groups, *social means* only address guidelines and consequences in case of failure to comply to them, i.e., privacy is not enforced, but (social) pressure is applied to motivate (privacy) compliant behavior.

We close this section by providing two quotes of Goldberg (et al.) related to the question if the focus should rather be on technological or social means to provide privacy.

"If we can guarantee privacy protection through the laws of mathematics rather than the laws of man and whims of bureaucrats, then we will have made an important contribution to society." (Goldberg et al. [60])

"With traditional privacy-enhancing technologies, the onus was entirely on the user to use whatever technology was available in order to protect himself. Today, there are other parties which need to be involved in this protection, since they store some of your sensitive information. Legislation, as well as other social constructs, such as contracts, help ensure that these other parties live up to their roles." (Goldberg [59])

The quotes are from two succeeding papers surveying privacy-enhancing technology for the Internet. In our opinion they perfectly show, how the general approach to address privacy moved its focus from technology to social means. This indicates, that society seems to have a stronger desire for collaborative support than for individual privacy.

5   A Qualitative Extension to Linear Temporal Logics

In this section we introduce a logical approach originally intended to specify processes on the basis of qualitative relational primitives. Before giving the definition of the language QLTL (Sect. 5.3) we introduce the domain of Qualitative Spatial and Temporal Representation and Reasoning (Sect. 5.1) and Linear Temporal Logic (Sect. 5.2). We will adapt QLTL in Sect. 6 in order to define a qualitative privacy description language (QPDL).

5.1   Qualitative Spatial and Temporal Reasoning

Humans communicate in natural language which is vague, coarse, and imprecise. By means of qualitative descriptions one can focus on distinctions between objects that make an important and relevant difference with respect to a given task [61]. *Qualitative Spatial and Temporal Representation and Reasoning (QSTR)* is concerned with capturing such distinctions about objects in the real world, also considered as commonsense knowledge, with a limited set of symbols, i.e., without numerical values [62]. These distinctions are captured by *relations*, which summarize indistinguishable cases into a single symbol. For example, in many cases it is sufficient to consider whether someone is `inside` a room or `outside`, the exact position in terms of coordinates does not matter.

Qualitative Calculi are based on sets of atomic relationships, called *base relations* $(\mathcal{BR})$, concerning a specific domain, e.g., topology or relative orientation. These base relations either represent themselves meaningful relations for the task at hand or allow these relations to be obtained by means of union of base relations. For the purpose of this paper it is sufficient that a qualitative calculus allows us to model binary[4] relations between entities using unions of base relations. The most widely considered knowledge representation for qualitative calculi is constraint-based. Given a set of variables $X = \{x_1, \ldots, x_n\}$ and a set of base relations $\mathcal{BR} = \{b_1, \ldots, b_m\}$, a knowledge base consists of constraints $(x_i \{b_{i_1}, \ldots, b_{i_k}\} x_j)$ which say that entities x_i and x_j are in relation $b_{i_1} \cup \ldots \cup b_{i_k}$. QSTR then provides us with (calculi-specific) algorithms to decide whether a constraint-satisfaction problem (CSP) consisting of such constraints is satisfiable or not [63]. A standard approach to this is by means of graphs, so called *qualitative constraint networks*, with objects as nodes and constraints attached as labels to the corresponding edges. The test of satisfiability also allows new constraints that follow from a given set of constraints to be inferred, similar to how resolution of logic formulas allows for deduction. For further details we refer to [63].

Topological distinctions are inherently qualitative in nature and they also represent one of the most general and cognitively adequate ways for the representation of spatial information [64]. Based on this inherent qualitative nature different qualitative calculi were developed, among them the Region Connection Calculus (RCC) [65]. Exploiting the connectivity of regions eight base relations are defined (see Fig. 1). In the following we exploit these relations in order to represent privacy issues. By considering the space that is covered by some object o, we are able to express that this object is (at least partially) in some region r:

$$\mathtt{in}(o, r) := \mathtt{PO}(o, r) \vee \mathtt{TPP}(o, r) \vee \mathtt{NTPP}(o, r)$$

5.2   Linear Temporal Logics

In *Linear Temporal Logic* (LTL) [66] it is possible to connect worlds, i.e., state descriptions, with modal operators like next or always. LTL was originally introduced in order to allow formal software verification. LTL is specifically known for being capable of expressing safety ('something bad never happens') and liveness properties ('something good eventually happens') in an efficient manner (e.g., [67]). Formulae can be built recursively over a set of atomic propositions $(a \in P)$ which can be true or false:

- a is a formula for every $a \in P$
- If ϕ is a formula, so is $\neg\phi$
- If ϕ, ψ are formulae, so is $\phi \otimes \psi$ with $\otimes \in \{\wedge, \vee, \rightarrow, \leftrightarrow\}$
- If ϕ is a formula, so is $M\phi$ with $M \in \{\circ, \square, \diamond\}$
- If ϕ, ψ are formulae, so is $\phi N \psi$ with $N \in \{U, R\}$

---

[4] In general relations with any arity are possible.

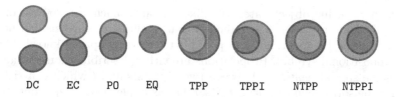

Fig. 1. The eight RCC base relations concerning two regions: disconnected (DC), externally connected (EC), partially overlapping (PO), tangential proper part (TPP), its inverse (TPPI), non-tangential proper part (NTPP), and its inverse (NTPPI)

With this it is possible to formalize change over time, i.e., defining constraints expressing which propositions have to be true or false in the next world or some future world. The task is to find an interpretation in a linear and discrete model of time. The semantics of modal operations in LTL are defined as follows:

$\circ\phi$	**(next)**	ϕ holds in the following world
$\Box\phi$	**(always)**	ϕ holds in the current and in all future worlds
$\diamond\phi$	**(eventually)**	ϕ holds in a future world ($\diamond\phi \leftrightarrow \neg\Box\neg\phi$)
$\phi\,U\,\psi$	**(until)**	ϕ holds at least until ψ holds, but they don't have to hold at the same time
$\phi\,R\,\psi$	**(release)**	ψ holds until and including the world in which ϕ first becomes true

Now, given observations of a system over time one can find out whether a set of LTL formulae is fulfilled by these observations or not. A prominent approach to this is model checking for which a variety of tools are available[5].

5.3 A Qualitative Linear Temporal Logic (QLTL)

In order to formalize traffic regulations or social conventions LTL was extended with qualitative primitives, i.e., relations from qualitative calculi, and sorts, resulting in QLTL [68]. We will adopt this approach in order to formalize privacy concerns. The syntax of QLTL is defined as follows:

- a set of spatial symbols $\mathcal{S}$. Let k be a number of sorts, then $S_i = \{s_{i_1}, s_{i_2}, \ldots\}$, $i = 1, \ldots, k$ are sets of spatial symbols and $\mathcal{S} := \bigcup_{i=1,\ldots,k} S_i$
- $\mathcal{R} = \{r_1, \ldots, r_n\}$ is a set of qualitative relation symbols
- $F = \{f_1, \ldots, f_l\}$ be a set of function symbols
- $G = \{g_1, g_2, \ldots\}$ is a set of propositional symbols for representing general, non-spatial knowledge
- The set of propositions P is defined as $P := G \cup \{r(s,t) | r \in \mathcal{R}, s, t \in (\mathcal{S} \cup \{f(s_i) | f \in F, s_i \in \mathcal{S}\})\}$.

---

[5] For an overview of tools we refer to https://en.wikipedia.org/wiki/List_of_model_checking_tools.

Sorts may define object categories like humans, machines, rooms, or even specific information pieces. It is intended that qualitative relations can be used in a rather natural manner, i.e., it is possible to represent spatial knowledge by a single propositional symbol. Propositions are either describing non-spatial facts (G) or some spatial relation r between two objects s and t which can either be sorts or some sort dependent aspect $f(s_i)$. For example, a sort dependent aspect may be the security range sec around some machine m. A human h being in this range could be expressed as $\text{in}(h, \text{sec}(m))$. QLTL formulae can then be defined recursively as regular LTL formulae with propositions $p \in P$ being valid formulae.

The semantics of QLTL is similar to LTL, i.e., an interpretation establishes an ordered sequence of worlds. Within each single world, all propositional symbols are mapped to truth values *true* or *false*, inducing the interpretation of formulae composed with logic conjuncts $(\land, \lor, \ldots)$. In QLTL we further require interpretations within all worlds to be *spatially consistent*, i.e., interpretations of given data must not be contradictory. This defines the *spatial semantics* of QLTL. This is, we filter out all spatially inconsistent interpretations as, for example, provided by SparQ [69].

Within one world, the interpretation of all (spatial) propositions $r(s_1, s_2)$ with $s_i \in S$ or $s_i = f_j(s)$ for some $f_j \in F, s \in S$ induces a qualitative constraint network with variables S and according constraints $r_i(x, y)$ where x, y are either the spatial symbols s_1, s_2 or the symbols obtained by application of $f_j(s_i)$. The spatial semantics of a relation r is defined by the respective qualitative calculus. In this work, we define that the set of qualitative relation symbols $\mathcal{R}$ is given by the RCC relations. Functions F are also assigned with a respective spatial semantics, e.g., mapping the security region of some machine m to the concrete extent of this specific machine.

6   Qualitative Privacy Description Language (QPDL)

We now present an approach which allows for formalizing different facets of privacy in a single framework, i.e., a qualitative privacy description language (QPDL), which is based on QLTL. In Fig. 2 we visualized the connectivities between the different aspects of privacy. In general it seems natural that privacy is an issue only in societies, i.e., groups of interacting humans. That is, a society has a certain understanding of the concept of privacy available to individuals or groups. These are often stated in the form of privacy policies that define rules expressing what is acceptable and what is not. In order to realize and enforce these policies, privacy-enhancing technologies are applied.

Privacy-enhancing technologies are often developed to accommodate an existing privacy concept. However, introducing new technology can also reshape the perception of a privacy concept, as specific functionality is included in the understanding of privacy of a society. In addition, the applied technologies also can have an effect on the society as they can influence the behavior of individuals or groups in specific ways. What technologies are applied is constrained by the

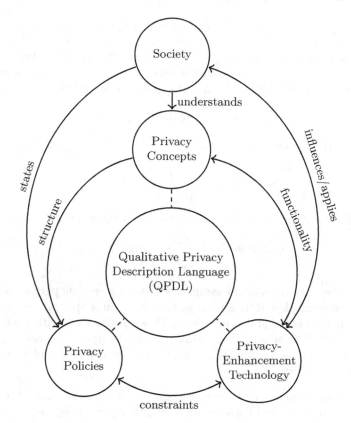

Fig. 2. Connectivities between the different perspectives of privacy

privacy policy applied. That is, a policy requires to restrict technological possibilities to what a society deems suitable. Furthermore, a privacy policy is most often modeled after the structure of a privacy concept in order to be understandable by society.

So far, these aspects are seen rather separate from each other. With QPDL we propose an approach which reflects an integrated view with the goal of being able to consider policies, technology, and concepts in a single language. This language is machine processable and designed to be based on cognitive aspects in order to be understandable for humans. In the following we exemplify how these aspects are reflected in formalizations.

6.1   Policy Definition in QPDL

A privacy policy is a set of rules that should be considered. Thus, a set of policies Π needs to be defined. We call the extension of QLTL with Π QPDL:

$$\Pi := \bigcup_{i=1,\dots,m} \pi_i$$

with $\pi_i = \{\phi_{i_1}, \phi_{i_2}, \ldots, \phi_{i_o}\}$ and m is the number of policies and o the number of rules included per policy. Simplified, each rule ϕ_{i_j} is an arbitrary QLTL formula itself, that a system should take care of in a specific manner. For reasons of simplicity we only consider a blacklist approach here, i.e., if a rule is evaluated true based on the currently available data, this rule is violated:

$$\phi_{i_j} \rightarrow violated(\phi_{i_j})$$

Furthermore, if a single rule of a policy is violated, the policy is violated in general:

$$violated(\pi_i) := \bigvee_{j=1,\ldots,l} violated(\phi_{i_j})$$

Respectively, the set of all policies is violated, if a single policy is violated:

$$violated(\Pi) := \bigvee_{i=1,\ldots,m} violated(\pi_i)$$

We now give some practical examples. Consider a specific person, e.g., Peter, who does not want that it is known wether he is in a specific room, e.g., the restroom. Then he could state the rule $in(Peter, Restroom)$ with $in(h, r)$ being modeled via RCC relations. If data about him being in the restroom would be available in some situation, this would result in a policy violation. Further examples may be that:

Ex.1 $knows(h_2, name(h_1)) \wedge knows(h_2, address(h_1))$: name and address of the same person must not be known by some other person (h_2) at the same time

Ex.2 $knows(h_2, name(h_1)) \wedge knows(h_2, address(h_1)) \wedge in(h_1, r) \wedge$
$in(h_2, r)$: name and address of a person must never be known to another person, unless both persons are in the same room at the same time

Ex.3 $stored(data) \wedge encrypted(data)$: all data stored must be encrypted

Ex.4 $\neg access(h, data) U \ valid\_code(h)$: no person can access data until a correct access code is entered

Ex.5 $(in(h_1, r) \wedge in(h_2, r)) \rightarrow \circ \ (show(data, t) \wedge in(t, r))$: only if two persons are in the room r, data is shown on a terminal t in this room

Again, in order to give these formulae a clear semantic, functions like $knows$ $(h, data)$ or $access(h, data)$ need to be grounded. For example, if an object (o) is in a region with respect to person (h), then o is known by h: $knows(h, o) :=$ $in(o, knowledge\_range(h))$. We note that data displayed on a screen is also an entity in space and can thus be handled in the same manner, i.e., territorial and informational privacy can be dealt with on the same basis.

That is, Ex. 1 can be seen as an informational policy and Ex. 2 as a territorial. Ex. 3–5 mainly reflect privacy enhancing technology, i.e., dealing with encryption and authorization. Especially Ex. 5 is interesting as it implies the requirement of two individuals being present, which adds a social component. In addition, Ex. 3 and 4 are stated from an informational perspective, Ex. 5 is stated from a territorial one.

6.2   System Affordances Definition in QPDL

Privacy policies always only state desired or assumed behavior or expectations, i.e., a system or human can decide to ignore or incorporate a given policy. That is, in order to get a society to trust that stated policies are observed, an individual or group has to provide respective evidence, e.g., provide transparent processes or process reviews. Another possibility is to formalize a system and analyze to what extent policies are observed or how violations are handled.

We differentiate between six system classes providing different privacy affordances [70], i.e., provide specific privacy considerations from the systems perspective[6] : *privacy oblivious systems, privacy aware systems, privacy repairing systems, privacy projecting systems, privacy conserving systems,* and *privacy shielding systems.*

Privacy oblivious systems do not care if a privacy policy is violated or not. That is, such a system does not provide any privacy-enhancing technology.

Privacy aware systems ensure that an individual is always informed if her privacy is violated[7]. Thus, these systems require at least some privacy-enhancing technology detecting violations. The QPDL formula

$$\Box\, (violated(\Pi_h) \rightarrow informed(h, violated(\Pi_h)))$$

expresses this property, with Π_h being the set of all policies π_h including violated rules addressing the individual h.

Privacy repairing systems are designed to actively take actions to return to a status where there is no privacy violation. That is, a system is able to apply privacy-enhancing technologies in order to traverse from a state with privacy violation to a future state without violations[8]. The QPDL formula

$$\Box\, (violated(\Pi) \rightarrow \diamond\, \neg violated(\Pi))$$

expresses this property[9].

Privacy projecting systems ensure that an individual is always informed before her privacy is possibly violated. That is, a system applies projection methods in combination with privacy-enhancing technologies to predict possible imminent violations. This can also include the detection of possible imminent violations that never actually occur. The QPDL formula

$$\Box\, (\circ\, violated(\Pi_h) \rightarrow informed(h, violated(\Pi_h)))$$

---

[6] We note that these are only categories of systems and do not address specific implementations.

[7] Depending on the implementation this can be a very general alert or a specific listing of all current (and possibly all previous) violations.

[8] A straight forward method to implement this behavior would be to delete all available knowledge when a violation is detected. However, this would most likely result in a system that is not very useful.

[9] The temporal horizon (when a violation has to be resolved) can be changed, e.g., to ensure the violation is resolved in the next world after its appearance: $\Box\, (violated(\Pi) \rightarrow \circ\, \neg violated(\Pi))$. The same holds also for the temporal horizons used in privacy projecting and privacy conserving systems.

expresses this property.

Privacy conserving systems are a combination of privacy projecting and privacy repairing systems. That is, they apply privacy-enhancing technology and prediction to ensure an individual is always informed before her privacy is possibly violated and that any violation is resolved along the line. The QPDL formula

$$\Box \left(\circ \, violated(\Pi_h) \rightarrow (informed(h, violated(\Pi_h)) \wedge \circ (\Diamond \neg violated(\Pi_h)))\right)$$

expresses this property.

Privacy shielding systems ensure that the provided privacy policies are never violated in any case. The QPDL formula

$$\Box \neg violated(\Pi)$$

expresses this property.

The formula expressing the general property of a system regarding its privacy affordance can be logically validated. That is, the entire system with all possible perceptions, actions, and states can be expressed in QPDL, as well as their respective properties. This is possible as QPDL is based on QLTL and thus LTL, which were designed explicitly for this purpose[10]. Thus, the possibility of applying system verification methods allows to proof that a system is, for example, privacy shielding through rigorous mathematical methods and by that (hopefully) installs some trust on the user side.

6.3   Applications and Properties

Until now, we only used QPDL to address theoretical systems. However, any privacy policy defined in QPDL can also be understood as a set of action- or business-rules. These in turn can be used in actual technological systems, as there exist algorithms able to evaluate such rule sets fast enough for online processing.

However, the theoretical analysis guarantees certain properties of these systems and of what states they can reach. The analytical questions are much more complex from a computational perspective as simply evaluating if a rule should fire in a given context. However, these analyses allow to identify conflicts, i.e., inconsistencies, of or within policies and provide a glimpse at the bigger picture of how a system deals with privacy in general.

7   Conclusion

We reviewed computer science literature with regard to three aspects which are currently considered rather independently: privacy concepts, privacy policy languages and their properties, as well as techniques in order to implement privacy

---

[10] QPDL allows to represent all aspects of privacy (concepts, policies, and privacy-enhancing technologies) and as a result we are confident that QPDL is expressive enough to model all reviewed privacy policy languages.

in technical systems (privacy enhancing technologies). In order to propose an integrated view on these three aspects we introduced QPDL (Qualitative Privacy Description Language), which is not only machine processable due to its clear semantic based on Linear Temporal Logic (LTL), but also aims at human comprehensibility due to acknowledgement of commonsense abstractions of space. We exemplified how policies can be stated and formalized different systems that deal with policy violations in specific manners, i.e., from ignoring policies to ensuring that policy violations never occur.

In the future we plan to provide methods for translation from the reviewed privacy policy languages to QPDL and back. This also includes theoretic investigations regarding the expressiveness of all languages in comparison to QPDL. In addition, we also plan to investigate possibilities for automated system evaluation, both on the side of a service provider as well as on the client side. Next to these very technical and application oriented ideas, we intend to research the effects and restrictions of applying different underlying temporal logics, e.g., utilizing computational tree logic (CTL) or alternating-time temporal logic (ATL) instead of LTL. Finally, the general discussion of how privacy is implemented and perceived within the society has to be addressed. That is, as privacy is not a technical problem at its core (e.g., [1,59]), but also has to be addressed on a social level in order to allow an agreed technical implementation and realization.

Acknowledgement. We acknowledge German Research Foundation (DFG) funding for project SOCIAL (FR 806/15-1). We thank the anonymous reviewers for their thoughtful and constructive comments.

References

1. Görlach, A., Heinemann, A., Terpstra, W.W.: Survey on location privacy in pervasive computing. In: Robinson, P., Vogt, H., Wagealla, W. (eds.) Privacy, Security and Trust within the Context of Pervasive Computing. The International Series in Engineering and Computer Science, vol. 780, pp. 23–34. Springer, Heidelberg (2005)
2. Nissenbaum, H.: Privacy as contextual integrity. Washington Law Rev. **79**, 119 (2004)
3. Schaub, F., Könings, B., Weber, M.: Context-adaptive privacy: leveraging context awareness to support privacy decision making. IEEE Pervasive Comput. **14**(1), 34–43 (2015)
4. Solove, D.J.: Understanding Privacy. Harvard University Press, Cambridge (2008)
5. Raab, C.D., Bennett, C.J.: Taking the measure of privacy: can data protection be evaluated? Int. Rev. Adm. Sci. **62**(4), 535–556 (1996)
6. Langheinrich, M.: A privacy awareness system for ubiquitous computing environments. In: Borriello, G., Holmquist, L.E. (eds.) UbiComp 2002. LNCS, vol. 2498, pp. 237–245. Springer, Heidelberg (2002)
7. Könings, B., Schaub, F.: Territorial privacy in ubiquitous computing. In: Eighth International Conference on Wireless On-Demand Network Systems and Services (WONS), pp. 104–108. IEEE (2011)

8. Könings, B., Schaub, F., Weber, M., Kargl, F.: Towards territorial privacy in smart environments. In: Intelligent Information Privacy Management, Papers from the 2010 AAAI Spring Symposium, Technical report SS-10-05, Stanford, California, USA, 22–24 March 2010. AAAI (2010)
9. Könings, B., Schaub, F., Weber, M.: Who, how, and why? Enhancing privacy awareness in ubiquitous computing. In: 2013 IEEE International Conference on Pervasive Computing and Communications Workshops, PERCOM 2013 Workshops, San Diego, CA, USA, 18–22 March 2013, pp. 364–367. IEEE (2013)
10. Wernke, M., Skvortsov, P., Dürr, F., Rothermel, K.: A classification of location privacy attacks and approaches. Pers. Ubiquit. Comput. 18(1), 163–175 (2014)
11. Kumaraguru, P., Cranor, L., Lobo, J., Calo, S.: A survey of privacy policy languages. In: SOUPS 2007: Proceedings of the 3rd Symposium on Usable Privacy and Security (2007)
12. Kasem-Madani, S., Meier, M.: Security and privacy policy languages: a survey, categorization and gap identification. CoRR abs/1512.00201 (2015)
13. Matheus, A., Herrmann, J.: Geospatial eXtensible Access Control Markup Language (GeoXACML) - Version 1 Corrigendum. Open Geospatial Consortium Inc., OGC (2011)
14. Herrmann, J.: Administration of (geo)xacml policies for spatial data infrastructures. In: Bertino, E., Damiani, M.L., Ghinita, G. (eds.) Proceedings of the 4th ACM SIGSPATIAL International Workshop on Security and Privacy in GIS and LBS, SPRINGL 2011, November 1st, 2011, pp. 53–59. ACM, Chicago (2011)
15. Barth, A., Datta, A., Mitchell, J.C., Nissenbaum, H.: Privacy and contextual integrity: Framework and applications. In: IEEE Symposium on Security and Privacy (S&P 2006), 21–24 May 2006, Berkeley, California, USA, pp. 184–198. IEEE Computer Society (2006)
16. Barth, A., Mitchell, J.C., Datta, A., Sundaram, S.: Privacy and utility in business processes. In: 20th IEEE Computer Security Foundations Symposium, CSF 2007, 6-8 July 2007, Venice, Italy, pp. 279–294. IEEE Computer Society (2007)
17. Dillaway, B., Hogg, J.: Security policy assertion language (SecPal) specification, version 1.0. Microsoft Research, 15 February 2007
18. Becker, M.Y., Fournet, C., Gordon, A.D.: Design and semantics of a decentralized authorization language. In: 20th IEEE Computer Security Foundations Symposium, CSF 2007, 6-8 July 2007, Venice, Italy, pp. 3–15. IEEE Computer Society (2007)
19. Becker, M.Y., Fournet, C., Gordon, A.D.: SecPal: design and semantics of a decentralized authorization language. J. Comput. Secur. 18(4), 619–665 (2010)
20. Ni, Q., Trombetta, A., Bertino, E., Lobo, J.: Privacy-aware role based access control. In: Lotz, V., Thuraisingham, B.M. (eds.) SACMAT 2007, 12th ACM Symposium on Access Control Models and Technologies Proceedings, Sophia Antipolis, France, 20–22 June 2007, pp. 41–50. ACM (2007)
21. Ni, Q., Bertino, E., Lobo, J., Brodie, C., Karat, C.-M., Karat, J., Trombetta, A.: Privacy-aware role-based access control. ACM Trans. Inf. Syst. Secur. 13(3) (2010)
22. Becker, M.Y., Malkis, A., Bussard, L.: A framework for privacy preferences and data-handling policies. Technical report, Microsoft Research Cambridge Technical Report, MSR-TR-2009-128 (2009)
23. Azraoui, M., Elkhiyaoui, K., Önen, M., Bernsmed, K., De Oliveira, A.S., Sendor, J.: A-PPL: an accountability policy language. In: Garcia-Alfaro, J., Herrera-Joancomartí, J., Lupu, E., Posegga, J., Aldini, A., Martinelli, F., Suri, N. (eds.) DPM/SETOP/QASA 2014. LNCS, vol. 8872, pp. 319–326. Springer, Heidelberg (2015)

24. Benghabrit, W., Grall, H., Royer, J., Sellami, M., Azraoui, M., Elkhiyaoui, K., Önen, M., de Oliveira, A.S., Bernsmed, K.: A cloud accountability policy representation framework. In: Helfert, M., Desprez, F., Ferguson, D., Leymann, F., Muñoz, V.M., eds.: CLOSER 2014 - Proceedings of the 4th International Conference on Cloud Computing and Services Science, Barcelona, Spain, 3–5 April 2014, pp. 489–498. SciTePress (2014)
25. Reiff-Marganiec, S., Turner, K., Blair, L., Campbell, G., Wang, F.: Appel: An adaptable and programmable policy environment and language. Technical report, Technical report CSM-161, Department of Computing Science and Mathematics, University of Stirling, UK (2014)
26. Langheinrich, M.: A P3P preference exchange language (APPEL). W3C Working Draft (2001)
27. Agrawal, R., Kiernan, J., Srikant, R., Xu, Y.: XPref: a preference language for P3P. Comput. Netw. 48(5), 809–827 (2005)
28. Iyilade, J., Vassileva, J.: P2U: A privacy policy specification language for secondary data sharing and usage. In: 35 IEEE Security and Privacy Workshops, SPW 2014, San Jose, CA, USA, 17–18 May 2014, pp. 18–22. IEEE Computer Society (2014)
29. Chowdhury, O., Jia, L., Garg, D., Datta, A.: Temporal mode-checking for runtime monitoring of privacy policies. In: Biere, A., Bloem, R. (eds.) CAV 2014. LNCS, vol. 8559, pp. 131–149. Springer, Heidelberg (2014)
30. Chowdhury, O., Gampe, A., Niu, J., von Ronne, J., Bennatt, J., Datta, A., Jia, L., Winsborough, W.H.: Privacy promises that can be kept: a policy analysis method with application to the HIPAA privacy rule. In: Conti, M., Vaidya, J., Schaad, A. (eds.) 18th ACM Symposium on Access Control Models and Technologies, SACMAT 2013, Amsterdam, The Netherlands, 12–14 June 2013, pp. 3–14. ACM (2013)
31. Hada, S., Kudo, M.: XML access control language: provisional authorization for XML documents. Language Specification (2000)
32. Damianou, N., Dulay, N., Lupu, E., Sloman, M.: A language for specifying security and management policies for distributed systems. Technical report 20, Department of Computing, Imperial College, London (2000)
33. Damianou, N., Dulay, N., Lupu, E.C., Sloman, M.: The ponder policy specification language. In: Sloman, M., Lobo, J., Lupu, E.C. (eds.) POLICY 2001. LNCS, vol. 1995, p. 18. Springer, Heidelberg (2001)
34. Erlingsson, Ú., Schneider, F.B.: IRM enforcement of Java stack inspection. In: IEEE Symposium on Security and Privacy, Berkeley, California, USA, 14–17 May 2000, pp. 246–255. IEEE Computer Society (2000)
35. Hallam-Baker, P.: Security assertions markup language, 1–24, May 14 2001
36. Hughes, J., Maler, E.: Security assertion markup language (SAML) v2. 0 technical overview. OASIS SSTC Working Draft sstc-saml-tech-overview-2.0-draft-08 (2005)
37. Lalana, K.: Rei: A policy language for the me-centric project. Technical report, TechReport, HP Labs (2002)
38. Bauer, L., Ligatti, J., Walker, D.: A language and system for composing security policies. Technical report, Princeton University (2004)
39. OASIS Standard: eXtensible Access Control Markup Language (XACML)version 2.0 (2005). http://docs.oasisopen.org/xacml/2.0/access_control-xacml-2.0-core-spec-os.pdf
40. Aktug, I., Naliuka, K.: ConSpec - a formal language for policy specification. Electr. Notes Theor. Comput. Sci. 197(1), 45–58 (2008)

41. von Oheimb, D., Mödersheim, S.: ASLan++ — a formal security specification language for distributed systems. In: Aichernig, B.K., de Boer, F.S., Bonsangue, M.M. (eds.) Formal Methods for Components and Objects. LNCS, vol. 6957, pp. 1–22. Springer, Heidelberg (2011)

42. Reagle, J., Cranor, L.F.: The platform for privacy preferences. Commun. ACM **42**(2), 48–55 (1999)

43. Cranor, L., Langheinrich, M., Marchiori, M., Reagle, J.: The platform for privacy preferences 1.0 (P3P1.0) specification. W3C Recommendation, April 2002

44. Bohrer, K., Holland, B.: Customer profile exchange (CPExchange) specification. public document

45. Karjoth, G., Schunter, M., Waidner, M.: Platform for enterprise privacy practices: privacy-enabled management of customer data. In: Dingledine, R., Syverson, P.F. (eds.) PET 2002. LNCS, vol. 2482, pp. 69–84. Springer, Heidelberg (2003)

46. Ashley, P., Hada, S., Karjoth, G., Schunter, M.: E-P3P privacy policies and privacy authorization. In: Jajodia, S., Samarati, P., (eds.) Proceedings of the 2002 ACM Workshop on Privacy in the Electronic Society, WPES 2002, Washington, DC, USA, 21 November 2002, pp. 103–109. ACM (2002)

47. Ashley, P., Hada, S., Karjoth, G., Powers, C., Schunter, M.: Enterprise privacy authorization language (EPAL 1.2). Submission to W3C (2003)

48. May, M.J., Gunter, C.A., Lee, I.: Privacy APIs: access control techniques to analyze and verify legal privacy policies. In: 19th IEEE Computer Security Foundations Workshop, (CSFW-19 2006), 5–7 July 2006, Venice, Italy, pp. 85–97. IEEE Computer Society (2006)

49. Vimercati, G., Paraboschi, S., Pedrini, E., Preiss, F.S., Raggett, D., Samarati, P., Trabelsi, S., Verdicchio, M.: Primelife policy language (2009)

50. Trabelsi, S., Sendor, J., Reinicke, S.: PPL: primelife privacy policy engine. In: POLICY 2011, IEEE International Symposium on Policies for Distributed Systems and Networks, Pisa, Italy, 6–8 June 2011, pp. 184–185. IEEE Computer Society (2011)

51. DeYoung, H., Garg, D., Jia, L., Kaynar, D.K., Datta, A.: Experiences in the logical specification of the HIPAA and GLBA privacy laws. In: Al-Shaer, E., Frikken, K.B. (eds.) Proceedings of the 2010 ACM Workshop on Privacy in the Electronic Society, WPES 2010, Chicago, Illinois, USA, 4 October 2010, pp. 73–82. ACM (2010)

52. Khandelwal, A., Bao, J., Kagal, L., Jacobi, I., Ding, L., Hendler, J.: Analyzing the AIR language: a semantic web (production) rule language. In: Hitzler, P., Lukasiewicz, T. (eds.) RR 2010. LNCS, vol. 6333, pp. 58–72. Springer, Heidelberg (2010)

53. Becker, M.Y., Malkis, A., Bussard, L.: A practical generic privacy language. In: Jha, S., Mathuria, A. (eds.) ICISS 2010. LNCS, vol. 6503, pp. 125–139. Springer, Heidelberg (2010)

54. Yang, J., Yessenov, K., Solar-Lezama, A.: A language for automatically enforcing privacy policies. In: Field, J., Hicks, M. (eds.) Proceedings of the 39th ACM SIGPLAN-SIGACT Symposium on Principles of Programming Languages, POPL 2012, Philadelphia, Pennsylvania, USA, 22–28 January 2012, pp. 85–96. ACM (2012)

55. Senicar, V., Jerman-Blazic, B., Klobucar, T.: Privacy-enhancing technologies - approaches and development. Comput. Stand. Interfaces **25**(2), 147–158 (2003)

56. Hafiz, M.: A pattern language for developing privacy enhancing technologies. Softw. Pract. Exper. **43**(7), 769–787 (2013)

57. Cherrueau, R., Douence, R., Südholt, M.: A language for the composition of privacy-enforcement techniques. In: IEEE TrustCom/BigDataSE/ISPA, Helsinki, Finland, 20–22 August 2015, vol. 1, pp. 1037–1044. IEEE (2015)
58. Fischer-Hübner, S.: Privacy and security at risk in the global information society. Inf. Commun. Soc. 1(4), 420–441 (1998)
59. Goldberg, I.: Privacy-enhancing technologies for the internet, II: five years later. In: Dingledine, R., Syverson, P.F. (eds.) PET 2002. LNCS, vol. 2482, pp. 1–12. Springer, Heidelberg (2003)
60. Goldberg, I., Wagner, D., Brewer, E.: Privacy-enhancing technologies for the internet. In: Proceedings, COMPCON 1997, pp. 103–109. IEEE, February 1997
61. Kuipers, B.: Qualitative Reasoning: Modeling and Simulation with Incomplete Knowledge. The MIT Press, Cambridge (1994)
62. Cohn, A.G., Hazarika, S.M.: Qualitative spatial representation and reasoning: an overview. Fundamenta Informaticae 46(1–2), 1–29 (2001)
63. Renz, J., Nebel, B.: Qualitative spatial reasoning using constraint calculi. In: Handbook of Spatial Logics, pp. 161–215 (2007)
64. Renz, J., Rauh, R., Knauff, M.: Towards cognitive adequacy of topological spatial relations. In: Habel, C., Brauer, W., Freksa, C., Wender, K.F. (eds.) Spatial Cognition 2000. LNCS (LNAI), vol. 1849, pp. 184–197. Springer, Heidelberg (2000)
65. Cohn, A.G., Bennett, B., Gooday, J.M., Gotts, N.: RCC: a calculus for region based qualitative spatial reasoning. GeoInformatica 1, 275–316 (1997)
66. Pnueli, A.: The temporal logic of programs. In: Proceeding of FOCS, pp. 46–57 (1977)
67. Sistla, A.P.: Safety, liveness and fairness in temporal logic. Formal Aspects Comput. 6(5), 495–511 (1994)
68. Dylla, F., Kreutzmann, A., Wolter, D.: A qualitative representation of social conventions for application in robotics. In: AAAI Spring Symposium Series (2014)
69. Wolter, D., Wallgrün, J.O.: Qualitative spatial reasoning for applications: new challenges and the SparQ toolbox. In: Hazarika, S.M. (ed.) Qualitative Spatio-Temporal Representation and Reasoning: Trends and Future Directions. IGI Global, Hershey (2011)
70. van de Ven, J., Dylla, F.: Privacy classification for ambient intelligence. In: Aarts, E., de Ruyter, B., Markopoulos, P., van Loenen, E., Wichert, R., Schouten, B., Terken, J., Van Kranenburg, R., Ouden, E.D., O'Hare, G. (eds.) AmI 2014. LNCS, vol. 8850, pp. 328–343. Springer, Heidelberg (2014)

An Information Privacy Risk Index
for mHealth Apps

Thomas Brüggemann[1], Joel Hansen[1], Tobias Dehling[2], and Ali Sunyaev[2(✉)]

[1] University of Cologne, Albertus-Magnus-Platz 1, 50931 Köln, Germany
mail@thomasbrueggemann.com, joel.hansen@pass-on.de
[2] University of Kassel, Mönchebergstraße 19, 34109 Kassel, Germany
{tdehling,sunyaev}@uni-kassel.de

Abstract. While the mobile application (app) market, including mobile health (mHealth) apps, is flourishing, communication and assessment of information privacy risks of app use has, in contrast, found only cursory attention. Neither research nor practice offers any useful and widely accepted tools facilitating communication and assessment of information privacy risks. We conduct a feasibility study and develop a prototypical instantiation of an information privacy risk index for mHealth apps. The developed information privacy risk index offers more detailed information than privacy seals without suffering from the information overload and inconsistent structure of privacy policies. In addition, the information privacy risk index allows for seamless comparison of information privacy risk factors between apps. Our research adds to the transparency debate in the information privacy domain by illustrating an alternative approach to communication of information privacy risks and investigating a promising approach to enable users to compare information privacy risks between apps.

Keywords: Information privacy · Risks · mhealth · Mobile health · Privacy enhancing technologies · Usable privacy

1 Introduction

In recent years, the growth of the consumer electronics market has seen a boost through the introduction of smartphones and tablet computers [17]. More and more users are now installing a variety of different applications (apps) on their mobile devices [2]. Among those apps are apps offering information and consultation on medication and other health-related topics [9] making mobile health care (mHealth) possible [17,18]. mHealth apps allow users, for example, to monitor health-related issues, understand specific medical conditions, or to achieve fitness goals [2]. By entering private and personal health information (e.g., medication intake, disease history, or blood values), users often expose sensitive personal information when using mHealth apps [14,18,19]. In return, users receive a tailored app experience offering relevant health-related information and functionality [11]. In the past, personal health information was managed and stored

© Springer International Publishing Switzerland 2016
S. Schiffner et al. (Eds.): APF 2016, LNCS 9857, pp. 190–201, 2016.
DOI: 10.1007/978-3-319-44760-5_12

solely in hospitals. Today, it is also collected and managed by mHealth apps and over the internet. Therefore, it is critical to protect users' personal information in order to reduce information privacy risks [17,18].

The risk to users is that personal health-related information can be misused [30]. Due to the fast growth of the mHealth app market, it is increasingly difficult to assess information privacy risks for each individual mHealth app [9]. Moreover, app providers offer only sparse and vague information on how personal user information is treated or stored. Users have to rely on privacy policies or information privacy seals [7] to acquire relevant information about privacy risks of mHealth apps. But privacy policies lack a standardized format [2], are typically written in formal legalese [23] and hard to understand for the majority of users [25]. Privacy seals aim at providing information about security and privacy of web services by issuing certificates [7]. Privacy seals fail at communicating details about the actual information privacy risks to users [7] and may not have an effect on user information disclosure at all [15]. Consequently, it is challenging for users to evaluate processing of their information by mHealth apps and to compare different apps with respect to information privacy before or while using mHealth apps. The required privacy information is either not available, hidden in legal language or not comprehensible for an averagely educated person [10].

We conduct a feasibility study on how to communicate information privacy risks in a clearer and more detailed way than privacy policies or privacy seals do. We identify six information privacy risk factors by downloading mHealth apps from the iOS and Android app stores and surveying them with respect to their information privacy risks. The six information privacy risk factors concern the input of personal information, sharing targets of collected personal information, a secure data connection, the ability to login to an app, use of analytics and advertising, and reasonableness of information collection [1]. The information privacy risk factors help to communicate the information privacy risks of individual mHealth apps to users more efficiently [26] and to improve the comparability between apps with respect to information privacy. We combine the information privacy risk factors into a factor weight equation [27] and represent the resulting information privacy risk score in a prototypical instantiation of a graphical user interface. The information privacy risk score and the graphical user interface are designed to enable users to better comprehend information privacy risks across multiple apps by providing a standardized communication medium for information privacy risk factors [22].

2   Communication of Information Privacy Risks

Privacy risks in the mHealth app context have been subject to various studies. Privacy risk assessment has been studied from different angles and various attempts were made to communicate privacy risks to users [2]. As users expose sensitive personal information when using mHealth apps [24], there is a vital need for accurate communication of information privacy risks. Currently, app providers' information privacy practices are predominantly communicated via their privacy policies.

The content of privacy policies of mHealth apps has been analyzed and evaluated, revealing that many popular apps do not provide privacy policies useful to users. The availability of privacy policies for mHealth apps has improved in recent years, but privacy policies are still difficult to comprehend for an averagely educated audience [10]. Users often agree to the privacy policies of popular apps on a basis of common trust [29] because reading them is highly time consuming [21]. Such user behavior does not foster user comprehension and understanding of information privacy risks, instead, it promotes exactly the opposite. Privacy seals represent an alternative approach, but can be misinterpreted. Users conclude, for instance, that a privacy seal indicates a high protection of personal information without paying attention to the service characteristics actually certified [20]. As a result, users may prefer web sites of providers featuring a privacy seal, even though there is no difference in privacy protection. Consequently, privacy seals can promote situations where users are misled in comparisons of online offerings with respect to information privacy risks. Even though studies have developed suggestions for enhancement [16,23], privacy policies and privacy seals cannot be considered effective tools for communication of information privacy risks of mHealth apps to users.

Other studies identified information privacy risks by downloading the apps. With this approach, information privacy risk factors, such as an insecure data transfer, geographic location and phone identifier leakage were identified [1,3–6,14]. These information privacy risk factors are mostly of a technical nature. Although the identification of information privacy risks has been enhanced through this procedure, attention to communication of identified information privacy risks is limited. In our study, we take a step further by downloading a sample of mHealth apps and identifying as well as analyzing information privacy risk factors of these apps. As a new and promising approach for communication of information privacy risks to users, we develop an information privacy risk index that communicates information privacy risk scores for mHealth apps through a publicly accessible graphical user interface.

3   Development of the Information Privacy Risk Index

Our study is based on a dataset of the 300 most often rated apps from the Google PlayStore and the 300 most often rated apps from the Apple AppStore in the app store categories 'Medical' and 'Health & Fitness'. Since our research approach requires the installation of the apps on our mobile devices, we excluded all apps not available free of charge (124 apps). The free apps are potentially more prone to information privacy violations than paid apps: The revenue model of free apps is often built around displaying personalized advertisements to users based on collected user information [1]. We downloaded every app available to our smartphones and identified six information privacy risk factors based on the resulting dataset and the information privacy risk factors proposed by Ackerman [1] and He, Dongjing, et al. [14].

Table 1. Personal information that had to be entered in the apps in our survey clustered in categories and assigned with their factor scores for the information privacy risk index equation

Category	Members of Category	Factor Scores[1]
Medication intake	Pills/recipes, medication dosage	0.147
Vital values	Blood pressure, heart rate, blood sugar, blood values etc	0.147
Diseases	Kind of disease	0.118
Symptoms	All acute, chronic, relapsing or remitting symptoms. For example: mood changes, rashes, swellings	0.118
Life status specs	Pregnancy, lifestyle (activity), smoking habits	0.106
Address	Country, state, street	0.088
Body specs	Weight, height, body frame, body fat, temperature etc	0.082
Family	Medical condition of children or ancestors, family size	0.059
Medical appointments	Date, doctor	0.053
Food intake	Calories, diet plan, drinks	0.035
Workout/Activities	goals, steps, distance covered/GPS tracking	0.029
Personality test	Questions about own behavior in certain situations	0.012
Sleep metrics	Sleep sound, dream description	0.006

3.1 Identification of Information Privacy Risk Factors

To identify information privacy risk factors and assess all apps in our dataset, we used a four-step procedure: First, we read the description of the app inside the app store to identify possible information privacy risks. App descriptions were assessed for indicators of information-privacy-related input fields. Second, we inspected the screenshots offered in the app store. The screenshots indicate information requested from users by showing text input fields for user information (e.g., medication intakes, disease history, blood values). Third, we downloaded the apps to our smartphones and used them. During app use, we checked the data transfer with the web debugging proxy application *Charles Proxy*[1]. *Charles Proxy* visualizes the HTTP connections the app uses and allows for the identification of data transfers between the app and third parties. Fourth, in an optional step, we read the privacy policy or terms of service to obtain information

---

[1] https://www.charlesproxy.com, visited 02/09/2016.

about the use of personal information. This step was only conducted when a data transfer displayed in the web debugging proxy application remained unclear.

Information Sharing Targets (T): We refer to information sharing targets as the target or host destination to which apps send users' personal information. Personal information can be sent directly to the app provider, research projects, social networks, analytics tools and marketing agencies [2]. Some apps may offer data storage and syncing on app providers' remote servers, which leads to a potential information privacy risk for users since, from the user perspective, the data vanishes on a non-traceable and non-retrievable remote server [2,14].

Personal Information Types (P): During app assessment, we extended the types of personal information input continuously as required. In total, we identified thirteen types of personal information input relevant for our research scope (see Table 1). For the sake of brevity, we only outline the most critical categories below. 'Life status specs' refer to user inputs revealing details about users' lifestyle (e.g., information about a pregnancy or smoking habits). Personal information inputs labeled 'medication intake' capture the amount and kind of medication consumed by the user. 'Vital values' represent health measurements (e.g., blood metrics or heart rate). 'Diseases' and 'Symptoms' are each assigned to single self-explanatory categories that represent the input of disease and symptom information [2,14]. The types of personal information inputs listed in Table 1 are limited to information inputs required by apps in our dataset. However, the personal information inputs align with the types of mHealth data inputs described by Kumar et al. [19].

Login (L): Furthermore, we distinguished between two assessments for login information. If a login is required [2], a user either has to register via a username or an email address, or otherwise via a social network login (e.g., Facebook). In the case that no login is required, apps were assessed with the value 'none'.

Connection Security (S): We classified data transfers as either an unencrypted or an encrypted HTTP data transmission. In case of an encrypted connection, we could only suspect, which data is actually being transferred.

Unspecific Information Transfer (U): We tested with the proxy application whether apps used click tracking analytics tools or contacted advertisement servers to display advertisement banners. We listed those findings under the information privacy risk factor 'Unspecific Information Transfer'. Due to encryption, we could not assess what personal information is being exchanged with these target hosts and whether transmitted information poses a threat to information privacy.

Reasonable Information Collection (R): For each identified personal information input, we coded the reasonableness of collection of personal information as a binary assessment. Some apps collected, for example, personal information that is not noticeably used by the app so that information collection seems fraudulent.

3.2   Calculation of the Information Privacy Risk Score

Based on the assessments of all apps in our dataset, we developed an algorithm for calculating an information privacy risk score that assigns each app with an information privacy score on a scale between 0.0 and 1.0. A privacy score of 0.0 indicates that the app poses no information privacy risk according to our app assessment. A privacy score of 1.0 on the other hand represents a strong information privacy risk. The information privacy risk score is the result of a factor weight equation based on the six information privacy risk factors we identified during app assessment. Triantaphyllou et al. [27] promote the use of a factor weight equation[2] as a decision making support tool. A factor weight equation is a suitable foundation for the information privacy risk index because the information privacy risk index serves as a decision support tool for app users. Additionally, using a simple factor weight equation makes the method of calculating the information privacy score comprehensible for possible future end-users. We determined default weights for the information privacy risk factors based on the risk assessment weights that Ackerman [1] proposed. Usually the reliability and validity of measures (such as the weights in our factor weight equation) are determined in research under controlled laboratory conditions [19]. To remedy this, the prototypical implementation of the information privacy risk index allows users to either use the default weights or to set their own weights [13].

$$PrivacyRiskScore_{App} = T_{App} * w(T) + P_{App} * w(P) + L_{App} * w(L) + \\ S_{App} * w(S) + U_{App} * w(U) + R_{App} * w(R) \tag{1}$$

where: T = Information Sharing Targets, P = Personal Information Types, L = Login, S = Connection Security, U = Unspecific Information Transfer, R = Reasonable Information Collection, $w(T)+w(P)+w(L)+w(S)+w(U)+w(R) = 1$

Scoring Model. After setting the weights for each information privacy risk factor, we developed the scoring models for each individual information privacy risk factor. For the binary information privacy risk factors connection security (S), unspecific information transfer (U) and reasonable information collection (R) no further scoring is necessary. As a special case, the information privacy risk factor connection security (S) will only be set to 1.0, if the connection is unencrypted and personal information is transmitted otherwise the encryption of the connection is of no relevance [19]. For the information privacy risk factor information sharing targets (T), we assigned default scoring values based on our discussion of relative importance in contribution to information privacy risks of mHealth app use. These values can be freely adapted by users. The scoring model for the information privacy risk factor personal information types (P) is

---

[2] The factor weight equation, as we call it, is often also referred to as the weighted sum model. We decided to us the term factor weight equation because our algorithm distinguishes between factor and weight variables.

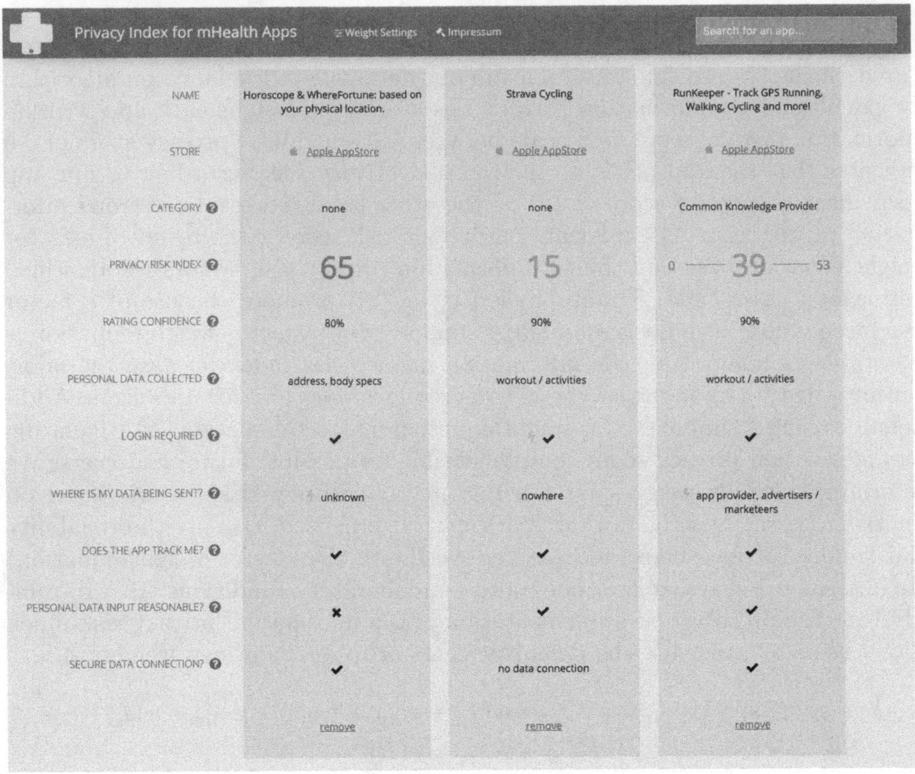

Fig. 1. Three apps have been selected and are listed in the comparison table view

slightly more elaborate. A single app can ask for multiple categories of personal information input and the scoring model would need to sum up the scores for each existing category to calculate the final score for personal information types (P). In total, we identified 13 types of personal information input but the maximum number of personal information input types identified for a single app was 5. This would lead to a single app never reaching the maximum score of 1.0. To remedy this, a correction factor is applied to the final privacy risk score.

3.3 Graphical User Interface

The information privacy risk assessment was complemented with a graphical user interface that enables users to make easy assessments of the information privacy risks that an app poses and seamlessly compare the information privacy risk factors of multiple apps. With the graphical user interface, users can get a fast overview about information privacy risks of individual mHealth apps and make a quick decision about selection and use of mHealth apps without having to read complicated privacy policies. The graphical user interface consists of two main views. Initially users are presented a weighting view in which the weights of all information privacy risk factors can be customized. Custom weights are stored in a client side cookie. The second view is the main apps table view. Inter-comparability between apps is achieved by listing the app rating results in a table view next to each other (see Fig. 1). Via a search bar, apps can be added to the table view. As soon as apps are added to the table view, information on the information privacy risk factors is displayed. Hovering a table view cell displays a small, black pop-up area offering detailed information on the respective information privacy risk factor. A little yellow bolt icon in front of a table view cell indicates the information privacy risk factor that has the most influence on the information privacy risk score of that app. The information privacy risk score itself is the large, color-coded (green, orange, red) number, which ranges from 0 to 100. This way the user can, in addition to understanding the number value of the information privacy risk score, compare the selected apps with just the glimpse of an eye, by looking at the colors. A click on the score value reveals a detailed view on how the information privacy score calculation was conducted. Dehling et al. [11] proposed the idea of clustering apps by assessments of potential damage through information security and privacy infringements into archetypes. If an app of our dataset is clustered within an archetype, the information-privacy-risk-score cell also displays the numbers of the lowest and highest privacy risk score apps from this archetype. These numbers are clickable in order to add the highest and lowest information privacy risk score apps to the table view. This creates an easy to use, fast and responsive graphical user interface, allowing users to customize the view with instantaneous reaction times [22] and tailor the graphical user interface to their needs [12]. Our graphical user interface is available to the public (https://privacy-risk-mhealth.herokuapp.com) and serves as a first step towards providing a comparison view on apps from the app stores with respect to their information privacy risks.

4   Findings

During the assessment of all 476 apps from our initial dataset, 178 apps were not available for download on the app stores. This reduced our dataset to 298 apps, 147 iOS and 151 Android apps. No apps in our sample have direct data transfers to research project hosts (or host names that we could identify as belonging to research projects) and research data use is only mentioned in three privacy policies. Two apps have data connections to social networks. 63 apps send personal information directly to the app provider. 27 apps potentially sent personal information to advertisers or marketing companies. The data connections potentially transferring personal data established a secure and encrypted HTTP connection within 42 apps, while 28 apps did not encrypt the data connection at all. In 228 cases, we could not identify whether the data connection was encrypted or the app did not send any data at all. 28 apps in our sample request personal information without noticeably using it. 105 apps request personal information and use it to tailor the app experience to users' preferences and needs. 165 apps require no information input at all. 51 apps require a login via username and

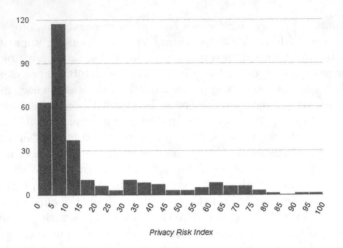

Fig. 2. Histogram of the information privacy risk score distribution

password or a social media account (e.g., Facebook, Twitter, Google) in order to be able to use the application or to tailor the app experience to the preferences and needs of the individual user.

Figure 2 shows a histogram of the distribution of information privacy risk scores we calculated for all apps, multiplied by 100 and rounded to the next integer value on the x-axis. The y-axis shows the amount of privacy risk scores in a certain cluster range. The histogram clusters index-values in increments of 5 and clearly shows that the majority of privacy risk scores are below 10. There are fewer apps with information privacy risk scores above 15. We see two increases in information privacy risk scores at values of 30 to 35 and 60 to 65.

5   Discussion

Our study revealed some interesting findings. 21 % of the apps in our dataset collecting personal information collect it without any noticeable use for it. Privacy-attentive apps should only collect information actually used by the app to provide the app functionality or tailor the app to user preferences and needs. Otherwise, information collection appears fraudulent and leaves a negative overall impression of the app. 40 % of the apps in our dataset transfer personal information without encryption. Even though use of a secure, encrypted data connection is not visible to users, a secure data connection should always be used by mHealth apps to guarantee confidentiality and integrity of personal data [14, 17]. A reason for the high number of low information privacy risk scores (Fig. 2) is the amount of apps that do not collect health information, but rather provide meditation sounds or medical dictionaries.

Overall, our publicly available information privacy risk index demonstrates the feasibility of providing users with an simple-to-use tool to establish an

overview of information privacy risks of mHealth apps and compare information privacy risk factors between apps. This constitutes a valuable contribution
right between extant approaches that either yield only very general information (i.e., privacy seals) or provide too much information in an inconsistent way
impeding information retrieval (i.e., privacy policies). Future research can make
use of our feasibility study and develop tools and frameworks to further enhance
communication and assessment of information privacy risks.

To scale up app assessment, future research can focus on automating app
assessments. For automated app assessments, apps could be automatically downloaded from the app stores, the source code could be decompiled and user inputs
and app information handling could be traced within the source code. This would
most likely be more feasible for Android apps, due to strict download regulations of the Apple AppStore. To circumvent such issues, the app survey process
may be integrated into the app stores by the store providers themselves. The
inclusion of the information privacy risk index by app providers bears the risk
that information privacy risk factors may not be sufficiently included in the survey of the app stores. Future research could focus on the necessary ruleset to
ensure that app providers or other instances include and implement a complete
and thorough information privacy survey, for instance, as proposed by the 'Data
protection impact assessment' of article 33 of the General Data Protection Regulation [8]. Our concept for a simple information privacy risk communication can
also be expanded by considering implications on other important parties such
as policy makers and consumer advocates. In this context, future research could
also address the development of business models regarding information privacy
risk assessment and information privacy risk communication.

Our research has some limitations. We were limited mainly in the tracking of
personal information transfers. If we were actually able to track what information
is transferred, the precision of mHealth app information privacy risk assessments
could be improved. Moreover, 178 apps in our dataset were already removed from
the app stores and not available for download. And the dataset included several
apps of app providers that only differ in their names but not in their functionality
(e.g., meditation sound apps). Even though we still examined a large amount
of apps, a larger dataset without the redundant apps could be more beneficial
for future research. A user study to evaluate the information privacy risk index
prototype was not conducted since it exceeded the scope of our study. Lastly, we
only examined free apps due to budget restrictions. Future research could also
study the information privacy risks of paid apps.

Nevertheless, this study demonstrates the feasibility of an information privacy risk index more informative than privacy seals and better structured than
privacy policies. The prototypical instantiation of the information privacy risk
index illustrates its utility to obtain an easy to use overview of the information privacy risks of mHealth apps and compare information privacy risk factors
between different apps. Our research investigates one potential approach to ease
the process of selecting the right app out of the overload of mHealth apps available to users [28]. Users can retrieve processed information about information

privacy risks of mHealth apps, which increases transparency of information privacy risks of mHealth apps [30]. Consequently, the information privacy risk index can, on the one hand, reduce uncertainty of information use by mHealth apps. On the other hand, the information privacy risk index empowers individual users to make better informed decisions about selection and use of mHealth apps.

References

1. Ackerman, L.: Mobile health and fitness applications and information privacy. In: Privacy Rights Clearinghouse, San Diego, CA (2013)
2. Adhikari, R., Richards, D., Scott, K.: Security and privacy issues related to the use of mobile health apps. In: Proceedings of the 25th Australasian Conference on Information Systems, 8th–10th December, Auckland, New Zealand. ACIS (2014)
3. Almuhimedi, H., et al.: Your location has been shared 5,398 Times! A field study on mobile app privacy nudging (CMU-ISR-14-116). In: Proceedings of the 33rd Annual ACM Conference on Human Factors in Computing Systems (2014)
4. Bal, G., Rannenberg, K., Hong, J.: Styx: design and evaluation of a new privacy risk communication method for smartphones. In: Cuppens-Boulahia, N., Cuppens, F., Jajodia, S., Kalam, A.A.E., Sans, T. (eds.) ICT Systems Security and Privacy Protection. IFIP, vol. 428, pp. 113–126. Springer, Heidelberg (2014)
5. Bal, G., Rannenberg, K., Hong, J.I.: Styx: privacy risk communication for the android smartphone platform based on apps' data-access behavior patterns. Comput. Secur. **53**, 187–202 (2015)
6. Balebako, R., et al.: Little BrothersWatching you: raising awareness of data leaks on smartphones. In: Proceedings of the Ninth Symposium on Usable Privacy and Security, p. 12. ACM (2013)
7. Beatty, P., et al.: P3P adoption on E-commerceweb sites: a survey and analysis. IEEE Int. Comput. **11**(2), 65–71 (2007). doi:10.1109/MIC.2007.45. ISSN: 1089-7801
8. EC European Commission. Proposal for a regulation of the european parliament and of the council on the protection of individuals with regard to the processing of personal data and on the free movement of such data (general data protection regulation). In: COM (2012) 11 final, 2012/0011 (COD), Brussels, 25 (2012), January 2012
9. de la Vega, R., Miró, J.: mHealth: a strategic field without a solid scientific soul. a systematic review of pain-related apps. PloS One **9**(7), e101312 (2014). ISSN: 1932-6203
10. Dehling, T., Gao, F., Sunyaev, A.: Assessment instrument for privacy policy content: design and evaluation of PPC. In: Proceedings of the Pre-ICIS Workshop on Information Security and Privacy. AIS, December 2014
11. Dehling, T., et al.: Exploring the far side of mobile health: information security and privacy of mobile health apps on iOS and android. JMIR mHealth uHealth **3**(1), e8 (2015)
12. Germonprez, M., Hovorka, D., Collopy, F.: A theory of tailorable technology design. J. Assoc. Inf. Syst. **8**(6), 351–367 (2007). ISSN: 1536-9323
13. Glasgow, R.E., Riley, W.T.: Pragmatic measures: what they are and why we need them. Am. J. Prev. Med. **45**(2), 237–243 (2013). ISSN: 0749-3797
14. He, D., et al.: Security concerns in android mHealth apps. In: Proceedings of the AMIA 2014 Annual Symposium, 15-19 November. AMIA, Washington, DC (2014)

15. Hui, K.-L., Teo, H.H., Tom Lee, S.-Y.: An exploratory field experiment. MIS Q. **31**, 19–33 (2007)
16. Gage Kelley, P., et al.: Standardizing privacy notices: an online study of the nutrition label approach. In: SIGCHI Conference on Human Factors in Computing Systems, New York, NY, USA. CHI 2010, pp. 1573–1582. ACM (2010). ISBN: 978-1-60558-929-9. doi:10.1145/1753326.1753561
17. Kim, J.T., et al.: Security of personal bio data in mobile health applications for the elderly. Int. J. Secur Appl. **9**(10), 59–70 (2015). ISSN: 1738-9976
18. Kotz, D.: A threat taxonomy for mhealth privacy. In: 3rd International Conference on Communication Systems and Networks. IEEE, ISBN: 1-4244-8952-0. doi:10.1109/COMSNETS.2011.5716518, January 2011
19. Kumar, S., et al.: Mobile health technology evaluation: the mhealth evidence workshop. Am. J. Prev. Med. **45**(2), 228–236 (2013). ISSN: 0749-3797
20. LaRose, R., Rifon, N.: Your privacy is assured of being disturbed: websites with and without privacy seals. New Media Soc. **8**(6), 1009–1029 (2006)
21. McDonald, A.M., Cranor, L.F.: The cost of reading privacy policies. J. Law Policy Inf. Soc. **4**, 540–565 (2008)
22. Palmer, J.W.: Web site usability, design, and performance metrics. Inf. Syst. Res. **13**(2), 151–167 (2002). ISSN: 1047-7047
23. Pollach, I.: What's wrong with online privacy policies? Commun. ACM **50**(9), 103–108 (2007)
24. Rohm, A.J., Milne, G.R.: Just what the doctor ordered: the role of information sensitivity and trust in reducing medical information privacy concern. J. Bus. Res. **57**(9), 1000–1011 (2004)
25. Sunyaev, A., et al.: Availability and quality of mobile health app privacy policies. J. Am. Med. Inf. Assoc. **22**, e1 (2015). doi:10.1136/amiajnl-2013-002605. PMID: 25147247, e28–e33. ISSN: 1067-5027
26. Tavani, H.T.: Philosophical theories of privacy: implications for an adequate online privacy policy. Metaphilosophy **38**(1), 1–22 (2007). ISSN: 1467-9973
27. Triantaphyllou, E., et al.: Multi-citeria decision making: an operations research approach. Encycl. Electr. Electron. Eng. **15**, 175–186 (1998)
28. van Velsen, L., Beaujean, D., van Gemert-Pijnen, J.: Why mobile health app overload drives us crazy, and how to restore the sanity. BMC Med. Inf. Decis. Making **13**(1), 1 (2013). ISSN: 1472-6947
29. Ran Yang, Y., Ng, J., Vishwanath, A.: Do social media privacy policies matter? evaluating the effects of familiarity and privacy seals on cognitive processing. In: Proceedings of the 48th Hawaii International Conference on System Sciences. Washington, DC, USA: IEEE Computer Society (2015), pp. 3463–3472. ISBN: 978-1-4799-7367-5
30. Zubaydi, F., et al.: Security of mobile health (mHealth) systems. In: Proceedings of the 15th IEEE International Conference on Bioinformatics and Bioengineering (BIBE), pp. 1–5 (2015)

Author Index

Beyerer, Jürgen 135
Bieker, Felix 21
Bier, Christoph 135
Bistolfi, Camilla 71
Bolognini, Luca 71
Brüggemann, Thomas 190
Büscher, Niklas 96

Cha, Shi-Cho 153
Chien, Li-Da 153
Costantino, Gianpiero 3

Dehling, Tobias 190
Dylla, Frank 171

Fischer, Mathias 96
Friedewald, Michael 21

Gambardella, Carmela 3
Ghernaouti, Solange 115

Hansen, Joel 190
Hansen, Marit 21

Knittl, Silvia 38
Krumay, Barbara 48
Kühne, Kay 135

Länger, Thomas 115
Liu, Tzu-Ching 153

Manea, Mirko 3
Matteucci, Ilaria 3
Mifsud Bonnici, Jeanne Pia 81
Milaj, Jonida 81

Obersteller, Hannah 21
Ozdeniz, Anil 3

Petrocchi, Marinella 3
Pöhls, Henrich C. 115

Rost, Martin 21
Ruiz, Jose Fran. 3

Schiffner, Stefan 96
Shiung, Chuang-Ming 153
Sialm, Gion 38
Sunyaev, Ali 190
Syu, Sih-Cing 153

Tsai, Tsung-Ying 153

van de Ven, Jasper 171

Printed in the United States
By Bookmasters